FARNBOROUGH : SALISBURY

Basingstoke : Reading. Romsey : Salisbury. Salisbury : Westbury

INTRODUCTION

Taking the place of a Merchant Navy Pacific, West Country 4-6-2 34030 'Watersmeet' waits for the right-away from Salisbury with a Waterloo - West of England express on the 16th May 1964. The engine was one of 50 that were never rebuilt, the programme being suspended in 1961 partly because of widespread electrification in Kent but also because the rebuilt locomotives were barred from many routes west of Exeter. 34030 was built in May 1946 and withdrawn in September 1964, most of its existence being spent at Exmouth Junction.

"Discuss unto me; art thou officer? Or art thou base, common, and popular?"

Of all the railways in the land, the Southern was probably the most difficult to categorise. Seen from the viewpoint of Victoria, Charing Cross or Cannon Street it seemed to be something of an outer-suburban system even though the Ramsgate trains had all the accoutrements of long distance trains, whilst the electrified suburban service was something unique to the system. The stranger to the south saw nothing inferior in the Charing Cross to Hastings expresses yet to their regulars they occupied some intermediate status between that of express and stopping train. Only at Waterloo did elements of the railway start to fall into well defined slots - the West of England expresses conceded nothing to the Anglo-Scottish services of Euston and Kings Cross - although one worried as to where the Portsmouth trains stood in relation to things; equipped with dining cars and corridor coaches yet running for only an hour and a half before retracing their tracks with none of the usual intermediate terminal ceremonies.

However for this, the first of a series covering the Southern of the 1950's, no such distractions arise. The area covered - Farnborough to Salisbury - was no less a main line than any other and has been selected to commence the series because it is a convenient district in which to describe the sum of the South Western's ex-

Unless otherwise stated all references to engine diagrams and train workings are for the early part of 1953.

press services, all of which ran over the section of line under review.

The matter covered in this series differs from previously published history in that it deals almost exclusively with matter not before covered: the train service and the engines that worked it, using the working timetables, engine workings and a solid injection of experience based upon a railway career, part - perhaps the happiest - of which was spent on the line. Matters such as constructional dates and years of opening have, except in the briefest of terms, been omitted since these subjects have been more

Acknowledgements for assistance with text and illustrations are due to:
R. Bell, S. Symes, A.J. Somers, P. Webb, P. Hay, M Bentley, J.Edgington, A Lilleywhite and W.S.Becket.

than adequately dealt with elsewhere by writers whose expertise lies in that direction. This series in concerned solely with the operational aspects of the line: in which the author, if not an expert, at least played a part.

There is, in these pages, an element of repetition which is difficult to avoid since many of the trains and engines mentioned are common to two or more chapters and it has proved difficult to limit mention of some workings to a single part of the book.

The fact that motive power depots existed at Basingstoke, Andover Junction and Salisbury is common knowledge but how much is known of the actual work that each of these depots had to perform? We know, for example, that Basingstoke had an allocation of about twenty engines for most of the 1950's and a host of published works tell us which engines they were. What these works have not told us is how many of the allocation were in daily use, which trains they worked and how far from their home shed each engine travelled and it is with detail of this nature that this series is concerned; describing in detail the work of each of those engines: the time they came off shed, the time they returned and what they did in between.

To support these workings full details of the timetable is given together with the details of engines which worked into the district from the adjacent areas in the hope that the reader will be well placed to reconstruct the events that made the South Western such an interesting line during the 1950's.

The workings quoted in the text are for 1953, unless stated otherwise, and although workings were amended from time to time, generally speaking the timetable changed very little during the course of the decade and the greater number of engine workings remained static during that time. The reader may safely assume that the line as described in 1953 saw out the decade more or less unchanged.

In addition to the engines based at Basingstoke, Andover Junction and Salisbury, similarly detailed information is given in respect of visiting engines of which a wide variety could be seen at the three sheds in question.

Although the line to Salisbury came to be regarded as the trunk route of the LSWR, the promoters of the route initially concentrated on Southampton, because of its maritime activities, and the line between the two, completed in a rather piecemeal fashion, was completed fairly quickly, the section from Nine Elms to Winchfield opening in 1838 and the remainder two years later.

The original intention had been for the West of England to be reached via Southampton using a projected extension from Dorchester to the west but in the event a more direct route was substituted, opening between Worting Junction and Andover Junction in 1854 and being extended to Salisbury three years later.

The first half-century of operation coincided with the mechanisation of the merchant navy which, in turn, resulted in a dramatic increase in the tonnage of traffic dealt with at Southampton and by the turn of the century it become increasingly apparent that the original double line was barely adequate for the needs of both the Wessex, Southampton and Exeter flows of traffic which all shared the same set of metals between London and Worting Junction. The remedy matters the company embarked upon a huge programme of expansion which included the quadrupling of the route from London to Worting together with the installation of air-operated track circuit block signals, the uniform symmetry of which became for many a hallmark of the line. These plans were completed between 1903 and 1904 and bequeathed to us the railway we now have.

A generation later saw the electrification of the suburban service - culminating in the extension of the third rail as far afield as Portsmouth - yet for all its efforts to modernisation, which included a mammoth coach renewal programme, the South-Western remained for many years a system of contrasts both in terms of planning and equipment.

By the late 1930's its long distance trains were well equipped, moderately fast and often very weighty yet the motive power had more in common with what could be seen at Liverpool Street rather than Paddington. Efforts to produce a class of engine the equal of a Royal Scot or a Castle had not been successful and most trains were handled by rather modest two-cylinder 4-6-0's which remained the norm until the arrival of the Bulleid Pacifics.

Standardisation extended to the timetable - at least in the down direction - with the majority of services, fast and slow, leaving Waterloo at fixed intervals: on the hour (odd) for the West of England, half past (most hours) for Bournemouth, fifty minutes past the hour to Port-

LSWR (1953) : DOWN SERVICES (FARNBOROUGH : BASINGSTOKE)								
Train	Engine	Line	F'boro	Fleet	W'field	Hook	B'STOKE	Destination
22.45 Feltham	*S15 4-6-0*	*L*	*00/10*				*00/57*	*Bournemouth (C)*
00.23 Woking	H15 4-6-0	L	00/35				01.25	Exmouth Jcn
23.25 Nine Elms	LN 4-6-0	T	00/40				01.08	Southampton Docks
23.58 Feltham	*S15 4-6-0*	*T*	*01/15*				*02/04*	*Exmouth Junction*
14.58 Gravesend (Milk)	*N15 4-6-0*	*L*	*01/40*				*02.00*	*Yeovil (Town)*
00.45 Nine Elms	H15 4-6-0	L	01/57				02.37	Eastleigh
01.25 WATERLOO	MN 4-6-2	T	02/08				02/24	PLYMOUTH
02.10 Clapham Jcn (Fish)	*N15 4-6-0*	*T*	*02/49*				*03.10*	*Fratton*
00.55 Feltham	*S15 4-6-0*	*L*	*02/52*				*03/32*	*Southampton (Docks)*
02.40 WATERLOO	MN 4-6-2	T	03/29				03.47	BOURNEMOUTH (C)
03.45 Waterloo	N15X 4-6-0	L	04.30					-
Vans	*N15X 4-6-0*	*L*	*04.45*				*05.10*	-
04.07 Feltham	*S15 4-6-0*	*T*	*05/24*				*06.13*	*Southampton (Docks)*
05.32 Woking	0395 0-6-0	L	05.57					-
05.40 WATERLOO	LN 4-6-0	T	06/32				06.50	WEYMOUTH
06.33 Woking	N15 4-6-0	L	06.54	07.02	07.10	07.18	07.28	Templecombe
07.31 Woking	U 2-6-0	L	07.48	07.54	08.01	08.07	08.16	Southampton (T)
01.30 Hoo Junction	*U 2-6-0*	*T*	*07/51*				*08/32*	*Eastleigh*
07.20 Waterloo	N15 4-6-0	L	08.15	08.22	08.29	08.35	08.44	Salisbury
08.45 Woking	N15 4-6-0	L	09.01	09.08	09.14	09.20	09.28	-
08.30 WATERLOO	MN 4-6-2	T	09/18				09.37	WEYMOUTH
07.43 Clapham Jcn (Pcls)	*H15 4-6-0*	*L*	*09.21*				*09.51*	*Eastleigh*
09.00 WATERLOO	MN 4-6-2	T	09/47				10.04	PLYMOUTH
09.52 Woking	0395 0-6-0	L	10.17					-
09.30 WATERLOO	WC 4-6-2	T	10/19				10.39	BOURNEMOUTH (W)
09.54 Waterloo	H15 4-6-0	L	10.45	10.52	10.59	11.05	11.14	Southampton (C)
09.45 Feltham	*S15 4-6-0*	*L*	*11/06*				*11/45*	*Eastleigh*
10.30 WATERLOO	MN 4-6-2	T	11/09				11/24	WEYMOUTH
11.00 WATERLOO	MN 4-6-2	T	11/37				11/48	PADSTOW
10.54 Waterloo	LN 4-6-0	L	11.45	11.52	11.59	12.05	12.14	Salisbury
11.30 WATERLOO	LN 4-6-0	T	12/07				12.27	BOURNEMOUTH (W)
10.45 Feltham	*S15 4-6-0*	*L*	*12/08*				*12.57*	*Exmouth Junction*
11.54 Waterloo	WC 4-6-2	L	12.45	12.52		13.02	13.11	Salisbury
03.20 Ashford (Kent)	*S15 4-6-0*	*L*	*13/00*				*13/37*	*Eastleigh*
12.30 WATERLOO	MN 4-6-2	T	13/09				13/23	BOURNEMOUTH (W)
Pick up Goods	*N15X 4-6-0*	*L*	*13.33*	*13.41*				
13.00 WATERLOO	MN 4-6-2	T	13/42				13/57	PLYMOUTH
12.54 Waterloo	N15 4-6-0	L	13.45	13.52	13.59	14.05	14.14	-
Pick up Goods	*N15X 4-6-0*	*L*		*14.00*	*14.09*			
13.30 WATERLOO	WC 4-6-2	T	14/09				14.27	WEYMOUTH
09.45 Tonbridge	*H15 4-6-0*	*T*	*14/20*				*14.54*	*Exmouth Junction*
Pick up Goods	*N15X 4-6-0*	*L*			*14.40*	*14.47*		
13.54 Waterloo	N15X 4-6-0	L	14.45	14.52	14.59	15.05	15.14	-
Pick up Goods	*N15X 4-6-0*	*L*				*15.15*	*15/36*	*West Yard*
15.00 WATERLOO	MN 4-6-2	T	15/37				15.55	PLYMOUTH
14.54 Waterloo	N15 4-6-0	L	15.45	15.52	15.59	16.05	16.14	-
15.20 WATERLOO	WC 4-6-2	T	15/57				16/14	WEYMOUTH
15.30 WATERLOO	WC 4-6-2	T	16/12				16.30	BOURNEMOUTH (W)
14.45 Feltham	*S15 4-6-0*	*L*	*16/12*				*16/59*	*Southampton Docks*
15.54 Waterloo	WC 4-6-2	L	16.45	16.52	16.59	17.05	17.14	-
15.54 Clapham Jcn (Milk)	*MN 4-6-2*	*L*	*16/57*				*17.25*	*Exeter (C)*
16.35 WATERLOO	WC 4-6-2	T	17/12				17/27	WEYMOUTH
17.00 WATERLOO	MN 4-6-2	T	17/46				18.04	EXETER (C)
17.09 Waterloo	N15 4-6-0	L	17.56	18.03	18.10	18.16	18.25	-
17.30 WATERLOO	WC 4-6-2	T	18/07				18.25	BOURNEMOUTH (W)
17.39 Waterloo	N15 4-6-0	L	18.29	18.36	18.43	18.51	19.00	Salisbury
18.00 WATERLOO	MN 4-6-2	T	18/37				18.55	PLYMOUTH
18.09 Waterloo	N15 4-6-0	L	18.56	19.03	19.10	19.16	19.25	-
18.30 WATERLOO	WC 4-6-2	T	19/09				19/23	WEYMOUTH
18.54 Waterloo	S15 4-6-0	L	19.45	19.52	19.59	20.05	20.14	Yeovil (Town)
18.42 Waterloo (Pcls)	*H15 4-6-0*	*L*	*20/01*				*20.38*	*Eastleigh*
19.30 WATERLOO	WC 4-6-2	T	20/07				20.25	BOURNEMOUTH (W)
19.54 Waterloo	N15 4-6-0	L	20.45	20.52	20.59	21.05	21.14	-
19.25 Nine Elms	*H15 4-6-0*	*T*	*20/50*				*21.40*	*Southampton Docks*
21.00 WATERLOO	LN 4-6-0	T	21/39				21.56	SOUTHAMPTON DOCKS
20.54 Waterloo	N15 4-6-0	L	21.44	21.51	21.58	22.04	22.13	Salisbury
21.10 Nine Elms	*MN 4-6-2*	*T*	*22/05*				*22/34*	*Plymouth*
19.35 Kensington (Pcls)	*H15 4-6-0*	*L*	*22/41*				*23.15*	*Poole*
22.00 Nine Elms	*MN 4-6-2*	*T*	*23/00*				*23/26*	*Exmouth Junction*
22.45 Woking	*S15 4-6-0*	*L*	*23/05*				*23/48*	*Eastleigh*
22.30 WATERLOO	LN 4-6-0	T	23/19				23.42	DORCHESTER (S)
22.40 Waterloo	H15 4-6-0	L	23.32	23.39	23.46	23.52	00.01	-
22.20 Feltham	*S15 4-6-0*	*T*	*23/35*				*00/06*	*Southampton Docks*
22.38 Nine Elms	*H15 4-6-0*	*T*	*23/40*				*00/20*	*Weymouth*

Express services in bold print. Goods & Parcels trains in italics. "/" = passing time. L : local line, T : through (fast) line.

Although very ordinary in appearance - especially after the arrival of the Bulleid Pacifics - the King Arthur 4-6-0's were capable of rousing performances and none more so than 30777 'Sir Lamiel' which in 1936 set up a 'record of records' by paring over seventeen minutes from the 90-minute schedule between Salisbury and Waterloo. Although relegated from the express passenger links from 1945 onwards, the N15's continued in service for a further fifteen years at the head of semi-fast services from Waterloo. 30777 is seen at Eastleigh MPD on the 14th May 1949 in readiness to work a Southampton (Docks) to Waterloo boat express.

	LSWR (1953) : DOWN SERVICES (OAKLEY : SALISBURY)										
Train	Engine	Oakley	Overton	W'church	Hurstb'n	A.JCN	Grateley	Idmiston	Porton	SALISBURY	Destination
00.23 Woking	*H15 4-6-0*	*00/47*				*02.22*					
01.25 WATERLOO	**MN 4-6-2**	**02/29**				**02.48**			**03.11**		**PLYMOUTH**
00.23 Woking	*H15 4-6-0*					*03.03*			*03.48*		*Exmouth Jcn*
14.58 Gravesend (Milk)	*N15 4-6-0*	*02/45*				*03.25*			*04.07*		*Yeovil (T)*
23.58 Feltham	*S15 4-6-0*	*03/02*				*03/48*			*04.35*		*Exmouth Jcn*
03.30 Basingstoke	*S15 4-6-0*	*03/49*				*04.45*			*05.40*		*West Yard*
05.30 Basingstoke	*700 0-6-0*	*05/50*				*06.46*	*07.25*				*Bulford*
06.33 Woking	N15 4-6-0	07.42	07.49	07.57	08.02	08.17	08.27	08.36	08.40	08.49	Templecombe
Light Engine	*M7 0-4-4T*						*07.48*		*08.12*		-
07.45 Basingstoke	*U 2-6-0*	*08.06*									*Pick-up*
07.45 Basingstoke	*U 2-6-0*	*08.26*	*08.34*								
Light Engine ex Amesbury	*700 0-6-0*								*09/30*	*09/44*	*MPD*
07.20 Waterloo	N15 4-6-0	08.59	09.05	09.12	09.17	09.27	09.37	09.46	09.49	09.58	-
07.45 Basingstoke	*U 2-6-0*		*09.20*	*09.30*							
07.45 Basingstoke	*U 2-6-0*			*10.00*	*10.06*						
09.00 WATERLOO	**MN 4-6-2**	**10/14**				**10.29**				**10.50**	**PLYMOUTH**
07.45 Basingstoke	*U 2-6-0*				*10.40*	*10.50*					
10.45 Basingstoke	N15 4-6-0	10.54	11.00	11.07	11.11	11.21	11.31	11.40	11.43	11.52	-
11.00 WATERLOO	**MN 4-6-2**	**11/53**				**12/04**				**12.23**	**PADSTOW**
10.54 Waterloo	LN 4-6-0	12.26	12.32	12.38	12.43	12.53	13.03	13.12	13.15	13.24	-
11.54 Waterloo	WC 4-6-2	13.22	13.28	13.34	13.39	13.49	13.59	14.08	14.11	14.20	-
13.00 WATERLOO	**MN 4-6-2**	**14/02**				**14.18**				**14.39**	**PLYMOUTH**
14.45 Amesbury	*700 0-6-0*								*15/10*	*15.25*	*Fisherton*
10.45 Feltham	*S15 4-6-0*	*14/19*				*14/54*				*15.44*	*Exmouth Jcn*
14.48 Basingstoke	N15 4-6-0	14.57	15.04	15.11	15.16	15.27	15.37	15.47	15.51	16.00	-
09.45 Tonbridge	*H15 4-6-0*	*15/15*				*15/50*	*16.11*				
15.00 WATERLOO	**MN 4-6-2**	**16/05**				**16.20**				**16.42**	**PLYMOUTH**
09.45 Tonbridge	*H15 4-6-0*						*16.45*			*17.19*	*Exmouth Jcn*
Passenger	M7 0-4-4T						17.19	17.30	17.32	17.41	-
16.48 Basingstoke	N15 4-6-0	16.57	17.04	17.11	17.16	17.28	17.38	17.48	17.51	18.00	-
15.54 Clapham Jcn (Milk)	*MN 4-6-2*	*17/39*				*18/00*				*18.27*	*Exeter (C)*
17.00 WATERLOO	**MN 4-6-2**	**18/17**	**18.20**	**18.27**		**18.39**				**19.00**	**EXETER (C)**
18.00 WATERLOO	**MN 4-6-2**	**19/05**				**19.22**				**19.44**	**PLYMOUTH**
17.39 Waterloo	N15 4-6-0	19.15	19.21	19.28	19.33	19.47	19.57	20.06	20.09	20.18	-
19.04 Basingstoke	*S15 4-6-0*	*19/24*				*20.35*				*21.25*	*Plymouth*
18.54 Waterloo	S15 4-6-0	20.44	20.51	20.58	21.03	21.14	21.24	21.33	21.37	21.46	Yeovil (T)
20.54 Waterloo	N15 4-6-0	22.25	22.30	22.36	22.41	22.51	23.01		23.10	23.20	-
21.10 Nine Elms	*MN 4-6-2*	*22/44*				*23/08*				*23.37*	*Plymouth*
22.00 Nine Elms	*MN 4-6-2*	*23/38*				*00.05*				*00.40*	*Exmouth Jcn*
	Express services in bold print. Goods & Parcels trains in Italics. "/" = passing time										

3

DOWN TRAINS. WEEK-DAYS.	MX ★		MXQ 11.30 p.m. SXQ Chichester.		MX 2.10 a.m. Bevois Pk. ★		SXQ Empty Stone Train Exmth Jc.		SO SF ★		*[NE71 1+5 SF]* ★		MX *[NE79]*		MO ★		MX *[F146]*	
	arr. a.m.	dep. a.m.	arr. a.m.	dep. a.m.	arr. a.m.	dep. a.m.	arr. a.m.	dep. a.m.	arr. a.m.	dep. a.m.	arr. a.m.	dep. a.m.	arr. a.m.	dep. a.m.	arr. a.m.	dep. a.m.	arr. a.m.	dep. a.m.
Nine Elms M.P. Shed																		
Loco. Jc.																		
Nine Elms Yard										12 10		12 25		12 45				
Nine Elms "A" Box									12 14		12 29		12 49					
Queen's Road									12 17T		12 32T		12 52L					
Clapham Jc.									12 22		12 37		12 59					
Wimbledon Pk. Sdgs.															1 15			1 50
Wimbledon "A" Box																		2 0L
Wimbledon Station																1 20L		
Wimbledon West Yard															1 25			
Wimbledon "C" Box																		
Raynes Park																		
Surbiton																		
Hampton Crt Jc.									12 40L	12 56		1 17						2 15
Esher																		
Walton																		
Feltham Marsh'ng Yd.		12 15																
Feltham East Box	12 20																	
Staines Central	12 32																	
Virginia Water	12 46																	
Chertsey	12 54	1 9																
Addlestone	1 16																	
Addlestone Jc.	1 24																	
Weybridge		1 29L																2 34
Byfleet Jc.	*To Wimbledon*																*To Brentford Ctl.*	
West Byfleet																		
Woking East																		
Woking													1	42				
Woking Down Yd.							12 23	25L										
Woking Jc.							12	25L	1	10	1	17						
Brookwood																		
Sturt Lane Jc.																		
Farnborough									*To Fratton.*		*To Fratton.*							
Fleet																		
Winchfield									*Will not run on Saturdays 13th June to 19th Sept.*									
Hook																		
Brick & Tile Co.'s Sdg.																		
Basingstoke							1 25	1 33					2 37	2 44				
Basingstoke West Box																		
Basingstoke West Yard													2 49	3L 14				
Worting Jc.							1	43						3 28				
Micheldever																		
Weston Box													3 52					
Wallers Ash Box														4 32				
Winchester Jc.													4	42				
Winchester City																		
Shawford																		
Allbrook													5	2				
Eastleigh East Jc.																		
Eastleigh Yd. East Sdgs.													5 6					
Eastleigh Yard (Field)																		
Eastleigh Yd. (Tipton)																		
Eastleigh East Jc.			*Not available on Friday nights/Saturday mornings 13th June to 19th Sept.*										*Will not run on Sats. 13th June to 19th Sept.*					
Eastleigh																		
Swaything																		
St. Denys																		
Bevois Park																		
Northam Yard																		
Northam Jc.	*MX 12.20 a.m. Eastleigh to Exmouth Jc.*																	
Southampton Jc.																		
Southampton Term.																		
Sou'ton Dock Gates																		
Oakley																		
Overton																		
Whitchurch North																		
Hurstbourne	★																	
Andover Town	arr. a.m.	dep. a.m.																
Andover Jc.							2 22	3 3										
Grateley																		
Bulford																		
Amesbury																		
Newton Tony																		
Newton Tony Jc.																		
Amesbury Jc.																		
Porton																		
Salisbury Milford	1	21	2	2	3	33												
Tunnel Jc.	1	25	2	8	3	38	3	44										
Salisbury East Yard	1 30	1 31	2 13	2 15	3 43	3 44	3 48	3 55										
Salisbury	1 45	4 30	A		3 58													
Salisbury West Yard			A															
Salisbury Fisherton			A															

A.—To West Yard or Fisherton due 2.30 a.m. as required.

4

An extract from the 1953 LSWR freight working timetable showing the down services between London and Salisbury/Southampton. As an aide memoire the columns relating to regular trains have been annotated with the engine workings, something that saved wading through pages of diagrams during times of crisis. 'Q' trains ran as required and their paths were included in the timetable simply for the sake of convenience. These trains only ran when specially authorised by prior advice from Waterloo HQ.

Train	Engine	Line	B'STOKE	Hook	W'field	Feet	F'Boro	Destination
17.18 Sidmouth Jcn (Milk)	*N15 4-6-0*	*L*	*00.02*				*00/32*	*Waterloo*
21.56 Bevois Park (S'ton)	*S15 4-6-0*	*L*	*00.08*				*00/50*	*Feltham*
22.30 Southampton Docks	*U 2-6-0*	*L*	*00/47*				*01/20*	*Feltham*
12.45 Torrington	*N15 4-6-0*	*T*	*01/24*				*01/45*	*Nine Elms*
19.50 Dorchester	*H15 4-6-0*	*T*	*01/57*				*02/30*	*Nine Elms*
21.55 WEYMOUTH	LN 4-6-0	L	02.20				02.38	WATERLOO
17.00 Torrington	*MN 4-6-2*	*T*	*02/47*				*03/05*	*Nine Elms*
00.45 Eastleigh	*H15 4-6-0*	*L*	*02/52*				*03/33*	*Feltham*
00.50 Fratton	*S15 4-6-0*	*T*	*03/22*				*03/55*	*Feltham*
13.55 Meldon	*H15 4-6-0*	*L*	*04.16*				*05/05*	*Woking*
03.10 Bevois Park (S'ton)	*S15 4-6-0*	*L*	*05/04*				*05/50*	*Woking*
Engine and Brake	*0395 0-6-0*	*L*					*06.30*	*Brookwood*
	H15 4-6-0	L	06.37	06.47	06.53	07.00	07.07	Waterloo
04.40 Eastleigh	*H15 4-6-0*	*T*	*06/45*				*07/25*	*Feltham*
06.04 Southampton (T)	LN 4-6-0	L	07.11	07.20	07.26	07.33	07.40	Waterloo
21.30 Okehampton	*H15 4-6-0*	*T*	*07.10*				*08/10*	*Woking*
06.45 Salisbury	WC 4-6-2	L	08.02	08.11	08.17			(Waterloo)
07.03 SOUTHAMPTON DOCKS	LN 4-6-0	T	08.10				08/24	WATERLOO
(06.45 Salisbury)	WC 4-6-2			08.17	08.24	08.32		Waterloo
03.20 Bournemouth (C)	*S15 4-6-0*	*L*	*08/14*				*08/46*	*Feltham*
	N15 4-6-0	L	08.25	08.34	08.40	08.47	08.55	Waterloo
08.41 Basingstoke Up Yard	*N15X 4-6-0*	*L*	*08/43*	*08.57*				
06.35 Bournemouth (C)	N15X 4-6-0	L	09.02	09.11	09.17			(Waterloo)
07.20 BOURNEMOUTH WEST	WC 4-6-2	T	09/14				09/25	WATERLOO
(06.35 Bournemouth (C))	N15X 4-6-0	L			09.17	09.23	09.31	Waterloo
08.15 SALISBURY	MN 4-6-2	T	09.15				09/32	WATERLOO
17.21 Plymouth	*N15 4-6-0*	*L*	*09/20*				*09/52*	*Feltham*
08.41 Basingstoke	*N15X 4-6-0*	*L*		*09.48*	*09.55*			
07.10 Yeovil Town	N15 4-6-0	L	10.00	10.08	10.14	10.20	10.27	Waterloo
07.34 WEYMOUTH	WC 4-6-2	T	10/04				10/15	WATERLOO
07.30 EXETER (C)	MN 4-6-2	T	10/22				10/33	WATERLOO
	WC 4-6-2	L	10.35	10.44	10.50	10.56	11.03	Waterloo
08.41 Basingstoke	*N15X 4-6-0*	*L*			*11.10*	*11.18*		
08.35 BOURNEMOUTH WEST	WC 4-6-2	T	10.59				11/15	WATERLOO
06.30 EXETER (C)	MN 4-6-2	T	11.21				11/37	WATERLOO
Light engine	*0395 0-6-0*						*12.08*	*Woking*
09.20 WEYMOUTH	LN 4-6-0	T	12/02				12/14	WATERLOO
	N15 4-6-0	L	12.02	12.11	12.17	12.23	12.31	Waterloo
08.41 Basingstoke	*N15X 4-6-0*	*L*			*12.40*	*12.48*	-	
11.05 BOURNEMOUTH WEST	WC 4-6-2	L	13.20				13/36	WATERLOO
08.15 PLYMOUTH	MN 4-6-2	T	13/22				13/34	WATERLOO
	N15 4-6-0	L	13.33	13.42	13.48	13.55	14.02	Waterloo
13.48 West Yard	*H15 4-6-0*	*L*	*13/50*				*14/25*	*Feltham*
11.30 WEYMOUTH	WC 4-6-2	T	14/02				14/13	WATERLOO
13.00 Salisbury	S15 4-6-0	L	14.14	14.22	14.28	14.35	14.43	Waterloo
13.15 Eastleigh (Pcls)	*H15 4-6-0*	*L*	*14.40*	*14.50*	*14.55*	*15.00*	*15.20*	*Clapham Jcn*
Light Engine	*S15 4-6-0*	*L*	*14.45*				*15.23*	*-*
10.30 ILFRACOMBE	MN 4-6-2	T	14/54				15/04	WATERLOO
11.36 Bournemouth West	H15 4-6-0	L	15.01	15.10	15.16	15.23	15.31	Woking
13.05 BOURNEMOUTH WEST	MN 4-6-2	T	15.17				15/33	WATERLOO
13.20 Southampton Docks	*S15 4-6-0*	*L*	*15/25*				*16/00*	*Feltham*
13.25 WEYMOUTH	WC 4-6-2	T	16/02				16/14	WATERLOO
	S15 4-6-0	L					16.20	Woking
15.15 Salisbury	N15 4-6-0	L	16.15	16.24	16.29	16.36	16.42	Waterloo
15.05 BOURNEMOUTH WEST	MN 4-6-2	T	17.29				17/45	WATERLOO
16.05 Salisbury	LN 4-6-0	L	17.37	17.46	17.51	17.58	18.07	Waterloo
12.20 ILFRACOMBE	MN 4-6-2	T	17/39				17/51	WATERLOO
16.34 BOURNEMOUTH WEST	MN 4-6-2	T	18/04				18/15	WATERLOO
17.15 Salisbury	N15 4-6-0	L	18.37	18.46	18.52	18.59	19.06	Waterloo
16.20 Southampton Docks	*S15 4-6-0*	*L*	*18/47*				*19/23*	*Feltham*
17.05 BOURNEMOUTH WEST	LN 4-6-0	T	19.19				19/35	WATERLOO
14.20 ILFRACOMBE	MN 4-6-0	T	19.27				19/43	WATERLOO
	WC 4-6-2	L	19.40	19.49	19.55	20.06	20.13	Waterloo
17.35 WEYMOUTH	MN 4-6-2	T	20/03				20/15	WATERLOO
15.50 PLYMOUTH	MN 4-6-2	T	21.02				21/21	WATERLOO
18.55 Southampton Docks	*N15 4-6-0*	*T*	*21.08*				*21/40*	*Nine Elms*
	U 2-6-0	L	21.15	21.24	21.30	21.37	21.44	Woking
17.40 Yeovil Town (Milk)	*N15 4-6-0*	*L*	*21.42*				*22/08*	*Gravesend*
18.30 WEYMOUTH	WC 4-6-2	T	21.58				22/14	WATERLOO
19.45 Eastleigh (ECS)	*H15 4-6-0*	*T*	*22.01*				*22/26*	*Waterloo*
20.50 Salisbury	N15 4-6-0	L	22.08	22.17	22.23	22.30	22.37	Woking
22.25 Up Yard	*S15 4-6-0*	*L*	*22/27*				*23/00*	*Feltham*
21.15 Eastleigh	*S15 4-6-0*	*L*	*22.36*				*23/30*	*Feltham*
21.05 Templecombe (Milk)	*MN 4-6-2*	*T*	*23.12*				*23/33*	*Clapham Jcn*
19.55 Bournemouth West (Pcls)	*N15X 4-6-0*	*T*	*23.26*				*23/50*	*Waterloo*

Express services in bold print   Goods & Parcels trains in Italics   "/" = passing time

smouth (electric) and fifty-four minutes past for most stations to Basingstoke. (The Wessex expresses were further sub-divided in that those from Waterloo at thirty minutes past the even hour ran fast with no more than a couple of intermediate calls to Bournemouth before proceeding on to Weymouth whilst the other trains ran as semi-fasts and terminated at Bournemouth West. Even most of the day-time goods trains from Feltham joined the main line at thirty-nine minutes past the hour to fit in with the running of passenger trains.

In contrast to the tidiness of the timetable was the exceptional post-war variety of motive power which meant that one could observe a considerable number of successive trains, each of which had a different type of locomotive at its head.

Attempts to standardise motive power had been de rigeur for many years before the Bulleid regime tried - and failed - to run everything with his unmistakable products. Before the war the N15 (King Arthur) 4-6-0's could be seen at the head of almost every train of distinction between Folkestone in the east and Exeter in the west, whilst Drummond, Urie and Maunsell had all done their utmost to see that the line could be worked with the smallest number of classes possible yet, in the process, produced a range of motive power whose variety was unparalleled anywhere else in the country. The situation was compounded during the post-war years when 140 Bulleid Pacifics were added; a feature that was expected to herald the withdrawal of some of the older 4-6-0's. In fact the older engines not only continued in full-time employment but remained on some of the most important services until the dawning of the 1960's. The Merchant Navy and West Country Pacifics instead of diluting the variety simply served to increase it.

Goods traffic was less intense than that of over lines - the South Western had no collieries and therefore none of the trip working that made the NER, for instance, such an interesting system - but there was a respectable service of trains from Feltham, where traffic from other regions arrived on the LSWR, and Nine Elms where most of the London goods traffic was centred. In addition to the through trains from London, a considerable amount of goods arrived on the system at Basingstoke from Reading and the West Midlands.

The greater part of the through goods workings were handled by H15 and S15 4-6-0's although advantage was taken of the fast services from Nine Elms to return a number of unbalanced Merchant Navy Pacifics to their home sheds. King Arthur 4-6-0's were also to be found on goods trains whilst absent to a great degree was the large fleet of 2-6-0's whose appearances on the main line tended to be few and far between. 0-6-0 engines were similarly uncommon although a number of '700' class 0-6-0's could be found on local workings in the Salisbury and Basingstoke area's whilst a rather venerable '0395' 0-6-0 made a couple of appearances daily at Farnborough on local services from Woking.

From the motive power point of few, perhaps the most interesting services east of Salisbury were the stopping trains between Waterloo and Basingstoke which were entrusted to the N15x 4-6-4T rebuilds; engines which had once been the pride of the Brighton line but had been rebuilt into 4-6-0 tender engines when the LBSCR electrification of 1933 made them redundant. The rebuilds were supposed to have

Although Drummond produced one of the best 4-4-0 classes seen on the LSWR his attempts to emulate the Great Western Railways's success in developing the four-cylinder 4-6-0 were less successful and of the several classes built only the T14 class of 1911 achieved any sort of reputation for sustained performance although most of their existence was passed in the shadows of the N15 4-6-0's. After being rebuilt by Urie the ten T14's spent most of their lives working from Nine Elms providing power for relief West of England and Dorset services. Nine members of the class - one was destroyed during the war - survived nationalisation although all were withdrawn during the very early 1950's.

Train	Engine	SALISBURY	Porton	Idmiston	Grateley	A.JCN	H'bourne	W'church	Overton	Oakley	Destination
17.00 Torrington	MN 4-6-2	*01.40*				*02/15*				*02/35*	*Nine Elms*
13.55 Meldon	H15 4-6-0	*02.20*				*03/10*				*03/50*	*Woking*
17.21 Plymouth	N15 4-6-0	*04.35*				*05.40*				*06/21*	*Feltham*
21.30 Okehampton	H15 4-6-0	*04.55*			*05.45*	*06/00*				*06/37*	*Woking*
	700 0-6-0	06.10	06.25								*Bulford*
	WC 4-6-2	06.45	06.56	06.59	07.07	07.19	07.29	07.35	07.43	07.51	Waterloo
Workmans	M7 0-4-4T	07.20	07.31	07.35	07.43						
	MN 4-6-2	08.15				08.40		08.53		09/02	WATERLOO
07.10 Yeovil Town	N15 4-6-0	08.42	08.53	08.56	09.05	09.16	09.26	09.33	09.39	09.47	Waterloo
07.30 EXETER (C)	MN 4-6-2	**09.33**				**10.00**				**10/15**	**WATERLOO**
06.30 Exeter (C)	MN 4-6-2	10.01	10.12		10.22	10.35	10.46	10.52	11.00	11.07	Waterloo
Pick up	S15 4-6-0	*10.42*	*10.58*								
Pick up	S15 4-6-0		*11.39*		*11.55*						
Pick up	S15 4-6-0				*12.30*	*12.45*					
08.15 PLYMOUTH	MN 4-6-2	**12.34**				**13.00**				**13/15**	**WATERLOO**
Light Engine	U 2-6-0					*13.08*			*13.28*		
	S15 4-6-0	13.00	13.11	13.13	13.22	13.33	13.43	13.49	13.55	14.02	Waterloo
Pick up	S15 4-6-0					*13.43*			*14.10*		
Pick up	S15 4-6-0								*14.20*	*14/28*	*Basingstoke*
10.30 ILFRACOMBE	MN 4-6-2	**14.03**				**14/26**				**14/47**	**WATERLOO**
	S15 4-6-0	14.25				15/12				15/47	*Basingstoke*
	N15 4-6-0	15.15				15.41				16/00	WATERLOO
	U 2-6-0								16.33	16.51	*Basingstoke*
	LN 4-6-0	16.05	16.16	16.18	16.27	16.40	16.51	16.58	17.06	17.13	Waterloo
Light Engine	M7 0-4-4T	*16.35*			*16.55*						
12.20 ILFRACOMBE	MN 4-6-2	**16.51**				**17.17**				**17/32**	**WATERLOO**
16.35 Amesbury	700 0-6-0				*17.15*	*17.30*					
	N15 4-6-0	17.15	17.26	17.29	17.38	17.51	18.02	18.08	18.16	18.23	Waterloo
16.35 Amesbury	700 0-6-0					*18.00*				*18/38*	*Basingstoke*
14.20 ILFRACOMBE	MN 4-6-2	**18.33**				**18.59**				**19/16**	**WATERLOO**
Light engine	BR4 2-6-0	*19.30*				*20.05*					
15.50 PLYMOUTH	MN 4-6-2	**20.09**				**20.35**				**20/52**	**WATERLOO**
17.40 Yeovil Town (Milk)	N15 4-6-0	*20.37*				*21/06*				*21/27*	*Gravesend*
	N15 4-6-0	20.50	21.01	21.03	21.12	21.23	21.33	21.39	21.47	21.54	Woking
21.05 Templecombe (Milk)	MN 4-6-2	*22.05*				*22/38*				*22/55*	*Clapham Jcn*
17.18 Sidmouth Jcn (Milk)	N15 4-6-0	*22.40*				*23.16*				*23/39*	*Waterloo*
	H15 4-6-0	*22.50*				*23/40*				*00/28*	*Basingstoke*
12.45 Torrington	N15 4-6-0	*23.52*				*00/53*				*01/13*	*Nine Elms*

LSWR (1953) : UP SERVICES (SALISBURY : OAKLEY)

Express services in bold print. Goods & Parcels trains in Italics. "/" = passing time.

formed a sub-section of the successful King Arthur class but in fact never rose to the heights of performance that were the hallmark of the N15's.

Apart from its distinctive atmosphere, another difference between the Southern and the other regions was that it disliked the system of centralised management that had been generally accepted elsewhere. North of the Thames almost every section of main line was remotely scrutinised from strategic points, information regarding each trains progress being relayed currently to district controllers by telephone from stations and signal boxes with directions on train and traffic working being issued from each central point to the staff concerned.

None of the three northern systems used identical methods and the degree of control varied from district to district but there was never any doubt as to where the ultimate responsibility for decisions lay.

The Southern, on the other hand, had never used the traffic control system, as it was understood elsewhere, believing that it was an expensive form of duplication, and instead required its station masters and their inspectors to be au fait at all times with the running of trains and to be ready to respond to any problems before they became serious. During the second world war, because of the unique circumstances that it brought, the Southern introduced, for a short time, a control system but abandoned it shortly afterwards, putting in its place a small number of train supervision offices which were manned by clerical staff who lacked the authority of traffic controllers. Although spawned by the wartime control system the supervision offices were in reality a recognition of the use of telephones and enabled each headquarters office to receive statistical information concerning the running of trains rather more quickly than had been the case when information was sent in writing from each station.

A legacy from earlier times which survived for many years was the dictum of Sir Herbert Walker who exhorted his staff never to use the telephone if a letter could be written instead.

Over the years a myth has developed giving the impression that the South Western was the leading component of the Southern and that the other elements regarded it from the viewpoint of inferiority. This may have been true of the former SECR - who tended to look up to everybody - but in truth the prima donna of the Southern was the LBSCR, whose staff - especially in the higher echelons - saw themselves as something of a race apart. They operated the densest passenger service - all electric - of any line and made no bones about their disdain for anyone who worked outside a thirty mile radius of Three Bridges.

The South Western, however, had the consolation of being a long-distance railway and put up a good fight with the Great Western in terms of traffic to the West Country, especially as regards Exeter whose first day service to Paddington did not reach London until after midday, in contrast to the Southern whose 07.30 express reached Waterloo more than an hour earlier.

Although the Southern found it difficult to compete in terms of speed for Plymouth traffic, it more than matched Paddington in terms of frequency and, at the same time, ran an extraordinary variety of through coaches to its branches in Devon and North Cornwall; a feature that gave it an edge over the (usually faster) Great Western who usually required a change of trains en route.

(In fact the Southern ran so many through sections on its West of England trains that it had difficulty in deciding which was the main portion. In its timetables and circulars, down trains were usually described as going to Plymouth whilst up trains were usually referred to as coming from Ilfracombe.)

If there was one weakness in South Western operations, it lay in the lack of a decent night train to the west; an omission that was surprising given that the midnight from Paddington was so sought after it was often difficult to get a seat and one long suspected that a corresponding service from Waterloo would have spread the load more evenly.

As it was the 01.25 Waterloo - Plymouth was the only night train from Waterloo to the west country and even this operated primarily for the benefit of the newspaper trade although the fact never seemed to deter the heavy complement of passengers who turned up nightly, many of whom seemed to travel through to Plymouth. An ideal arrangement - perhaps a fantasy - would have been a sleeping car attached to the 22.30 Dorchester express as far as Eastleigh and the 01.45 Eastleigh to Yeovil to Salisbury where it could have been attached to the 01.25. A Plymouth car would have been filled ten times over whilst another to Padstow would have been an ideal way of travelling overnight to the West country. Objections on the grounds of demand (in the case of Padstow) were often countered with the example of the service between Kings Cross and Fort William but the proposal

SERVICES (1953) ROMSEY : SALISBURY									
Train	Route	Engine	ROMSEY	K. Jcn	D'bridge	Dean	A. Jcn	SALISBURY	Destination
00.20 Eastleigh	C. Ford	Q1 0-6-0	*00/45*	*00/53*			*01/19*	*01.45*	
01.55 Eastleigh	C. Ford	U 2-6-0	*02/10*	*02/14*			*02/26*	*02.36*	Yeovil Town
02.10 Bevois Park	C. Ford	S15 4-6-0	*02/47*	*02/55*			*03/23*	*03.58*	
03.58 Bevois Park	C. Ford	H15 4-6-0	*04/38*	*04/45*			*05/12*	*05.37*	
06.07 Eastleigh	C. Ford	M7 0-4-4T	06.23						
06.40 Eastleigh	C. Ford	L1 & M7	07.05						
	C. Ford	L1 4-4-0	07.30	07/40					Andover Jcn
07.30 Eastleigh	C. Ford	LM2 2-6-2T	07.44						
07.14 Broadstone		T9 4-4-0					08/09	08.19	
05.58 Portsmouth	Southampton	U 2-6-0	07.59	08/04	08.07	08.15	08/22	08.31	
07.56 Eastleigh	C. Ford	M7 0-4-4T	08.13	08/18					Andover Jcn
07.42 B'mouth (C)		2 x T9 4-4-0					09/01	09.10	
06.55 Portsmouth	Southampton	T9 4-4-0	08.32						
07.29 Portsmouth	C. Ford	H15 4-6-0	08.43	08/48	08.51	09.01	09/08	09.16	Bristol
08.33 Southampton (T)	C. Ford	T9 4-4-0	09.12	09/17					Andover Jcn
07.20 Chichester	C. Ford	S15 4-6-0	*09/15*	*09/23*			*09/49*	*10.29*	
09.03 PORTSMOUTH	Southampton	U 2-6-0	10.18	10.23			10/33	10.41	
10.10 Southampton (T)	Southampton	43xx 2-6-0	10.32	10/37					Cheltenham
09.33 PORTSMOUTH	Southampton	BR4 2-6-0	10.42	10/47			10/57	11.05	**CARDIFF**
10.04 B'mouth (W)		T9 4-4-0					11/28	11.37	
09.30 Eastleigh	C. Ford	BR4 2-6-0	*10/50*	*10/58*			*11/24*	*12.05*	
11.10 Eastleigh	C. Ford	M7 0-4-4T	11.25						
10.34 Portsmouth	Southampton	BR4 2-6-0	11.48	11/53	11.55	12.03	12/10	12.18	Bristol
10.23 Bevois Park	C. Ford	H15 4-6-0	*12/06*	*12/14*			*12/40*	*12.52*	
11.30 Bevois Park	C. Ford	43xx 2-6-0	*12/21*	*12/29*					Andover Jcn
12.00 Southampton (T)	C. Ford	M7 0-4-4T	12.35						
11.19 Portsmouth	Southampton	LM2 2-6-2T	12.47	12/52					Andover Jcn
11.00 BRIGHTON	Southampton	WC 4-6-2	13/08	13/12			13/22	13.31	**CARDIFF**
11.30 BRIGHTON	Southampton	WC 4-6-2	13/35	13/39			13/49	13.58	**PLYMOUTH**
12.24 Eastleigh	C. Ford	M7 0-4-4T	13.40						
13.03 Portsmouth	C. Ford	T9 4-4-0	14.05	14/10	14.12	14.20	14/27	14.35	
		45xx 2-6-2T	14.12	14/20					Andover Jcn
13.20 B'mouth (W)		T9 4-4-0					14/48	14.59	
15.14 Nursling	S'ton	T9 4-4-0	15.24						
14.33 Portsmouth	Southampton	U 2-6-0	15.36	15/41	15.44	15.52	15/59	16.08	Bristol
15.45 Portsmouth	C. Ford	T9 4-4-0	16.49						
16.36 Southampton (T)	Southampton	Manor 4-6-0	17.00	17/05					Cheltenham
17.16 Eastleigh	C. Ford	M7 0-4-4T	17.31						
14.20 Weymouth	C. Ford	T9 4-4-0	18.00	18/05					Andover Jcn
16.52 B'mouth (W)		T9 4-4-0					18/13	18.22	
16.45 Portsmouth	Southampton	U 2-6-0	18.17	18/22	18.25	18.33	18/40	18.49	
17.16 Fawley	C. Ford	T9 4-4-0	18.45						
17.45 PORTSMOUTH	Southampton	BR4 2-6-0	19.01	19/06			19/16	19.25	**CARDIFF**
		T9 4-4-0	19.07	19/12					Andover Jcn
19.20 Eastleigh	C. Ford	M7 0-4-4T	19.35						
19.04 S'ton Docks	Southampton	43xx 2-6-0	*20/09*	*20/18*					Andover Jcn
15.35 Wimborne		700 0-6-0					*20/20*	*20.37*	
18.50 Wimborne		700 0-6-0					*20/45*	*21.02*	
19.43 B'mouth (W)		T9 4-4-0					*21/01*	*21.10*	
19.17 Portsmouth	C. Ford	T9 4-4-0	20.45	20/50	20.53	21.01	21/08	21.17	
20.50 Eastleigh	C. Ford	Q1 0-6-0	*21/15*	*21/23*			*21/50*	*22.25*	
19.45 Portsmouth	Southampton	T9 4-4-0	21.24	21/29					Andover Jcn
21.44 Eastleigh	C. Ford	43xx 2-6-0	22.03	22/08	22.11	22.19	22/27	22.36	

Express services in bold print. Goods & Parcels trains in Italics "/" = passing time

The prewar SR mainline classes had been difficult to identify at a difference and matters did not change much with the Bulleid regime. Apart from the shape of the nameplate it was only the rather bulbous shape of the boiler cladding that distinguished between a Merchant Navy and one of the light Pacifics. To enthusiasts in the London area, the Exmouth Junction Merchant Navy's were the most welcome of the class since, even though through workings from Exeter had been introduced in 1950, only a very limited number were visible on any given day. The up Atlantic Coast Express was a booked Exmouth Junction turn and, if for no other reason, keenly observed as on September 6th 1956 aqt Fleet when 35002 'Union Castle' was the booked engine. 35002 was for many years an Exmouth Junction engine, remaining there - apart from a brief stay at Bournemouth during the Spring of 1954 - until May 1958 when, after rebuilding, it was transferred permanently to Bournemouth. Its final days, from November 1960, were spent at Nine Elms.

Stopping trains in the home counties were usually the preserve of nondescript 4-6-0 or 2-6-4T's, generally considered ten-a-penny. Connoisseurs of short train journeys were therefore more than normally grateful to the Southern who diagrammed 'namers' to most of their outer-suburban workings. N15 30457 'Sir Bedivere' pulls away from Fleet in September 1956 with the 12.54 Waterloo to Basingstoke.

UP TRAINS. WEEK-DAYS.	MX		MX		MXQ		MX		MXQ		MX		MO		MX		MO		MXQ	
			5.0 p.m. Torring-ton SX.		10.15 p.m. SXQ Millbrook.		Two Engines.		Engine.		12.50 a.m. Fratton.				3.35 a.m. Farnham.		4.15 a.m. Guildford Shed.			
	★		SF★								SF★		★						SF	
	arr.	dep.	arr.	dep.	arr.	dep.	arr.	dep.	arr.	dep.	arr.	dep.	arr.	dep.	arr.	dep.	arr.	dep.	arr.	dep.
	a.m.	a.m.	a.m.	a.m.	a.m.	a.m.	a.m.	a.m.	a.m.	a.m.	a.m.	a.m.	a.m.	a.m.	a.m.	a.m.	a.m.	a.m.	a.m.	a.m.
Salisbury West Yard	...	...	...	...	...	...	...	...	...	...										
Salisbury	...	1 35	1 32	1 40	...	...	...	...							...	...	...	...	...	...
Salisbury East Yard	...		...		...	...	...	...							...	...	...	...		
Tunnel Jc.	1	39	1	44	...	...	...	...							...	...	...	...		
Salisbury Milford	1	42	...	...	...	...	...	...							...	...	...	...		
Porton	...	...	...	...	...	...	...	...							...	...	...	...		
Amesbury Jc.	...	...	...	...	...	...	...	...							...	...	...	...		
Newton Tony Jc.	To		...	...	...	...	...	...							...	...	...	...		
Newton Tony	Eastleigh.		...	...	...	...	...	...							...	...	...	...		
Amesbury	...	...	...	...	...	...	...	...							...	...	...	...		
Bulford			...	...	...	...	...	...							...	...	...	...		
Grateley	...	...	...	...	...	...	...	...	...	...					...	...	...	...	...	...
Andover Jc.	...	...	2	15	...	...	...	...	...	...					...	...	...	...	...	...
Andover Town	...		...	...	...	...	...	...	...	...					...	...	...	...		
Hurstbourne	...	...	...	...	...	...	...	...	...	...					...	...	...	...		
Whitchurch North	...	...	...	...	...	...	...	...	...	...					...	...	...	...		
Overton	...	...	...	...	◄		...	...	...	...					...	...	...	...		
Oakley	...	...	...	...			...	...	...	...					...	...	...	...		
Southampton Docks Shunting Grd.	...	...	...	...	...	...	...	...	...	...	...	1 40	...		...	...	...	...	...	2 10
Sou'ton { Dk. Gates { Terminus	...	...	...	...	...	...	...	...	...	...	1	43	...		...	...	...	...	2	18
Northam Jc.	...	...			...	...	...	...	...	...	1	56	...		...	...	...	...	2	25
Bevois Park	...	...			...	...	...	...	...	...	...	...	...		...	...	...	...	...	30
St. Denys	...	...			...	...	...	...	...	...	...	...	...		...	...	...	...	2	30
Eastleigh	...	...			A	1 A40	...	...	...	...	1C53	2C 5	2	10	...		...	...	2	40
Eastleigh East Jc.	...	...			...	...	...	...	...	...					...		...	...		
Eastleigh Yard (Field)	...	...			1	45	...	...	...	...	2	12	...		...		...	...		
Allbrook	...	...			1	45	...	...	...	...					...		...	...		
Shawford	...	...			...	...	...	...	...	...					...		...	...		
Winchester City	...	...			...	...	...	...	...	...	2W29	2 36			...		...	...	3	5
Winchester Jc.	...	...			2	12	...	...	...	...	2	42	2	37	...		...	...	3	5
Wallers Ash Box	...	...			...	...	...	...	...	...	...	...	...		...		...	...	...	...
Weston Box	...	...			...	...	...	...	...	...					...		...	...		
Micheldever	...	...			...	...	...	...	...	...					...		...	...		
Worting Jc.	...	...	2	40 T	2	45L	...	...	...	...	3	14 T	3	10 L	...		...	...	3	35L
Basingstoke West Box	...	...	...	...	...	...	...	...	...	...	...	...	...		...		...	...	...	...
Basingstoke Up Yard	...	...			...	...	...	...	...	...					...		...	...	...	...
Basingstoke	...	...	2	47	2 57	3 10	...	...	...	...	3	22	3W18	3 26	...		...	...	3 45	3 53
Basingstoke East Box	...	...	...	...	...	...	...	...	...	...	...	...			...		...	...	...	...
Barton Mill Sidings	...	...	...	...	...	...	...	...	...	...					...		...	...		
Hook	...	...	...	...	To		...	...	...	...					...		...	...		
Winchfield	...	...	...	...	Reading		...	...	...	...					...		...	...		
Fleet	...	...	...	...	West Jct.		...	...	...	...					...		...	...		
Farnborough	...	...	...	...			...	...	...	...					...		...	...		
Sturt Lane Jc.	...	...	...	...			...	...	...	...					...		...	...		
Brookwood	...	...	...	...			...	...	...	...					4	7 L	...	...		
Woking Jc.	...	...	...	...			...	...	...	...					...		4	32 L	...	...
Woking Up Yard	...	...	...	...	...	...	T	3 45	L	3 55	4	7	4	19	4	19	...	...	4	44
Woking	...	...	3	20	...	...	T	3 45	L	3 55	4	7	4	19	4	19	...	...	4	44
Woking East	...	...	...	...	...	...	...	...	...	...	...	...	...	...	...		...	...	...	...
West Byfleet	...	...	...	...	...	...	...	...	...	...	4	16	4	32	4	32	...	...	4	57
Byfleet Jn.	...	...	...	...	...	...	...	...	...	...	4	16	4	32	4	32	...	...	4	57
Weybridge	...	...	...	...	...	...	...	...	4 15	4 20	...	...	...	...	...		...	...	...	...
Addlestone Jc.	...	...	...	...	...	...	...	...	4 22	4 24	4	19	4	35	4	35	...	...	5	0
Addlestone	...	...	...	...	...	...	...	...	...	...	...	...	...	...	...		...	...	...	...
Chertsey	...	...	...	...	...	...	...	...	...	...	4	27	...		...		...	...	5	15
Virginia Water	...	...	...	...	...	...	...	...	...	...	...	...	4	50	4	50	...	...	5	15
Egham	...	...	...	...	...	...	...	...	...	...	4	47	5	2	5	2	...	...	5	27
Staines Central	...	...	...	...	...	...	...	...	...	...	4	47	5	2	5	2	...	...	5	27
Ashford	...	...	...	...	...	...	...	...	...	...	5	1	5	14	5	14	...	...	5	39
Feltham "E" Box	...	...	...	...	...	...	...	...	...	...	5	1	5	14	5	14	...	...	5	39
Feltham Up Reception Sidings	...	...	...	...	...	...	...	...	...	...	5 3	...	5 17	...	5 17	...	...	...	5 42	...
Walton	...	...	...	...	...	...	...	...			...	...	...	...	...	...	...	...	...	...
Esher	...	...	...	...	...	...	...	...	To		...	...	...	...	...	...	...	...	...	...
Hampton Crt. Jc.	...	...	3	40	...	...	4	7 L	Salisbury.		...	...	...	...	...	...	...	...	...	...
Surbiton	...	...	...	...	...	...	4 10	G			...	...	...	...	...	...	4 55		...	...
Malden	...	...	...	...	...	...	...	...			...	...	...	...	...	...	...	...	...	...
Raynes Park	...	...	...	...	...	...	...	...	Not avail-		...	...	...	...	...	...	...	...	...	...
Wimbledon "C" Box	...	...	...	...	...	...	...	...	able on		...	...	...	...	...	...	...	...	...	...
Wimbledon West Yard	...	...	...	...	...	...	...	...	Saturdays		...	...	...	...	...	...	...	...	...	...
Wimbledon	...	...	...	...	...	...	...	...	13th June		...	...	...	...	...	...	...	...	...	...
Earlsfield	...	...	...	...	...	...	...	...	to		...	...	...	...	...	...	...	...	...	...
Clapham Jc.	...	...	3	55	...	...	...	...	19th Sept.		...	...	...	...	...	...	...	...	...	...
Queen's Road	...	...	3	58	...	...	...	...			...	...	...	...	...	...	...	...	...	...
Nine Elms "A" Box	...	...	4	3	...	...	...	...			...	...	...	...	...	...	...	...	...	...

A—No. 1 Up Goods Line.
C—No. 2 Up Goods Line.
G—For Freight shunting.

Goods services from Dorset and the west on their way to London during the early hours (1953).

9

met with no enthusiasm and nothing was ever done. To fall asleep at Micheldever and to awake at somewhere like Camelford would have been a journey for the imagination to conjure with.

Working on the South Western could be a happy experience - especially outside the larger cities - and it was the author's luck to be in charge of a section of it many years ago; an episode which gave him the best eighteen months of his railway career. One member of his staff was so wedded to the company that after a successful career on the footplate at Eastleigh ('no engine like a Nelson, guv'), he came back in retirement as a car park attendant whilst another who worked in a rural booking office would cheerfully take orders for tickets on the telephone and, his sense of service coming before the strictest interpretation of the accountancy regulations, deliver them on his bicycle.

Another of the stations was manned by ex-matelots with one of the inspectors having been a chief petty officer. At ten sharp each morning there would be a knock on the door followed by the entrance of the Inspector, saluting with his cap tucked under his arm.

"Permission to serve tea. Sir!"

"Carry on."

And, as per Monsignor's chocolate, six 'other ranks' would file in, one with a tray, another with a cup and so on…all for the 'guvnors' tea.

Most of the staff worked conscientiously to make things run smoothly but not everyone fully understood the facilities provided. A Travelling Ticket Inspector was waiting on a local station for a delayed Portsmouth bound train to arrive from Southampton and to while away the time sat on a seat chatting away to the porter. The warning bell, operated by the signalman, rang and the Inspector stood up, commenting that his train was aproaching.

"How do know the train's coming?" asked the porter in all innocence.

The Inspector gave him a long look and indicated the platform bell.

"Well I go to hell," said Paddy, "I've been at this station twenty years and never knew that's what that bell was for…."

To the public and the enthusiast however it was the trains and their engines that constituted the railway and to give an introduction to what follows in the succeeding chapters, the scheduled workings for each of the sections covered are given, showing the trains that ran and the engines that were booked to work them. Goods and parcels services are shown in italics and an oblique sign indicates a passing time. Although the workings are those for 1953, there was little change of significance to the workings during the decade and for the most part the only noticeable change was the replacement of a number of older engines, chiefly M7 0-4-4T's and N15 4-6-0's, by standard BR classes from 1955 onwards.

Of the sections dealt with in this book, the Farnborough - Basingstoke stretch was the busiest and had to accommodate not only the Wessex and West of England services but, in addition, the hourly outer-suburban stopping trains which left Waterloo at 54 minutes for Basingstoke (some being extended on to Salisbury). On top of the passenger services was a respectable volume of goods traffic from Feltham or Nine Elms to Southampton and the West Country, not all of which was able to run during the relatively quiet night hours.

The Oakley to Salisbury section illustrates the much lighter service west of Worting Junction and consists of the West of England trains together with the occasional Waterloo stopping train extended beyond Basingstoke. A particular point of interest lies in the number of King Arthur N15 4-6-0's that were still at work in relation to the use made of the Bulleid light Pacifics. A particularly interesting service was the daily sight of a Lord Nelson 4-6-0 on a Waterloo - Salisbury slow; the engine filling-in during a Bournemouth - Waterloo working. The Nelsons had at one time been the chosen instrument for the principal West of England expresses but had been supplanted by the Merchant Navy class to such an extent that the 4-6-0's were post-war stangers to the line west of Worting.

Connecting the two main lines of the South Western was the secondary line from Salisbury to Eastleigh and its branch from Romsey to Southampton. This route presented something of a dilemma for the timetable planners since the regular service of trains between Bristol and Portsmouth could be operated in shorter time if they were routed via Chandlers Ford and

Train	Locomotive	SALISBURY	A Jcn	Dean	D'bridge	K Jcn	ROMSEY	Route	Destination
	U 2-6-0	01.35	01/56			02/22	02/30	C. Ford	Eastleigh
	Q1 0-6-0	03.03	03/51			04/17	04/25	C. Ford	Chichester
	T9 4-4-0	03.52	03/56						Weymouth
	700 0-6-0	04.05	04/26						B'mouth (C)
	Q1 0-6-0	04.25	04/46			05/12	05/20	C. Ford	Eastleigh
	M7 0-4-4T						06.43	C. Ford	Eastleigh
06.45 Andover Jcn	T9 4-4-0	07.15	07/26						
	T9 4-4-0					07/26	07.30	Southampton	Portsmouth
	700 0-6-0	07.37	08/04						Wimborne
	LM2 2-6-2T						08.00	C. Ford	Weymouth
07.30 Andover Jcn	43xx 2-6-0					08/04	08.08		
	T9 4-4-0	07.47	07/57	08.03	08.11	08/12	08.16	Southampton	Portsmouth
	43xx 2-6-0						08.32	C. Ford	Portsmouth
	T9 4-4-0						08.52	Southampton	Portsmouth
04.10 Cheltenham	43xx 2-6-0					09/02	09/10	Southampton	S'ton Docks
	H15 4-6-0	08.45	09/06			09/32	09/40	C. Ford	Eastleigh
09.30 Andover Jcn	M7 0-4-4T					10/04	10.08	C. Ford	Eastleigh
	T9 4-4-0	09.25	09/36						B'mouth (W)
	U 2-6-0	09.47	09/58	10.00	10.12	10/13	10.17	Southampton	Portsmouth
	M7 0-4-4T						10.35	C. Ford	Eastleigh
08.10 Bristol	U 2-6-0	10.37	10/48	10.50	11.02	11/03	11.07	Southampton	Portsmouth
Light engine	M7 0-4-4T						11.35	C. Ford	Eastleigh
Pick up	H15 4-6-0	11.18	11/39	11.50					
11.25 Andover Jcn	T9 4-4-0					11/59	12.03	C. Ford	Eastleigh
	S15 4-6-0	11.27	11/48			12/14	12/22	C. Ford	Eastleigh
10.27 Bristol	BR4 2-6-0	12.44	12/54			13/02	13/06	Southampton	PORTSMOUTH
	M7 0-4-4T						13.15	Southampton	Portsmouth
	T9 4-4-0	12.58	13/10						B'mouth (W)
06.48 Cheltenham	45xx 2-6-2T					13/15	13.23		
	T9 4-4-0	13.06	13/17	13.20	13.30	13/32	13.36	C. Ford	Southampton (T)
10.11 Cheltenham	Manor 4-6-0					13/38	13.42	Southampton	Southampton (T)
10.30 CARDIFF	BR4 2-6-0	13.28	13/38			13/46	13.50	Southampton	PORTSMOUTH
Pick-up	H15 4-6-0			13.45	14.00				
	M7 0-4-4T						14.05	C. Ford	Eastleigh
12.14 Fullerton	T9 4-4-0					14/08	14.16		
	T9 4-4-0						14.35	S'ton	Nursling
11.00 PLYMOUTH	WC 4-6-2	14.55	15/05			15/13	15/17	Southampton	BRIGHTON
Pick-up	H15 4-6-0			15.10		15/17	15.25	C. Ford	Eastleigh
	43xx 2-6-0	15.07	15/28			15/54	16.02	Southampton	S'ton Docks
13.00 CARDIFF	WC 4-6-2	15.57	16/07			16/15	16/19	Southampton	BRIGHTON
16.12 Andover Jcn	LM2 2-6-2T					16/46	16.50		
	LM2 2-6-2T						17.03	C. Ford	Southampton (T)
	H15 4-6-0	16.18	16/39			17/05	17/13	C. Ford	Eastleigh
13.56 Cheltenham	43xx 2-6-0					17/18	17.22	Southampton	Southampton (T)
	T9 4-4-0	17.07	17/17	17.23	17.31	17/32	17.36	Southampton	Portsmouth
	T9 4-4-0	17.20	17/31						B'mouth (W)
	T9 & M7						17.50	C. Ford	Eastleigh
	T9 4-4-0						18.05	C. Ford	Eastleigh
18.40 Andover Jcn	L1 4-4-0					19/12	19.17		
16.32 Bristol	U 2-6-0	18.57	19/07	19.13	19.20	19/21	19.25	Southampton	Portsmouth
	L1 4-4-0						19.35	C. Ford	Eastleigh
ECS	M7 0-4-4T						19.50	C. Ford	Eastleigh
16.35 CARDIFF	U 2-6-0	19.45	19/55			20/04	20.08	Southampton	PORTSMOUTH
19.35 Andover Jcn	T9 4-4-0					20/14	20.18	C. Ford	Eastleigh
16.35 Exeter	S15 4-6-0	20.16	20/26	20.32	20.39	20/42	20.46	C. Ford	Portsmouth
	T9 4-4-0	20.22	20/33						B'mouth (C)
15.20 Cheltenham	BR4 2-6-0					21/52	22/00	C. Ford	Eastleigh
19.10 Bristol	S15 4-6-0	22.00	22/11	22.18	22.25	22/27	22.31	Southampton	Eastleigh
16.40 PLYMOUTH	BR4 2-6-0	23.10	23/21			23/31	23/35	C. Ford	EASTLEIGH

Goods & Parcels trains in Italics. "/" = passing time

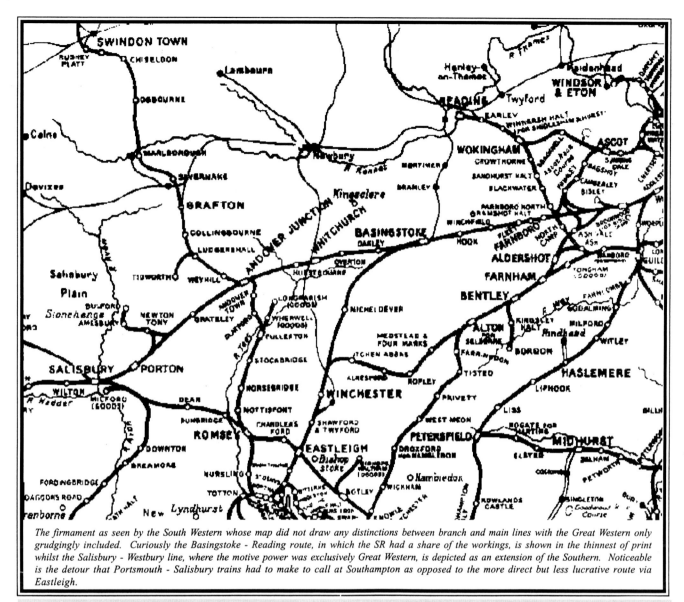

The firmament as seen by the South Western whose map did not draw any distinctions between branch and main lines with the Great Western only grudgingly included. Curiously the Basingstoke - Reading route, in which the SR had a share of the workings, is shown in the thinnest of print whilst the Salisbury - Westbury line, where the motive power was exclusively Great Western, is depicted as an extension of the Southern. Noticeable is the detour that Portsmouth - Salisbury trains had to make to call at Southampton as opposed to the more direct but less lucrative route via Eastleigh.

As the 1950's passed, the ranks of the 4-4-0 classes - not so long before the universal passenger locomotive - thinned dramatically, especially as the programme of BR standard types got into its stride. Paradoxically the Southern - in many respects the most modern of systems with its high proportion of electrification and 140 postwar Pacifics - provided the best chance in the country of seeing 4-4-0's in regular service and the T9 'Greyhounds' could be seen in large numbers on the Portsmouth - Southampton - Salisbury axis throughout the 1950s in spite of the arrival of Standard 2-6-0's and 'Hampshire' diesel multiple units. The scene above was taken in 1957 but could have been witnessed any time in the preceding sixty years. 30300 and a rake of LSWR coaches form the 11.19 Portsmouth & Southsea to Andover Junction at Stockbridge.

READING - BASINGSTOKE (1953)						
Train	Locomotive	RDG (W)	Mortimer	Bramley	B'STOKE	Destination
19.10 Victoria Basin	Hall 4-6-0	02/45			03/15	West Yard
03.15 Reading (Pcls)	61xx 2-6-2T	03/17			03.40S	
06.50 Reading	Hall 4-6-0	06.56	07.07	07.17	07.27S	Southampton (T)
07.58 Reading	61xx 2-6-2T	08.01	08.12	08.20	08.30W	
02.15 Oxley	43xx 2-6-0	08/07			08/47	West Yard
09.12 Reading	Hall 4-6-0	09.16	09.27	09.36	09.47S	Portsmouth
09.15 Reading West	28xx 2-8-0	09/19	10.06			
09.15 Reading West	28xx 2-8-0		10.15	10.25		
10.17 Reading	N15X 4-6-0	10.21	10.32	10.40	10.51W	
09.15 Reading West	28xx 2-8-0			10.52	11/08	West Yard
09.40 Moreton Sdgs	N15 4-6-0	10/29		11.10	11/25	West Yard
12.15 Reading	BR4 2-6-0	12.19	12.30	12.37	12.46S	Portsmouth
13.48 Reading	Hall 4-6-0	13.52	14.03	14.12	14.22S	Portsmouth
09.30 BIRKENHEAD	N15 4-6-0	14.58			15.24S	B'MOUTH (W)
15.10 Reading	61xx 2-6-2T	15.13	15.23	15.30	15.40W	
08.37 NEWCASTLE	LN 4-6-0	16.16			16.38S	B'MOUTH (W)
17.10 Reading	U 2-6-0	17.14	17.24	17.30	17.43S	Southampton (T)
17.50 Reading	61xx 2-6-2T	17.53	18.04	18.11	18.21W	
19.00 Reading	N15X 4-6-0	19.04	19.14	19.20	19.30S	Southampton (T)
Light engine	U 2-6-0	19/20			19.54W	
20.38 Reading	61xx 2-6-2T	20.42	20.52	21.00	21.10W	
21.17 Reading	Hall 4-6-0	21.21	21.31	21.37	21.47W	
Light engine	Hall 4-6-0	21/36			22.02W	
16.55 Worcester (Pcls)	Hall 4-6-0	21/55			22.20W	Eastleigh
22.05 Reading West	Hall 4-6-0	22/08			22/50	West Yard
23.00 Reading	BR4 2-6-0	23.03	23.13	23.19	23.29S	
S : Southern platforms. W : GWR platforms						

Eastleigh whilst the route via Southampton served a greater population but resulted in a longer journey.

No greater contrast with the Waterloo - Salisbury could be imagined and where one had a regular service of modern trains with the latest in motive power, the other was a haunt of pregrouping types with many of the through trains being worked by T9 4-4-0's and (until early 1953) a D15 4-4-0. Sharing the workings were a number of U class 2-6-0's and a handful of BR standard class 4 2-6-0's, newly allocated as a replacement for some of the older 4-4-0's.

With a little luck a D15 4-4-0 could be caught on a Portsmouth - Salisbury passenger although their last diagrammed duty, the 10.34 and 17.45 workings from Portsmouth, had been taken over by BR 4MT 2-6-0's in the summer of 1953.

The route was also the only part of the LSWR reviewed in this book which saw the ugly 'clockwork' Q1 0-6-0 engines, a couple from Guildford working through to Salisbury with goods trains from Chichester.

There were signs of a new order but these were slight enough to be regarded as novelties. A number of LMS Ivatt 2-6-2 tanks worked a handful of services between Eastleigh and Romsey and were complemented by the larger BR 3MT version which were making slow inroads into the workings on the M7 0-4-4 tanks.

Allied to the Romsey - Southampton section was the MSWR, and full details of the service and engine workings are given for the southern section of the line. Generally reckoned to be something of a backwater, it may come as a surprise to discover that a relatively heavy service of goods trains used the route which, as its promoters intended, provided a useful link between the west Midland area of the Midland Railway and Southampton docks. Motive power on the route was exclusively Great Western - 43xx 2-6-0's and 45xx 2-6-2T's - with a small number of locomotives being out-shedded at Andover Junction to handle early morning workings at the south end of the line.

Another line which saw an interestingly varied selection of motive power was the Great Western route from Basingstoke to Reading which, although dominated by GWR classes, saw a number of booked workings by SR locomotives.

Most of the trains on the line were worked by Halls 4-6-0's and 61xx tanks although the daily pick-up goods made an interesting spectacle as it wound its way up and down the branch behind a 28xx 2-8-0 from Reading MPD. The Halls were common enough on GW metals and little notice was taken of them but at Basingstoke they acquired a certain rarity status. Other regular visitors to the line were based at Wolverhampton, working through to Basingstoke from the west Midlands, and were not examples commonly found in the London area.

The two express services, the Bournemouth to Birkenhead and York trains, were worked by the Southern as were a minority of the stopping trains. Curiously Basingstoke only had a single duty on the line - a pair of local trains for which a Remembrance N15X 4-6-0 was provided - whilst two of the other locals were worked by 2-6-0's from Guildford shed. The most unusual engine on the line was the Nine Elms H15 4-6-0 which started its day with the 09.54 Waterloo - Eastleigh and later worked a late-night passenger from Basingstoke to Reading. The engine returned to London via the SECR branch with a working to Feltham.

The Great Western also ran into Salisbury and the route across to Westbury was wholly GWR in character with no foreign influence other than the fact that the GWR shed at Salisbury had been closed in 1950, the complement being transferred to the Southern MPD which also provided accommodation for the handful of Great Western engine which stabled between workings.

As usual on the Great Western the most familiar engines to be seen were the Hall 4-6-0's although there were four daily departures from Salisbury for which a pair of Castle and Star 4-6-0's were provided. The Stars at the time were fading fast, having been replaced on the main line by recent batches of Castles and Britannia Pacifics, and it was becoming increasingly difficult to find them on express passenger work. The Salisbury services did not, of course, allow much scope for sustained output but it did offer the facility for regularly seeing these historic machines at work in their twilight years.

BASINGSTOKE - READING (1953)						
Train	Locomotive	B'STOKE	Bramley	Mortimer	RDG (W)	Destination
	Hall 4-6-0	00.30N			01/12	Hinksey (Oxford)
	Hall 4-6-0	02.10N			02/40	Oxley (Wolves)
	Hall 4-6-0	04.30N			04/58	Crewe
05.10 West Yard	61xx 2-6-2T	05/13S			05/46	Woodford (GC)
	Hall 4-6-0	06.57W	07.08	07.15	07.24	Reading General
	N15 4-6-0	07.38W	07.47	07.54	08.03	Reading General
	N15X 4-6-0	08.24W	08.33	08.40	08.49	Reading General
08.20 Eastleigh	BR4 26-0	09.40S	09.49	09.56	10.05	Reading General
09.50 West Yard	61xx 2-6-2T	09/53S			10/34	Reading West Yard
10.13 Southampton (T)	Hall 4-6-0	11.22S	11.32	11.39	11.48	Reading General
09.20 B'MOUTH (W)	N15 4-6-0	11.35S			12.01	BIRKENHEAD
Pick up Goods	28xx 2-8-0	13.05N	13.19			
11.16 B'MOUTH (W)	LN 4-6-0	13.27S			13.54	YORK
12.31 Southampton (T)	U 2-6-0	13.45S	13.54	14.01	14.10	Reading General
Pick up Goods	28xx 2-8-0		14.05	14.25	15/08	Reading West Yard
	N15X 4-6-0	15.55W	16.05	16.12	16.21	Reading General
14.45 Portsmouth	Hall 4-6-0	16.45S	16.55	17.02	17.11	Reading General
ECS	61xx 2-6-2T	16.55W	17.05			
	61xx 2-6-2T		17.10	17.16	17.25	Reading General
	U 2-6-0	18.05W	18.15	18.23	18.32	Reading General
17.17 Portsmouth	BR4 2-6-0	19.40W	19.49	19.56	20.05	Reading General
	61xx 2-6-2T	19.55N			20/35	Scours Lane
18.35 Bournemouth (W)	H15 4-6-0	21.20S	21.29	21.36	21.45	Reading General
	43xx 2-6-0	21.45N			22/13	Oxley (Wolves)
	61xx 2-6-2T	22.35W	22.44	22.51	23/01	Reading General
21.45 Eastleigh (Pcls)	Hall 4-6-0	23.40S			00.06	Crewe
19.48 Weymouth	Hall 4-6-0	23.55S	00.04		00.18	Reading General
W : GWR platforms ; S : SR platforms. N : North Yard						

Train	Locomotive	W'BURY	Dilton	W'minster	Hey'bury	Codford	Wylye	Wishford	Wilton	SARUM	Destination
					WESTBURY : SALISBURY (1953)						
22.00 Avonmouth	43xx 2-6-0	02.45AB		03.09DB						04/25	East Yard
19.45 Bassaleg	28xx 2-8-0	03.45AB		04.09DB						05/40	East Yard
01.00 Cardiff	Hall 4-6-0	06.20AB		06.39DB						08/05	East Yard
05.25 Swindon	Hall 4-6-0	07.02	07.25	07.41	07.50	07.56	08.04	08.13	08.19	08.25	
Pick up	43xx 2-6-0	07.35		07.56							
21.15 Aberdare	Hall 4-6-0	07.55		08/15						09/40	East Yard
Pick up	43xx 2-6-0			08.45	09.15						
Pick up	43xx 2-6-0				09.35	09.43					
08.06 Devises	P&P	08.46	08.51	08.59							
02.35 Radyr	72xx 2-8-2T	09.00		09/20				10.00			
08.10 Bristol	Star 4-6-0	09.29	09.34	09.45	09.53	09.59	10.07	10.16	10.22	10.27	Portsmouth
02.35 Radyr	72xx 2-8-2T								10.27	10/55	East Yard
Pick up	43xx 2-6-0					10.09	10.23				
Pick up	43xx 2-6-0						10.35	10.49			
Pick up	43xx 2-6-0							11.02	11.10		
Pick up	43xx 2-6-0								11.25	12/20	East Yard
10.27 Bristol	Hall 4-6-0	11.47	11.52	12.02	12.09	12.14	12.20	12.28		12.37	Portsmouth
06.45 S.T. Jcn	72xx 2-8-2T	11.55		12/15						13.11	East Yard
10.30 Cardiff	Castle 4-6-0	12.41		12.56						13.32	Portsmouth
10.55 Bristol	Hall 4-6-0	14.15		14/35						15.36	East Yard
Pick up		14.30		14.50	15.08	15.18					
13.00 Cardiff	Castle 4-6-0	15.08		15.22						15.47	Brighton
15.40 Bradford		16.01	16.06	16.16	16.23	16.29	16.37	16.46	16.51	16.56	Portsmouth
16.10 Trowbridge	P&P	16.20	16.25	16.34							
16.32 Bristol	Hall 4-6-0	17.56	17.51	18.04	18.12	18.18	18.26	18.35	18.40	18.45	Portsmouth
16.35 Cardiff	Hall 4-6-0	18.53		19.07						19.37	Portsmouth
19.10 Bristol	Hall 4-6-0	20.38	20.43	20.56	21.04	21.10	21.18	21.27	21.32	21.38	Eastleigh
16.10 S.T. Jcn	72xx 2-8-2T	21.20AB		21.44DB	22.08						
20.45 Bristol	Star 4-6-0	21.56		22.11						22.41	
16.10 S.T. Jcn	72xx 2-8-2T					22.35				23.20	Fisherton
21.50 Bristol	Grange 4-6-0	22.55AB		23.14DB						00/20	East Yard
			AB : Attach banking engine. DB : Detach banking engine.								

Together with the train service, which is liberally tabulated and illustrated, the engine workings (or diagrams) for every engine that worked into the district are given in full. These diagrams were the single most important element of the operating world since they represented the easiest way of ordering the hundreds of engines and sets of men that ran the service. The general practice was for senior operating staff to annotate their working timetables with the engine diagrams for each train, giving an easy reference to the key components for each working. Thus if the 17.50 goods from Bevois Park to Basingstoke, for example, suffered a delay of, say, ninety minutes it was a simple matter to consult the working timetable which would show the train being worked by No. 68 engine,

a Nine Elms H15 4-6-0, and that the engines' next working was the 21.20 Basingstoke to Reading passenger with a break of only 62 minutes at Basingstoke. The diagrams also showed the men who manned each engine, in this case, a Reading (GW) set who travelled out to Basingstoke and relieved the H15 on arrival. In this instance, because a delay of 30 minutes could not be countenanced, Basingstoke MPD would be asked to turn out another engine for the 21.20 Reading and the rest of the diagram, whilst arrangements would have to be made to work the late running H15 later in the night to a suitable point where it could get back into its diagram and release the substituted Basingstoke engine.

It was the practise on the Southern for engines to display their diagram number on one of

the directional discs in order to simplify the matter of identifying light engines as they ran from the shed to pick up their trains. Given the large number of engines that ran light from Nine Elms to Waterloo, a single identifying number was very useful and prevented much of the confusion that existed, for example, on the Great Northern where engines running light from Hornsey to Kings Cross were often stopped several times by signalmen who could not always be sure what each engine for for. (It is surprising how many light engines ended up in the wrong place simply because signalmen were unsure of their destination). The diagram numbers were also useful in identifying trains at places such as Eastleigh and Basingstoke where two otherwise identical trains often stood side by side, heading in the same direction. A quick glance at the engine workings was all that was needed to distinguish one from the other.

Thus it is hoped that this book and the series it commences gives the most detailed operating scenario yet produced about the LSWR. To add a new dimension to railway matters, interspersed in the pages are examples of actual running performances by the various classes that operated the line with the difference that drawbar outputs have been included in the tabulations together with a horsepower weighting which reconciles the effect that speed has on output.

An examination of the schedule tables, particularly those of the Farnborough - Worting section, reveals the remarkably small proportion of trains which were booked to be worked by light Pacifics; the engines being generally confined to a handful of Wessex workings with very few of the class operating between Basingstoke and Salisbury and beyond to Exeter. This begs the question why, with 110 of the class on its books, so many trains remained in the hands of older machines such as the King Arthur 4-6-0's and Lord Nelsons.

The answer lies in the appalling maintenance difficulties that the class presented - for some reason the larger Merchant Navy locomotives were either immune from the same difficulties or received especial mechanical attention - which deterred the authorities from maximising the utility of the engines and thus kept in main line employment a large number of locomotives which, by general standards, should have been put out to grass. (Matters reached such a state at one depot that LBSCR Atlantics had to be resurrected for an express service as late in the day as 1956).

The Bulleid Pacifics continue to have an enthusiastic following but - from the managerial perspective - perhaps one is entitled to ask whether or not a class of engine with suffers under utilisation for ten years and then has to be expensively rebuilt is the success that some would claim. Had the original engines been conventional in appearance one suspects that the affection the class has generated, especially amongst those who knew them from a distance, might have been a little muted. It is not the first time that appearances have interfered with judgement - many a marriage has been proposed on similar grounds - and one recalls, as a parallel, the wild enthusiasm that was created by the Duplex 4-4-4-4 locomotives of the Pennsylvania RR. The adoration continues but for the other side of the coin, the comments of those who had to maintain and operate them can be quite colourful.

Train	Locomotive	SARUM	Wilton	Wishford	Wylye	Codford	H'bury	W'minster	D. Marsh	WESTBURY	Destination
					SALISBURY - WESTBURY (1953)						
	72xx 2-8-2T	01.10						02.15		02.29	S.T. Jcn
	Star 4-6-0	02.55						03.27		03.35	Bristol
	Grange 4-6-0	03.10						04.06		04.14	Avonmouth
	43xx 2-6-0	03.30						04.35		04.49	Avonmouth
	Hall 4-6-0	07.25	07.32	07.38	07.47	07.56	08.02	08.15	08.22	08.25	Bristol
	P&P							09.04	09.11	09.14	Devizes
07.29 Portsmouth	Hall 4-6-0	09.34	09.41	09.47	09.55	10.04	10.16	10.19	10.29	10.30	Bristol
09.33 PORTSMOUTH	Hall 4-6-0	11.17						11.52		12.00	CARDIFF
10.34 Portsmouth	Star 4-6-0	12.45	12.52	12.58	13.06	13.14	13.20	13.32	13.39	13.42	Bristol
10.23 Bevois Park	72xx 2-8-2T	13.08						14.05		14.20	Rogerstone
11.00 BRIGHTON	Hall 4-6-0	13.52						14.26		14.34	CARDIFF
pick up							15.30	15.42			
14.33 PORTSMOUTH	Castle 4-6-0	16.20						16.54	17.00	17.03	BRISTOL
	28xx 2-8-0	16.35				17.16					
ECS	P&P							17.05		17.15	
	Hall 4-6-0	17.02	17.09	17.15	17.23	17.31	17.37	17.48	17.55	17.58	Cardiff
16.35 Salisbury	28xx 2-8-0					17.40		18.04		18.18	S. T. Jcn
Pick up							18.30			18.51	
	43xx 2-6-0	18.00	18.09								
18.00 Salisbury	43xx 2-6-0			18.27	18.49						
18.00 Salisbury	43xx 2-6-0				18.59	19.13					
17.45 PORTSMOUTH	Castle 4-6-0	19.38						20.12		20.20	CARDIFF
18.00 Salisbury	43xx 2-6-0					20.13		20.36			
	Hall 4-6-0	20.15	20.22	20.28	20.37	20.45	20.51	21.00	21.07	21.10	Cardiff
18.00 Salisbury	43xx 2-6-0							21.10		21.32	
	Hall 4-6-0	23.15						00.25		00.34	Aberdare

MOTIVE POWER

Although the original Urie N15 4-6-0's were modified to conform with the Maunsell locomotives of 1925, the performance of the earlier engines never quite approached that of the later locomotives and a number of palliatives were attempted in order to rectify matters, one such being the fitting of five Urie engines with multiple jet blastpipes. The experiment did not extend to the other fifteen locomotives of the batch but was useful to enthusiasts since the wide diameter chimney allowed an additional means of identifying some of the original engines at a glance. 30736 'Excalibur' with its wide chimney and steam pipe casing peeping out from underneath the smoke deflector, rests at Eastleigh MPD in 1954.
The N15 class did not end with the Urie/Maunsell machines but were increased in number by the addition of thirty additional engines in 1925, built by the North British Co. in Glasgow and known as the 'Scotch Arthurs' together with a further fourteen in 1926 constructed at the company's works in Eastleigh.

In spite of its status as a passenger railway - goods traffic accounted for only about one third of its revenue - the South Western seemed to be plagued with difficulties in its attempts to design a successful six-coupled express passenger locomotive and even though a start was made under Drummond during the early years of the century, it was not until several years after the grouping that any lasting success was achieved and, even then, few successive designs could claim to be free from controversy.

Part of the problem stemmed from a lack of appreciation of the advances that had been achieved at Swindon - not that the LSWR was alone in failing to fully understand the advantages of long-lap valve events and superheating - together with an obsession for fire-tube boilers and four cylinder drives. Fortunately the contemporary four-coupled locomotives had been solidly built on traditional principles and were sufficiently powerful and fast to maintain the timetable for the time being.

To compound matters, Drummond was a character whose length of service, experience and reputation made it difficult for any effective dissension to be voiced and remedial engineering had to wait until 1912 when Urie succeeded to the post on Drummond's death.

The final decade of Drummonds period of office was, in some ways, a testing time for the LSWR since the general acceptance of bogie coaches had considerably increased the weight of trains whilst, in 1906, the Great Western had reduced the distance between Paddington and Exeter by twenty miles and, at a stroke, greatly

narrowed the competitive relationship between the two companies.

Urie was immediately faced with the dual charge of transforming Drummond's experiments and reappraising the line's motive power requirements in order to bring the fleet up to the condition necessary to meet the changed circumstances that had arrived during the Edwardian years. These in themselves were daunting responsibilities yet within two years of taking office the far heavier burden of producing locomotives equal to the war effort added to Urie's problems.

It became clear from early in his reign that Urie had little time for his predecessor's love of

Right: The big one. The diagram for the engine of the Atlantic Coast Express which in railway parlance was referred to as simply 'number five'. It is interesting to note that after working the heaviest duty on the line - the ACE was in a class of its own in every sense - the Pacific returned to London by taking over a stopping train from Padstow as far as Templecombe, finishing the working on a milk train to Clapham Junction. The 00.30 QV service from Clapham Junction to Nine Elms ran when required if any goods traffic was on hand which had not been dealt with by any other working. Having no night trains the SR was unable to work all its Exeter link engines on express trains throughout and hence several Merchant Navy Pacifics returned to their home stations on whatever service happened to be available.

Despite the Bulleid programme of Pacifics, the archtypal Southern express passenger locomotive in the eyes of most SR enthusiasts (and railwaymen) was the N15 King Arthur 4-6-0: a simple and rugged two cylinder machine which was both reliable and capable of astonishing performances. This state of affairs was not reached without difficulty and the N15 design evolved over a considerable period of time starting with the rather sluggish N15 4-6-0's of 1918 which were not a significant advance on the 4-4-0 classes which had been produced at the turn of the century. In 1925 ten of the Drummond 4-cylinder G14 locomotives were completely rebuilt as two-cylinder locomotives incorporating many recent developments in design whilst at the same time the twenty original N15's were similarly modified; the two batches of engine being absorbed into the same, N15, classification. Notwithstanding their very different origins the two components of the class were difficult to distinguish visually from each other, the most obvious sign being the bulbous steam piping of the original Urie 4-6-0's.

The subtle difference in appearance can be seen in the two illustrations, the upper view showing one of the 1925 Maunsell series, 30454 'Queen Guinevere' as it waits to leave Salisbury in 1952 with the 17.15 stopping train for Waterloo. The lower view pictures one of the original Urie engines, 30740 'Merlin', at Eastleigh in 1954 with the 17.27 to Portsmouth & Southsea.

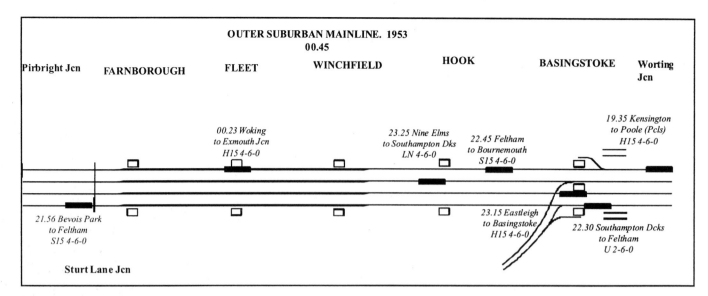

OUTER SUBURBAN MAINLINE. 1953
00.45

Pirbright Jcn   FARNBOROUGH   FLEET   WINCHFIELD   HOOK   BASINGSTOKE   Worting Jcn

00.23 Woking
to Exmouth Jcn
H15 4-6-0

23.25 Nine Elms
to Southampton Dks
LN 4-6-0

22.45 Feltham
to Bournemouth
S15 4-6-0

19.35 Kensington
to Poole (Pcls)
H15 4-6-0

21.56 Bevois Park
to Feltham
S15 4-6-0

23.15 Eastleigh
to Basingstoke
H15 4-6-0

22.30 Southampton Dcks
to Feltham
U 2-6-0

Sturt Lane Jcn

---

experiment and in 1914, on the eve of war, one of the Drummond 4-cylinder 4-6-0's appeared from Eastleigh rebuilt as a two-cylinder mixed traffic locomotive - the first of the H15 class - followed shortly afterwards by seven similar engines to Urie's own design. What, perhaps, was especially significant about the H15 4-6-0's was the fact that they set the trend of design for successive main-line classes and heralded the element of standardisation for which the Southern in later years became well known.

These new locomotives, which possessed the blessings of mechanical simplicity and good steaming characteristics, took some of the weight from the shoulders of the '0395' and '700' class goods 0-6-0's but were not numerous enough to cope with the requirements of war-time passenger traffic, for which Urie had to content himself with the hurried superheating of the engines he had inherited until matters reached such a pass that authority was finally given to proceed with a six-coupled express locomotive.

As it happened the war ended before the new class could make any impression but, similar in detail to the H15 class of 1914, the N15 engines of 1918, for all their early weaknesses, were the cornerstone of SR express motive power and held their place as the principal choice for express passenger working for almost thirty years.

Twenty of these 4-6-0's, sufficient for most of the Exeter and Dorset services, were produced but in spite of their design simplicity, they did not steam well and the Drummond T14 4-6-0's - the best of Drummond's large engines although much modified by Urie - remained in the foreground for some years to come.

Whilst the LSWR had invested considerably in the resignalling and quadrupling of the line between Waterloo and Basingstoke during the

PRINCIPAL LOCOMOTIVE
DEVELOPMENTS (LSWR)

Date	Detail
1913	Rebuilding of C14 0-4-0T
1914	Rebuilding of Drummond 4-6-0 to H1
	New H15 4-6-0
1915	D15 4-4-0 Superheated
	L12 4-4-0 rebuilt
	T14 4-6-0 rebuilt
1918	New N15 4-6-0
1920	S11 4-4-0 superheated
	700 class 0-6-0 superheated
	New S15 4-6-0
1921	New G16 4-8-0T
	New H16 4-6-2T
1922	T9 4-4-0 rebuilt
1924	Additional H15 locomotives
1925	Additional N15 locomotives
1926	New LN 4-6-0
1927	Additional S15 locomotives
1928	2-6-0 moguls from 2-6-4T
1929	New Z 0-8-0T
1930	New V 4-4-0
1931	New W 2-6-4T
1934	N15X from LBSCR 4-6-4T
1938	New Q 0-6-0
1941	New MN 4-6-2
1942	New Q1 0-6-0
1945	New WC 4-6-2
1948	New Leader (aborted)
1956	Pacific rebuilding started

early years of the century, little had been done to improve upon methods of handling goods services; an omission brought to light during the war when the increase in goods traffic - especially that from other companies - all but saturated the localised exchange sidings which tended to be situated in and around the Clapham Junction area.

The company battled on as best it could during the war and the lessons learnt solidified in the form of a scheme for the for the centralisation of cross-London traffic which in 1922 materialised as the hump marshalling yard at Feltham which not only directed the flow of traffic into one single location but also relieved the main lines in the London area of the congestion that had been caused by the earlier method of working.

In anticipation of this development Urie was instructed to produce motive power to serve the new arrangements and in 1920/1 introduced three new types of locomotive: the G16 4-8-0T and H16 4-6-2T for shunting the humps at Feltham and working cross-London trips respectively plus the S15 main line goods 4-6-0 which was based at Feltham to work the new timetable of long distance express freights to Salisbury and Wessex. To complement these designs Urie also increased the number of H15 4-6-0's and had the '700' 0-6-0 tender engines superheated.

Commentators of the LSWR have generally painted Urie's term of office in rather grey colours, seeing his decade in office as a rather dull interregnum between the strident days of Drummond and Maunsell; observations based more on the small number of new express passenger engines that appeared during the period rather than an appreciation of the prevailing difficulties of the time. What tends to be overlooked is

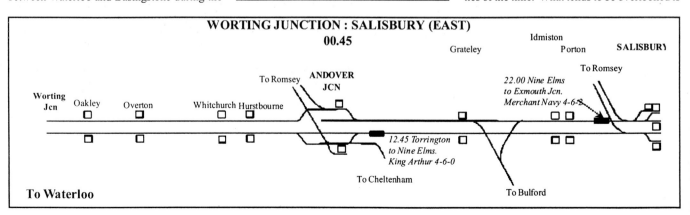

WORTING JUNCTION : SALISBURY (EAST)
00.45

Worting Jcn   Oakley   Overton   Whitchurch   Hurstbourne   ANDOVER JCN   Grateley   Idmiston   Porton   SALISBURY

To Romsey

To Romsey

22.00 Nine Elms
to Exmouth Jcn.
Merchant Navy 4-6-2

12.45 Torrington
to Nine Elms.
King Arthur 4-6-0

To Cheltenham

To Bulford

To Waterloo

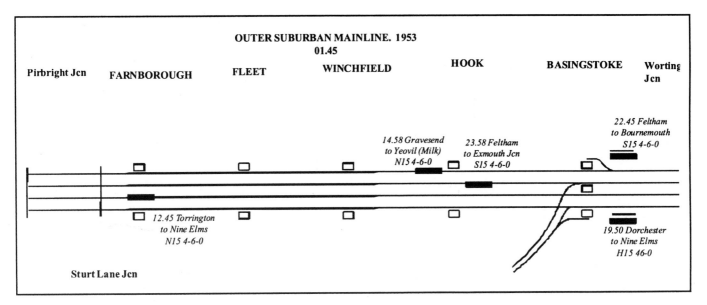

OUTER SUBURBAN MAINLINE. 1953
01.45

Pirbright Jcn   **FARNBOROUGH**   **FLEET**   **WINCHFIELD**   **HOOK**   **BASINGSTOKE**   Worting Jcn

22.45 Feltham
to Bournemouth
S15 4-6-0

14.58 Gravesend
to Yeovil (Milk)
N15 4-6-0

23.58 Feltham
to Exmouth Jcn
S15 4-6-0

12.45 Torrington
to Nine Elms
N15 4-6-0

19.50 Dorchester
to Nine Elms
H15 46-0

Sturt Lane Jcn

---

the fact that as Chief Mechanical Engineer, Urie by adopting a policy of simple but rugged two-cylinder locomotives, bequeathed to the Southern Railway the basis of a successful formula which remained in force for more than twenty-five years.

On the other hand what was unfortunate about the Urie period was that the circumstances of the day prevented him from having the luxury of being able to utilise the technical lessons learned by the Great Western Railway during the first decade of the century and had it not been for the Great War it is more than likely that the benefits of long-lap travel and high pressure systems would have been applied at Eastleigh considerably earlier than was the case.

As it was such developments had to wait until the arrival of the Southern Railway, who brought with it the Chief Mechanical Engineer of the SECR Richard Maunsell.

The fact that he had the LSWR in his dominion must have come as a breath of fresh air to Maunsell who, for ten years, had been constrained by axle-weight restrictions from giving the difficult SECR the power it needed for its express services between London and the Kent Coast. No such limitations applied to the main routes of the South Western yet the greater part of its express passenger fleet was dated by any reckoning and required attention so urgently that little time for innovative design was available.

D15 4-4-0. 30464. 7:225/245 tons . (1953)						
m.ch	Point	l/in	W.T.T.	Actual	mph	dbhp	pc
0.00	WATERLOO			0.00	0.00	-	- -
					pwc		
7.19	Wimbledon	2176		12.25	55.0	405	1
13.27	Hampton Court Jcn	-4205	18.00	19.10	63.5	332	2
19.12	Weybridge	2348		24.36	66.5	460	3
24.27	WOKING	676	30.00	29.32	58.5	347	2
				Signals			
33.17	Farnborough	467		40.57	64.0	424	2
36.38	Fleet	2852		44.02	64.0	381	2
					pwc		
42.13	Hook	789		50.49	53.0	199	1
47.60	BASINGSTOKE	684	54.00	59.26	52.0	237	1
50.23	Worting Jcn	260	57.00	62.15	58.0	866	5
52.31	Oakleigh	734		64.35	56.0	311	2
61.07	Hurstbourne	-429		72.45	69.0	-	-
66.19	ANDOVER JCN	-401	73.00	77.04	75.0	238	2
72.49	Grateley	275		83.03	55.0	451	3
78.19	Porton	-571		88.30	65.0	290	2
83.43	SALISBURY	-216	91.00	95.37	-	- -	

Hook - Porton. 36 miles 1/4999. 57 mph : 327 dbhp (pc 2)

Apart from occasional summer-Saturday turns on the London - Lymington Pier trains, by the 1950's the sight of a D15 on an express working had become a memory. In 1953, however, a seven coach enthusiasts special was run behind 30464 with Driver Hooker - of the exchange trials - at the regulator. Although beset with delays en route (plus an eight minute late start) the 4-4-0 succeeded in running to Salisbury in a net time of 90 minutes and the run generally emulated the circumstances of Edwardian times. The power outputs, however, make an interesting contrast with those of the 4-6-0's which took over from the grouping.

It has to be remembered that formation of the Southern Railway ushered in a new period of dynamic aims and that the weight of trains, if not their speeds, was considerably greater in

1924 than it had been a decade earlier. It was difficult to see how the ambitions of the new system were going to be met with engines that were all but obsolete and therefore, rather than experiment with three or four cylinder designs as he might otherwise have done, Maunsell contented himself with a simple two-cylinder 4-6-0, based to some extent on the Urie design of 1918 but incorporating the technical benefits attributed to Swindon.

The result was the N15 King Arthur class of 1925 which was not only highly successful for South Western purposes but quickly spread to the other constituent parts of the Southern Railway, giving the company possession of the first truly standard express passenger locomotive to be introduced onto a British system. The principals embodied in the Maunsell N15 design were simultaneously incorporated into the H15 and S15 goods engines - the former including a number of Drummond 4-6-0's - with the result that within a few years of the grouping the '15' family of classes not only handled most of the South Western's principal passenger and goods trains but enthusiasts on the line found their powers of observation were being tried to the limit since it was not at all easy to distinguish one type from another at any sort of distance.

Incorporated into the Maunsell 4-6-0's were the earlier Urie locomotives although even

---

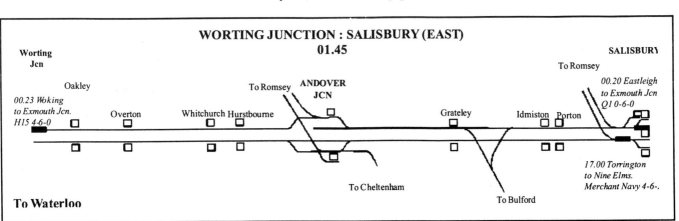

WORTING JUNCTION : SALISBURY (EAST)
01.45

Worting Jcn   Oakley   Overton   Whitchurch   Hurstbourne   **ANDOVER JCN**   Grateley   Idmiston   Porton   **SALISBURY**

To Romsey

To Romsey

00.20 Eastleigh
to Exmouth Jcn
Q1 0-6-0

00.23 Woking
to Exmouth Jcn.
H15 4-6-0

17.00 Torrington
to Nine Elms.
Merchant Navy 4-6-.

To Cheltenham

To Bulford

To Waterloo

For reasons that have never been satisfactorily resolved, the Southern appeared to show the greatest reluctance to roster its Bulleid light Pacifics, preferring to keep King Arthur, Lord Nelson and even H15 and S15 locomotives on main line passenger services even though 110 of the newer engines had been delivered. It was not until the rebuilding programme of 1957 was well under way that the Pacifics started to make serious inroads into the ranks of older types although even in the final days of steam a considerable amount of passenger working was carried out by BR 5MT 4-6-0's. Unrebuilt light Pacific 34102 'Lapford' arrives in Basingstoke with the 09.30 Birkenhead - Bournemouth (West) in 1961, the working only recently having been taken over from King Arthur N15 4-6-0's.

Although publicised - not unsuccessfully - by the Southern Railway as being the last word in express passenger engines, the sixteen Lord Nelson 4-6-0's were rather a disappointing class which in spite of numerous attempts at improvement, never rose to the distinction expected of them. Originally divided between the South-Western and the Eastern Divisions - they saw service on the Continental expresses from Victoria in prewar days - they were found a niche in the 1950's on the Southampton boat trains; a large batch being based at Eastleigh for the purpose. They were also regular performers on the Wessex night mails whilst non-nocturnal enthusiasts could usually track them to earth on the 10.54 and 11.30 departures from Waterloo to Bournemouth and Salisbury respectively. 30854 'Howard of Effingham' is hauled from Eastleigh works by E4 0-6-2T 35279

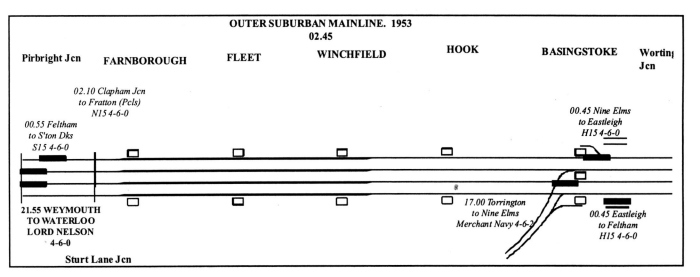

after rebuilding the 1918 King Arthurs never steamed as freely as the later engines.

Not all Maunsell's efforts were crowned with success and the latter part of the decade was dogged by misfortune when his plans to equip the SECR with modern 2-6-4 tanks as the standard locomotive for the Kent coast services were thrown into disarray by a crash by one of the class at Sevenoaks which, although primarily due to the state of the permanent way, cast a shadow on the new engines and resulted in their rebuilding as 2-6-0 tender engines, many of which found their way onto the ex-LSWR for duties on secondary freight and passenger services.

Successful as the King Arthur class became, they were still a relatively small engine and in order to provide a greater margin of power, and to meet the Southern Railway's growing aspirations, Maunsell attempted to augment them with a large three-cylinder express locomotive for the handful of exceptionally fast and heavy services such as the principal West of England services from Waterloo and the Continental expresses bewteen Victoria and Dover.

Introduced in 1926, the Lord Nelson 4-6-0's were huge four-cylinder locomotives which not only had a claim to be the most powerful engines in the country but inspired the LMS - who at the time were making desperate efforts to produce an express passenger locomotive - to beat a path to Waterloo in order to make enquiries about the design. In practice however they fell far short of their potential and at their very best were

no better - if as good - as a King Arthur N15. In their early days the class was divided between Nine Elms and Stewarts Lane, the latter allocation working the Dover boat trains from Victoria, but in post-1939 years the class was concentrated on the South Western, working mainly on the Wessex main line and especially on the Southampton boat trains.

H15 4-6-0 30475. 8:253/270 tons (1939)					
m.ch Point	1/in	W.T.T.	Actual mph	dbhp	pc
0.00 WATERLOO	-	0.00	0.00	-	-	-
3.74 Clapham Jcn	-3642	7.00	6.52 45	549	2
7.19 Wimbledon	752		11.00 52	535	3
19.12 Weybridge	11626		22.35 61.5	470	3
21.54 West Byfleet	6128		24.55 68	790	5
24.27 WOKING	367	29.00	27.50	-	-	-
0.00 WOKING	-	0.00	0.00	-	-	-
			p.w.c.		
6.53 MP.31	312		11.47 25	523	2
8.71 Farnborough	-946		15.00 52.5	769	3
12.11 Fleet	2852		18.20 64.5	799	5
23.33 BASINGSTOKE	733	27.00	29.00 62	556	4
25.76 Worting Jcn	260	29.00	31.35 55	549	3
31.15 Overton	2925		36.52 66.5	641	4
34.61 Whitchurch	-549		39.55 73.5	486	3
41.72 ANDOVER JCN	-369	45.00	45.58	-	-	-
Clapham Jcn - W. Byfleet 18 miles 1/3039 : 523 dbhp (pc 3)					
MP.31 - Overton. 24.5 miles 1/953 : 666 dbhp (pc 4) 59					

The usual engines to be found on West of England expresses before the war were Lord Nelson 4-6-0's on the main services with King Arthur 4-6-0's on any relief sections. When hard pressed for engines during the peak of the season mixed traffic engines were pushed into the limelight as on the occasion when 30475, an H15 4-6-0, found itself at the head of one of the sections of the 13.00 Waterloo - Plymouth which it worked as far as Salisbury. Under normal circumstances the H15's were generally to be found on goods and parcels services although they were booked (1953) to work the 09.54 and 22.40 stopping trains from Waterloo.

From time to time various attempts were made to improve the steaming weaknesses of the Lord Nelsons but they remained rather sluggish machines and with hindsight it could be suggested that the expenditure might have been put to better use had it been invested in a larger fleet of Schools 4-4-0's which appeared in 1930 and were beyond any question the most successful express passenger class the system had ever seen.

There is a certain irony in the fact that whilst the South Western and the Southern Railway seemed blighted in their quest to produce a powerful express passenger 4-6-0, the nearest they came to meeting the specifications was with a 4-4-0; a wheel arrangement all but redundant by 1930 but which successfully handled exceptionally heavy services between London and Bournemouth to timings which equalled almost anything in the country.

The Schools - or V - class had been designed with the limitations of the Charing Cross - Hastings route foremost in mind but the class was expanded to forty engines, sufficient to allow a number to be allocated to both Portsmouth and Bournemouth where they were retained for the principal business services to Waterloo until electrification, in the case of the former, and the war saw the concentration of the whole class on the SECR section. (In passing, it is often stated that the Schools engines were devoted exclusively to the Charing Cross - Hastings route. Whilst they certainly monopolised the Hastings trains until the arrival of diesel multiple units, they were also regularly used between Charing Cross and

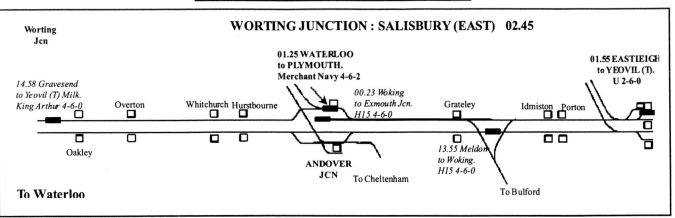

The advent of 140 brand new Pacifics did not prevent the Southern from taking acceptance of all five BR mainline diesels during the early 1950's, using them extensively on the routes to Bournemouth and Exeter. Their behaviour was erratic - a foretaste of things to come - and in 1955 they were returned to the London Midland where they remained until withdrawn in the 1960's. 10202, one of two SR 1750hp locomotives introduced in 1951, calls at Salisbury with a down West of England express in 1952.

Margate, via Dover, and over the LCDR between Victoria and Ramsgate where they had two workings a day until electrification. In addition they were also the regular engines for both Thanet sections of the through express to Birkenhead.)

With the Lord Nelson, Schools and King Arthur engines, by the early 1930's the Southern found itself with a fleet of locomotives which were just about adequate for their purposes and for the remainder of the decade the only passenger engines to make an appearance were the N15X 4-6-0's - a rather flawed rebuilding of the LBSCR 4-6-4 express tanks - which spent most of their lives in the Basingstoke backwater running stopping trains to and from Waterloo.

Maunsell was succeeded just before the war by Oliver Bulleid, a charismatic individual who, unlike Urie, was not only determined that, in spite of a world war, business should proceed as normal but managed to persuade the authorities to allow him to produce a revolutionary design of express passenger locomotive at a time when the country was crying out for goods engines. Describing them as a mixed traffic engine, the first of the Merchant Navy class appeared in 1941 followed by a smaller version four years later, the total amounting to no less than 140 locomotives which, it was hoped, would permit the withdrawal of almost all express locomotives older than the Schools 4-4-0's.

In the event the new engines worked side by side with the old - Drummond locomotives were still hard at work until the 1960's - a feature

that doubtless owed something to the temperamental nature of the Pacifics which, whilst they could haul extraordinary loads at very high speeds and could 'steam on egg-shells', were both difficult to maintain and unpredictable in performance.

Equalling anything the other railway's possessed in terms of power and size, the Merchant Navy Pacifics were rarely fully extended in service. The weight of trains forecast at the time of their introduction did not materialise whilst the Southern operators remained conservative in the matter of running times - it is a matter for regret that the introduction of a mile-a-minute timing was unnecessarily delayed five if not ten years whilst the economies latent in the Merchant Navy's potential for running independent sections of West of England trains as a single service were never fully realised. Initially the class operated the heavier services between Waterloo and Exeter and Bournemouth but in 1950 the Bournemouth allocation was transferred to Dover and Stewarts Lane, leaving the Wessex services to be operated by Nine Elms-based locomotives. At the same time the change of engines was eliminated at Salisbury - where the allocation was reduced from five to four engines - enabling the engines involved in the Exeter workings to achieve a daily mileage of almost 350 miles which, for such a large number of locomotives, probably set a new record for utilisation. (Engines on the east and west coast routes amassed similar mileages but not on such a great scale and only occasionally with continuous running. To achieve it, however, the South-

ern was obliged to use the Pacifics on balancing goods trains; the paucity of overnight passenger services from Waterloo being minimal).

The lightweight Pacifics, whose numbers ought to have seen them working every other service of consequence - did not enjoy the same level of utilisation, esteem or respect. Fitting staff damned them as being difficult to maintain and complained that even the most simple tasks required the dismantling of large sections of each locomotive; a factor which extended the time spent out of traffic for attention which, on any other class of engine, would have been dealt with rather more promptly. (Similar complaints applied to the Merchant Navy engines but their status as the only class 8P class on the system gave them a priority that the smaller engines did not enjoy).

Locomotive maintenance is not a subject that has been given much prominence in print yet it is a crucial element in the economic lives of locomotives. The numbers (and cost) of fitting staff is based on the time that it is calculated each maintenance task should take and if any particular class of engine consistently exceeds this average, the costs of maintenance - and the time the engine is out of traffic - not only soars alarmingly but a backlog of maintenance is created in respect of other engines. To add to the problems the post-war growth of the motor-car industry, and the tempting salaries it offered, severely hampered the railway's effort to maintain its complement of fitting staff. All too often, newly qualified mechanical staff would be lured away into the car industry, whose chief

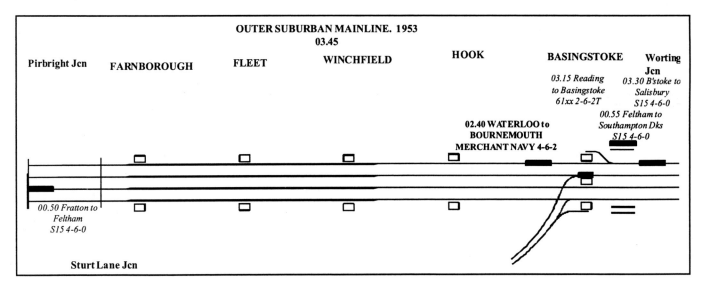

OUTER SUBURBAN MAINLINE. 1953
03.45

Pirbright Jcn   FARNBOROUGH   FLEET   WINCHFIELD   HOOK   BASINGSTOKE   Worting Jcn

03.15 Reading to Basingstoke 61xx 2-6-2T

03.30 B'stoke to Salisbury S15 4-6-0

02.40 WATERLOO to BOURNEMOUTH MERCHANT NAVY 4-6-2

00.55 Feltham to Southampton Dks S15 4-6-0

00.50 Fratton to Feltham S15 4-6-0

Sturt Lane Jcn

engineers regarded a railway apprenticeship as a qualification of considerable value. (Not a few of the famous names in car engineering learned their trade as premium apprentices on the railway).

The problems of maintenance combined with the variable running qualities of the light Pacifics ensured that they did not, in fact, replace to any worthwhile degree the older two-cylinder designs of the Urie/Maunsell years and, indeed, it may come as a surprise to those who have assumed the ubiquity of the light Pacifics to discover what a small proportion of trains in and out of Waterloo were regularly diagrammed to the class. (With the number of light Pacifics on its books and allowing for a percentage out of work for one reason or another, by the early 1950's the King Arthur and Lord Nelson 4-6-0's should only have seen the light of day on season special trains and the like. In fact not only were the N15x engines given full employment until the mid-50's, but an evening semifast from Waterloo to Yeovil was actually booked to an S15).

Instead, therefore, of becoming the standard engine of the system, as the rebuilt 7P 4-6-0's and A1 Pacifics were elsewhere, the SR not only found itself having to run trains with a variety of older locomotives but, incredibly, by the 1950's large numbers of light Pacifics - no less than fourteen in late 1953 - were being placed in store.

The position also found its way into the diagramming statistics where, on the LSWR, less than a third of the light Pacifics were being allo-

cated regular daily work. Nine Elms was only booked to use three out of its seventeen engines whilst Salisbury had no regular duties for four of its five West Country's. The nadir was to be found at Brighton whose three daily West Coast trains (to Bournemouth, Plymouth and Cardiff) were diagrammed to four West Country Pacifics of which, not infrequently, none were available to work. At one point in the 1950's the Bourne-

AVAILABILITY : BULLEID PACIFICS (1953)						
	MERCHANT NAVY		WEST COUNTRY		TOTAL	
Shed	Allocation	Diagrams	Allocation	Diagrams	Allocation	Diagrams	%
NINE ELMS	12	8	17	3	29	11	38
BOURNEMOUTH	-	-	9	6	9	6	67
SALISBURY	4	2	5	1	9	3	33
TOTAL	16	10	31	10	47	20	42

mouth service, for which a 2-6-4T was often substituted, was rediagrammed for an LBSCR Atlantic.

Neither did their propensity for catching fire - generally an unusual occurrence with a steam engine - enhance the reputation of the light Pacifics and one of the most spectacular Bulleid instances occurred on Chrismas Eve 1954 when 34095 'Brentor', after losing eighty minutes to Wool through poor running with the 13.30 Waterloo - Weymouth, caught fire and had to be rescued by a King Arthur 4-6-0 from Dorchester. The 13.30 eventually reached Weymouth all but four hours late whilst the reaction filtered back to eight other Weymouth-bound services, each of which arrived at least two hours behind time. Such happenings were not typical of the class - at times they could put up exhilerating performances - but the incidence of problems associated with the engines produced a situation that

could not be allowed to persist and eventually patience snapped, resulting in an expensive programme of rebuilding commencing in 1956 for the Merchant Navy engines and a year later for the light Pacifics.

The Bulleid Pacifics were not the only novelties to be seen at Waterloo in the early 1950's since in the fifteen month period from Christmas 1951 all four of BR's main line diesel locomotives were transferred to Nine Elms with the fifth - the 800 hp 10800 - working on the ex-LBSCR from Norwood Junction. The quartet of main line engines remained on the South Western for some time (and were joined in May 1954 by the 2000hp 10203), running on both the Exeter and Weymouth roads. Diesel's, at the time, were regarded very much as the motive power of the future and at first were regarded with considerable promise. The honeymoon, however, did not last long and before much time had passed, the main topic of comment concerned the frequency with which the diesels failed. Occasionally one would be regaled with tales of brilliant performances on the American Railways, who at the time were restocking with diesel locomotives as fast as the manufacturers could produce them. Given the experience of the five main line engines possessed by BR, one felt sorry for the United States.

The diesel locomotives remained with the Southern until 1955 when they returned to the London Midland and, coincidentally or not, more than a decade passed before a diesel engine was regularly seen at Waterloo again. No lessons were learnt from the experiment and, all in all, it

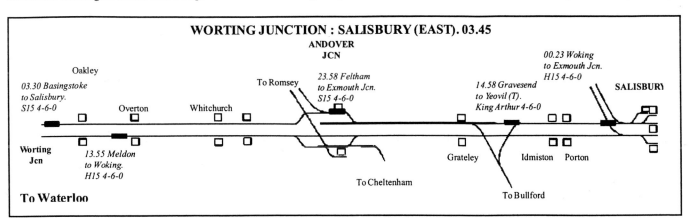

WORTING JUNCTION : SALISBURY (EAST). 03.45

ANDOVER JCN

Oakley

03.30 Basingstoke to Salisbury. S15 4-6-0

00.23 Woking to Exmouth Jcn. H15 4-6-0

23.58 Feltham to Exmouth Jcn. S15 4-6-0

14.58 Gravesend to Yeovil (T). King Arthur 4-6-0

SALISBURY

To Romsey

Overton   Whitchurch

Worting Jcn

13.55 Meldon to Woking. H15 4-6-0

Grateley   Idmiston   Porton

To Cheltenham

To Bullford

To Waterloo

The BR 5MT 4-6-0's arrived on the Southern (at Bath, Green Park) in June 1954 and were followed by a batch of ten which replaced the King Arthur 4-6-0's on the Victoria - Ramsgate services. Eleven more arrived at Nine Elms in November 1955 to replace the N15's on the stopping trains to Salisbury, the number rising to twenty-one from June 1959 when the Stewarts Lane allocation was made redundant by electrification. One of the former Stewarts Lane engines, 73087 'Linette', runs light from Salisbury shed to the station prior to working back to Waterloo. To add insult to injury some of the class were named after the N15's they had replaced, the nameplate being just visible on the engine's running plate. Z class 0-8-0T 30957 shunts in the background.

was rather a wasted exercise. Had the four engines been allocated to a small depot with a limited number of long distance express services - such as Holyhead - where they could have become almost the sole motive power, valuable lessons might have been learned in readiness for the following decade. Much experience might have been obtained had the four (later five) engines been based at Exmouth Junction and retained for the London workings but as it was the engines worked turn and turn about with steam locomotives, lacking the specific attention they required and returning very little in the way of experience. The result was that when diesel engines started to appear in large numbers during the early 1960's, they arrived as a completely alien form of traction.

The (theoretical) ability of diesel locomotives to remain in traffic for long periods of time without intermediate servicing did at least provide the system with a useful tool on Christmas Days when the engine of the 11.00 ex Waterloo had to start its homeward journey from Exeter after a turn-round of only fifty minutes. This was barely sufficient for a steam engine to run to and from Exmouth Junction and therefore for several years one of the diesels was always earmarked for the turn. By Christmas 1954, however, the availability of the five engines had sunk to such an ebb - during the autumn of that year only one of the quintet was normally in traffic - that the arrangement ceased with Merchant Navy 35017 being used in lieu.

The block allocation of diesels to the Southern started to break up from March 1955 when one of the LMS locomotives, 10001 was returned to its home metals in readiness for duties

KING ARTHUR N15 4-6-0 30450 'Sir Kay. 354/365 tons (1935)						
m.ch Point	1/in	W.T.T.	Actual	mph	dbhp	pc
0.00 SALISBURY	-	0.00	0	-	-	-
5.24 Porton	216		9.30	42	977	3
10.74 Grateley	572		16.20	59	875	4
17.24 ANDOVER JCN	-275	22.00	21.30	80	685	5
22.36 Hurstbourne	401		25.55	71	813	6
28.01 Overton	428		30.40	67	994	7
31.12 Oakley	2937		33.30	70	823	5
33.20 Worting Jcn	-734	39.00	35.22	65	116	1
35.63 BASINGSTOKE	-260	41.30	37.30	75	697	5
41.30 Hook	-762		42.05	69	207	1
47.05 Fleet	-674		46.40	76	702	5
50.26 Farnborough	-2852		49.20	75	579	4
52.43 MP 31	946		51.07	73	773	6
59.16 WOKING	-312	63.00	56.05	83	525	4
61.69 West Byfleet	-367		58.03	82	151	1
64.31 Weybridge	-6128		60.00	75	-	-
66.37 Walton	5242		61.35	76	1015	8
71.40 SURBITON	-4244	75.00	66.30	-	-	-

Porton - Oakley. 26 miles 1/1903. 65 mph. 833 dbhp (pc5)
Worting Jcn - Woking. 26 miles -1/563. 75 mph 529dbhp (pc4)

There can little doubt that by the time sufficient numbers of King Arthur 4-6-0's had been delivered to cover the principal Salisbury and Bournemouth trains, start to stop mile a minute averages could have become a matter of course. As it was the Southern preferred the conservative course of allowing its trains ample scope for recovering delays to a greater extent than was the case on the northern railways.

out of Euston. The remainder followed at intervals; the last to leave being 10203 which left Nine Elms for Camden on the 20th of July 1955.

Ironically, in view of the fact that the early 1950's saw several prolonged visits by the diesels, the LSWR was largely excluded from dieselisation when it took root in the early 1960's and was the last system to operate the steam status quo. GW Warship class diesel hydraulics started to appear on the West of England trains in 1965 whilst a few borrowed Class 47 diesel

electrics took a hand with some of the Bournemouth workings in the final months prior to electrification.

It is widely believed that because the SR invested so heavily in electrification between the wars it had little interest in steam traction but the reality was that - the LBSCR apart - its steam interests were as wide as those of the other companies since, except for the Portsmouth line, the third rail covered only the inner-suburban area and extended barely thirty miles on the main line. In fact the Southern spent a considerable sum on its steam fleet, the Schools and Lord Nelson classes were both post-electrification classes whilst the influx of Pacifics at the end of the war had no parallel anywhere else.

However because the suburban services had been electrified, there was no need to consider the introduction of modern six-coupled tank engines as the LMS, for example, had done and the Southern was unique in that almost all its outer-suburban steam services were operated with tender engines, the exception being the Tunbridge Wells service which, after the demise of the LBSCR 4-4-2 tanks in 1951, were handled by LMS and BR 2-6-4T's.

From the enthusiasts point of view, this made the South Western rather special - a ride from London on a limited budget behind a 'namer' was something of a treat and, on a personal note, one can only estimate the proportion of one's weekly pocket-money which found its way into Waterloo booking office in order to purchase half day returns to Woking in the quest for a run behind an N15 or an N15X. Indeed the South Western was the exact opposite from other regions in that one had to travel some little dis-

WATERLOO TO DORCHESTER JUNCTION.

BASINGSTOKE—Thorneycrofts Sidings.

ALL classes PROHIBITED except E.4, G.6, and Z. These engines may work over the approach and No. 1 siding as far as the timber shed but must not enter Nos. 2 or 3 sidings.

BASINGSTOKE—Park Prewett Sidings.

ALL classes PROHIBITED except G.6 and Z. These engines must not enter the top siding. Speed must not exceed 5 m.p.h. in these sidings.

One reason why the G6 0-6-0T's survived so long at Basingstoke - and elsewhere - was because they had an availability denied more modern engines. To have upgraded every nook and cranny visited by small shunting engines would probably have cost more than the replacement engines and thus longevity was assured. The clearance for the Z class 0-8-0's was not, so far as is know, utilised since the small number of engines in the class were usually occupied in marshalling yard duties.

tance from London in order to experience a trip behind a suburban tank engine. Eastleigh, where there were M7's galore, was the best bet although to those 'in the know' it was still possible in the 1950's to get a run on the main line behind an 0-4-4T.

It is interesting to speculate on what type of suburban engine the Southern would have used had they not electrified the London suburban network. The three other companies invested heavily in modern six-coupled express tank engines which were used to advantage whilst the SR - which had been the first to introduce the type - had its fingers badly burnt at Sevenoaks in 1927 and thereafter regarded the 2-6-4T with the greatest suspicion. (The fact that the permanent way rather than engine design had been responsible for the difficulties with the SECR 2-6-4 tanks never took root in the minds of SR management and twenty five years later when LMS engines - well proven elsewhere - were proposed for the Victoria - Tunbridge Wells workings, it was only after the most stringent trials that they were accepted). Whether the SR would have worked its inner workings for ever and a day with developments of the 0-4-4T is a

matter of conjecture but enthusiasts of the 1950's will be grateful that there was at least one main line which afforded some relief from the 2-6-4T monotony of other routes. Because of the electrification, which swept all but shunting and goods engines away from the London area, it was difficult to get a run behind a tank engine - those that remained were a few M7 0-4-4T's retained for empty stock duties between Waterloo and Clapham Junction - and one had to venture some distance from London to see large tanks engines regularly at work on main line passenger trains.

If the electrified suburban services may have had little to offer the enthusiast, the same could not be said of the main line, especially in postwar days when the South Western could offer the greatest imaginable variety of motive power. Bulleid Pacifics, heavy and light, Lord Nelson's, King Arthur's, H and S15's, Remembrance N15x's: examples of almost every post-grouping six-coupled type which made it possible to see a succession of half a dozen express services, each of which was powered by a different class of engine. Only the Drummond era was missing although, if one frequented the line at

the right times in the late 1940's, it was still possible to catch the Indian summer of the T14 Paddleboxes which received an unexpected fillip toward the very end of their long lives.

The five survivors of the class were brought back to life, after some time in store at Nine Elms, in the early summer of 1949 and the decision was taken to make the best possible use of them until each became due for shops, after which each would be withdrawn. For much of this last year of operation they could be found on the Nine Elms-based Basingstoke workings whilst on occasional summer Saturdays one of the class was turned out for the 13.00 West of England service as far as Salisbury where, at the time, all trains changed engines. The reprieve lasted for almost two years; the last two examples being withdrawn from traffic in the Spring of 1951.

The Paddleboxes, even after attempts by both Urie and Maunsell to improve them, had never been amongst the leading lights on the South Western but it was pleasing to see such an imposing class of engine go out on a positive note.

The old order: Drummond T14 'Paddlebox' 4-6-0 443 stands at Eastleigh shortly after being withdrawn from traffic in 1949. Standing on an adjacent road is K10 4-4-0 341 which was taken out of traffic shortly afterwards. Oil burning T9 4-4-0 713 survived for a little longer and worked until April 1951.

THROUGH SERVICES

Displaying a headcode that may have had the signalman scratching his head - Victoria to Brighton via Oxted - Rebuilt West Country 34044 'Dorchester' comes off the Southampton route at Worting Junction and heads for London on 1st August 1959. The train is probably an Ocean Liner Express from Southampton Docks to Waterloo.

Express services on the main line left London on the odd hour for the West of England and half past most hours for Southampton, Bournemouth and Weymouth, the latter including the all-Pullman Bournemouth Belle which ran daily between Waterloo and Bournemouth West.

A summer-only Pullman service had been tried between London and the West of England - which the SR regarded as marginally the more superior of the two express services - but failed to meet expectations. Known as the Devon Belle the fourteen coach express - which included an observation car in the Ilfracombe section - commenced operations in 1947, running at week-ends only until 1949 when its currency was extended to include a Thursday departure from Waterloo and a Tuesday departure from Ilfracombe and Plymouth. It was the first attempt, other than a short-lived GWR experiment in 1929, to run Pullman cars in the West of England.

Leaving Waterloo at mid-day the service ran non-stop to Wilton to change engines - the train was the first regular service ever to pass through Salisbury non-stop - since the absence of water troughs on the system precluded non-stop working between London and Exeter. The train was not a success and in 1950 the Plymouth section was withdrawn although this did little to increase the profitability of the service and by 1953 departures from Waterloo had been reduced to three per week, leaving at 12.00 on

KING ARTHUR (N15) 4-6-0. 30777 'Sir Lamiel' 10:328/345 ton					
m.ch Point	Gradient	W.T.T.	Actual	mph	dbhp pc
0.00 SALISBURY	-	0.00	0.00	-	- -
5.24 Porton	216		8.22	53.0	1266 5
10.74 Grateley	572		14.00	66.0	1070 6
17.24 ANDOVER JCN	-275		18.43	88.5	919 7
24.35 Whitchurch	370		24.24	72.5	788 6
28.01 Overton	549		27.20	72.5	1050 8
31.12 Oakley	2937		29.54	79.0	1185 9
33.20 Worting Jcn	-734	39.00	31.33	75.0	- -
35.63 BASINGSTOKE	-260	41.30	33.26	83.5	819 7
43.57 Winchfield	-762		39.15	82.0	494 4
47.05 Fleet	-674		41.33	85.0	897 8
50.26 Farnborough	-2852		44.00	80.5	376 3
59.16 WOKING	-467	62.30	50.26	88.5	617 5
61.69 West Byfleet	-367		52.15	90.0	491 4
64.31 Weybridge	-6128		54.05	82.0	- -
69.12 Esher	-1951		57.18	80.5	- -
71.40 Surbiton	1428		59.28	76.5	- -
73.61 New Malden	-7145		61.14	74.0	- -
76.24 Wimbledon	29803		63.20	69.0	- -
77.77 Earlesfield	-664		64.46	72.5	- -
83.43 WATERLOO	-3965	90.00	72.41	-	- -

Porton : Oakley 25.8 miles at 1/1904. 961 dbhp (pc 7): 72
Worting Jcn : West Byfleet 28.6 miles at -1/537. 581 dbhp (pc5
There cannot be many instances of an engine gaining nearly twenty minutes on an express schedule but N15 30777 'Sir Lamiel' succeeded whilst working an up West of England service in 1936.

Fridays, Saturdays and Sundays only. These contractions failed to reduce the losses and, in a last ditch attempt to turn loss into profit the departure time was altered from midday to 16.40 in the evening with an intermediate stop

at Salisbury which allowed, for the first time, the engine to work through to Exeter as had been the case with all other west of England trains since 1950. Sad to say none of the palliatives made any significant difference to the patronage of the service and at the end of the 1954 season the Southern decided that nothing more could be done and the train was withdrawn, the majority of its vehicles being transferred to the WR for the South Wales Pullman which commenced operations between Paddington and Swansea in 1955.

In many respects the Devon Belle was the odd-man out of the SR Pullman services; the remainder of the 'Belle' family were relatively successful and none more so than the Bournemouth Belle, which had commenced regular running in 1936 after a period as a Sunday-only working, and lasted until its withdrawal upon electrification in 1967. Leaving Waterloo at 12.30 it ran to Bournemouth West calling only at Southampton and Bournemouth Central, reaching its destination only eighteen minutes after the arrival of the preceding 11.30 from London. Unusually for a Dorset service, it had no subsidiary sections but ran as a complete unit, the stock and Nine Elms Merchant Navy Pacific returning from Bournemouth West at 16.34 and arriving in Waterloo at 18.50.

There was something undeniably special about the Pullman trains - the supplement was by no means excessive whilst the standard of service was generally beyond criticism - yet

When one recalls the trouble that the Southern went to in order to provide relatively humble cross-Channel boat trains with modern Pacifics - not to mention the gleaming Britannia which Parkeston Quay uniformly turned out for the Hook Continental - the sight of an S15 4-6-0 working an Ocean Liner Express from Southampton to Waterloo seems a little strange. The Ocean Liner schedules were not fast - 114 minutes for the 80 mile distance was the normal booking - and on 2nd August 1958, at the height of a very busy period, Eastleigh MPD was doubtless having difficulty in meeting demand. The unidentified member of the class drops off the Battledown flyover and crossed over to the up through line at Worting Junction.

neither SR Pullman service was regarded by the operators as being the premiere train of the line; that particular honour - insofar as it existed - being bestowed upon the Royal Wessex, the business express which ran up from Weymouth in the mornings, returning from Waterloo at 16.35.

Curiously the 'Wessex' - which was a fast and heavy service - was not a Merchant Navy duty for most of the 1950's, but was worked in both directions by Bournemouth West Country Pacifics, each engine working through from Weymouth to London and vice versa.

The Royal Wessex workings were nothing if not arduous for the engines involved; the engine of the up service, for example, coming off Bournemouth shed at 04.08 to relieve a T9 4-4-0 at Wimborne on the 03.52 Salisbury - Weymouth in order to get to its starting point which in those days was a Great Western location and, as such, played no part in the running of Southern services. The light Pacific then ran to London with the up 'Wessex', leaving Weymouth at 07.34 and getting to Waterloo at 10.50. The return working was not with the down 'Wessex', which left Waterloo at 16.35, but with the 13.30 express which the Pacific ran through to Weymouth before returning to Bournemouth with the 19.48 stopping train to Reading which it worked as far as

Bournemouth Central. The total time in steam for the diagram came to seventeen hours with 352 revenue miles operated.

The reason for the use of a light Pacific as opposed to a class 8 engine was that Bournemouth parted with its Merchant Navy allocation in 1950 - the engines being transferred to Stewarts Lane for the Victoria - Dover continental services - leaving only light Pacifics for

LORD NELSON 4-6-0. 30860 'Lord Hawke'. 417/445 tons (1931)							
m.ch	Point	1 in	W.T.T.	Actual	mph	dbhp	pc
0.00	WATERLOO		0.00	0.00	-	-	-
7.19	Wimbledon	2177		11.50	53.0	755	3
12.03	Surbiton	20774		16.55	66.0	924	5
19.12	Weybridge	8960		23.45	58.0	410	3
31.00	MP 31	408		36.20	53.0	907	5
36.38	Fleet	-4585		41.45	68.0	943	6
42.13	Hook	790		47.10	63.0	720	4
50.21	WORTING JCN	435	57.00	55.10	54.0	861	5
55.42	Overton	2925		60.50	66.0	879	5
66.19	ANDOVER JCN	-415	72.00	69.45	85.0	657	5
72.49	Grateley	275		75.20	53.0	456	3
78.19	Porton	-572		80.50	83.5	1199	7
83.42	SALISBURY	-216	90.00	86.40	-	-	-

Weybridge - Porton. 59 miles 1/1399 : 62 mph : 829 dbhp (pc 5)

The Lord Nelson 4-6-0's could slog away with heavy trains so long as exception speeds were not called for. 30860 'Lord Hawke' was recorded in 1931 at the head of the Atlantic Coast Express and whilst it succeeded in reaching Salisbury with more than three minutes in hand, on every instance of meeting an adverse gradient speed fell quite markedly. The run was generally representative of the class in its early days.

its principal services until early 1954 when three of the larger engines returned following complaints about the time-keeping of the Royal Wessex.

Next in line to the Royal Wessex was the Atlantic Coast Express, which left Waterloo at 11.00 and conveyed more separate portions in its load than any other train in the country. It was also a very fast train by Southern standards running to Salisbury in 83 minutes - the only service to do so non-stop - eclipsing the timing of the Devon Belle by some twenty minutes. Having portions for Plymouth and Ilfracombe (in addition to a spread of other locations) the Atlantic Coast was probably as significant a factor in the decline of the Devon Belle as anything; leaving London at much the same time of day with full dining facilities and being considerably faster but without the need for a supplementary fare. In addition there was the existence of the similarly timed Cornish Riviera from Paddington which also played a part in abstracting traffic from the Pullman.

Although the Atlantic Coast Express enjoyed the prestige of a mile-a-minute run between London and Salisbury, the remainder of the West of England services were not regarded as being particularly special and all made at least two stops before reaching Salisbury. These intermediate calls followed no particular

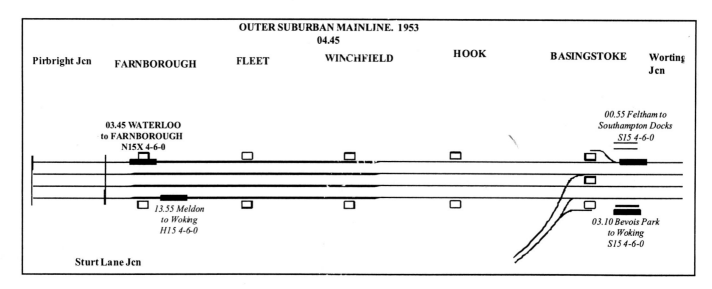

OUTER SUBURBAN MAINLINE. 1953
04.45

Pirbright Jcn • FARNBOROUGH • FLEET • WINCHFIELD • HOOK • BASINGSTOKE • Worting Jcn

03.45 WATERLOO
to FARNBOROUGH
N15X 4-6-0

00.55 Feltham to
Southampton Docks
S15 4-6-0

13.55 Meldon
to Woking
H15 4-6-0

03.10 Bevois Park
to Woking
S15 4-6-0

Sturt Lane Jcn

pattern, the 13.00 and 18.00 trains served Basingstoke and Andover Junction whilst the 09.00 called at Surbiton and Woking in addition. The 17.00 which ran no further than Exeter Central stopped at Woking and Basingstoke and then degenerated into something of a rural service by making calls at Overton and Whitchurch North before running into Salisbury two hours after leaving London.

All the West of England trains, fast and slow, were booked to be worked by 8P Merchant Navy Pacifics between Waterloo and Exeter Central, each engine working through following the abolition of the long standing change of engines at Salisbury in 1950. In addition each locomotive worked on an out and home basis, a system which gave rise to higher daily mileages than could normally be found on the other regions of BR. The LM, for example, would typically diagram an engine to work a distance of about 200 hundred miles with the return journey not being made until the next day whilst on the GN most trains changed engines at Grantham, 105 miles from Kings Cross. The Bulleid Pacifics on the West of England workings on the other hand were managing nearly 350 miles per day in revenue earning service which, given the number of engines concerned, probably represented the high point of motive power utilisation.

This high daily mileage reflected well upon the headquarters diagrammers who were faced with the task of obtaining this high degree of utilisation in the face of a passenger timetable which only operated for two shifts out of the three, making it very difficult to keep the locomotives operating during the night. The answer lay in balancing a number of Merchant Navy locomotives by diagramming them to operate selected night goods trains; a move that recalled their original description of a mixed traffic engine.

Three sheds played a part in the Exeter workings; Nine Elms and Exmouth Junction being responsible for three Waterloo departures each whilst Salisbury sent an engine to London with a morning train to work westwards with the 13.00 ex Waterloo, the only down Exeter train to be handled by that shed.

Altogether ten Merchant Navy locomotives were required to operate the West of England

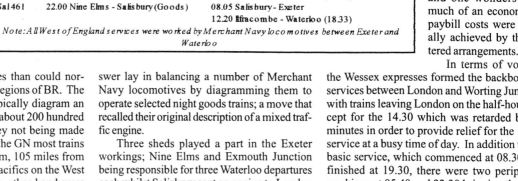

Engine	Down service	Balance
	LOCOMOTIVE WORKINGS : WEST OF ENGLAND EXPRESSES	
Ex Jcn 498	01.25 Waterloo : Plymouth	15.50 Plymouth : Waterloo (22.08)
N. Elms 4	09.00 Waterloo - Plymouth	14.20 Ilfracombe - Waterloo (20.25)
N. Elms 5	11.00 Waterloo - Plymouth	21.05 (Milk) Templecombe : Clapham Jcn (00.20)
Sal 431	13.00 Waterloo - Plymouth	08.15 Salisbury - Waterloo (10.08)
		16.40 Plymouth - Salisbury (22.52)
N. Elms 7	15.00 Waterloo - Plymouth	17.00 (Goods) Torrington - Nine Elms (04.03)
Ex Jcn 494	15.54 Clapham Jcn - Exeter (Milk)	06.30 Exeter - Waterloo (12.19)
Ex Jcn 496	17.00 Waterloo - Exeter	08.15 Plymouth : Waterloo (14.15)
Ex Jcn 495	18.00 Waterloo - Plymouth	07.30 Exeter - Waterloo (11.08)
Ex Jcn 497	21.10 Nine Elms - Exmouth Jcn (Goods)	10.30 Ilfracombe - Waterloo (15.40)
Sal 461	22.00 Nine Elms - Salisbury (Goods)	08.05 Salisbury - Exeter
		12.20 Ilfracombe - Waterloo (18.33)
Note: All West of England services were worked by Merchant Navy locomotives between Exeter and Waterloo		

workings although one of the workings - Exmouth Junction 494 - was a ready candidate for the substitution of a smaller engine in the event of a power shortage since turn in question worked up to London with the early morning slow service from Exeter - something like six hours being allowed - returning with the afternoon milk empties from Clapham Junction.

An interesting feature of the through workings between Waterloo and Exeter was the fact that Salisbury were required to maintain additional firemen at the station to pull coal forward in the tender whilst the mainline crews were being relieved and one wonders how much of an economy in paybill costs were actually achieved by the altered arrangements.

In terms of volume the Wessex expresses formed the backbone of services between London and Worting Junction with trains leaving London on the half-hour except for the 14.30 which was retarded by 50 minutes in order to provide relief for the 15.30 service at a busy time of day. In addition to the basic service, which commenced at 08.30 and finished at 19.30, there were two peripheral workings at 05.40 and 22.30 bringing the total to fourteen departures from Waterloo. The Weymouth services were also very heavy workings - twelve or thirteen coaches was quite normal - and consisted of at least two sections - Bournemouth West and Weymouth - with some

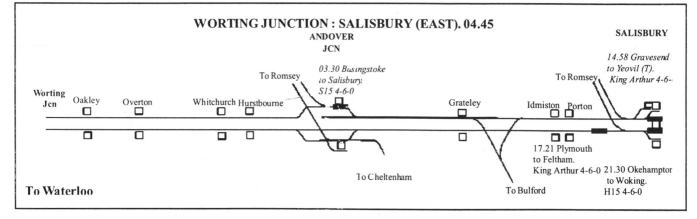

WORTING JUNCTION : SALISBURY (EAST). 04.45

ANDOVER JCN

SALISBURY

14.58 Gravesend
to Yeovil (T).
King Arthur 4-6-0

To Romsey

03.30 Basingstoke
to Salisbury.
S15 4-6-0

To Romsey

Worting Jcn • Oakley • Overton • Whitchurch • Hurstbourne • Grateley • Idmiston • Porton

To Cheltenham

17.21 Plymouth
to Feltham.
King Arthur 4-6-0

To Bulford

21.30 Okehampton
to Woking.
H15 4-6-0

To Waterloo

26

Whilst the regular London - Exeter services were all booked for Merchant Navy haulage an exception was made for the daily Plymouth - Brighton express which was diagrammed to be worked throughout by West Country Pacifics with a change of engine at Salisbury. Unrebuilt light Pacific 34066 'Spitfire' rolls the heavy up service into the west end of Salisbury in 1964. Until the Kent Coast electrification of 1962, 34066 had been a South Eastern engine, based at Stewarts Lane for workings to Ramsgate and the Continental boat trains. It had not had a happy career and was the locomotive involved in the St Johns disaster of December 1957 when it ran through signals in heavy fog and collided with a stationery multiple unit, an incident which resulted in the death of 90 passengers. The locomotive was never rebuilt and remained in its original state until being taken out of traffic in September 1966.

Rebuild 34032 'Camelford' eases a train of stock from slow to main and into Salisbury station during carriage shunting operations. The engine had worked into the area with the night goods from Exmouth Junction and returned west with the 12.56 slow train to Yeovil Junction; the service which conveyed a through portion brought from London in the Atlantic Coast Express.

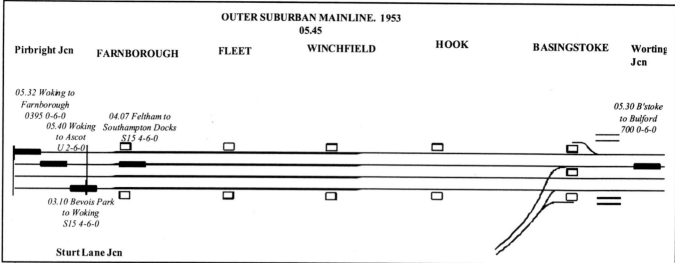

OUTER SUBURBAN MAINLINE. 1953
05.45

Pirbright Jcn   FARNBOROUGH   FLEET   WINCHFIELD   HOOK   BASINGSTOKE   Worting Jcn

05.32 Woking to Farnborough
0395 0-6-0
05.40 Woking to Ascot
U 2-6-0

04.07 Feltham to Southampton Docks
S15 4-6-0

05.30 B'stoke to Bulford
700 0-6-0

03.10 Bevois Park to Woking
S15 4-6-0

Sturt Lane Jcn

trains conveying a through portion for Swanage in addition. Two trains of particular interest were the 02.40 Waterloo to Bournemouth Central which conveyed a section for Portsmouth - the only London service via Basingstoke to do so - whilst the 19.30 from Waterloo conveyed two sections for Bournemouth West, the first arriving at 22.38 behind a Bournemouth West Country 4-6-2 and the second, detached at Brockenhurst to serve intermediate stations, at 23.03 behind an M7 0-4-4 tank.

Although the natural terminating point of the Wessex trains was Weymouth, operations were complicated by the fact that the line west of Dorchester belonged to the Western whilst the nearest SR operating point of any importance was Bournemouth, nearly 35 miles to the east. The London trains were therefore either worked on an out and home basis by Nine Elms shed or by Bournemouth engine and men which worked locally between Bournemouth and Weymouth. For most of the decade Weymouth MPD played no part in SR operations and existed only to provide GWR motive power for services to Westbury and Paddington.

Strangely, in view of their importance and weight, only three of the fourteen services were

handled by Merchant Navy locomotives (the 08.30, 10.30 and the 12.30 Pullman) whilst the majority were worked by West Country light Pacifics with three trains (the 05.40, 11.30 and 22.30) being allocated to Lord Nelson 4-6-0's.

The 11.30 was something of a scheduled swan-song for the Lord Nelson class since it was their last booked express service, the train making only two stops - Basingstoke and Win-chester - before reaching Southampton at 13.19. The two other LN-worked services were semi-fast trains of a less demanding nature but it was nevertheless pleasing at the time to see the pre-Bulleid generation of engines retaining a foothold on express duties so long after the Merchant Navy and West Country Pacifics had

taken over the lions share of front line work. It should not be thought that the Lord Nelsons had in any way been mothballed and in fact they remained hard at work on the frequent although unscheduled Ocean Liner expresses which operated between Waterloo and Southampton Docks. It was, however, disappointing to find that the King Arthur 4-6-0's - little if at all inferior to the Lord Nelsons - had been ousted from both the Wessex and West of England expresses even though a large number of them remained at work on the stopping services between Waterloo and Salisbury.

Only one Merchant Navy locomotive was booked to cover the entire route to Weymouth and that was the Nine Elms Pacific which covered the 143 miles in stages by starting out from London with the 02.40 departure to Bournemouth Central, continuing forward with the 10.30 ex Waterloo after running an intermediate trip to Bournemouth West (which including bringing the Bournemouth west section of the Royal Wessex to the Central station). The engine's final working was with the 17.35 Weymouth - Waterloo.

Without an allocation of engines at Weymouth, it proved impossible to work all the

Engine	Engine	From London	Balance
N.Elms 30	MN 4-6-2	02.40 Waterloo - Bournemouth (C)	17.35 Weymouth - Waterloo (20.50)
N.Elms 31	LN 4-6-0	05.40 Waterloo - Weymouth	10.33 Bournemouth (C) - Waterloo (12.50)
N.Elms 32	MN 4-6-2	08.30 Waterloo - Weymouth	13.05 Bournemouth (W) - Waterloo (16.09)
N.Elms 33	WC 4-6-2	09.30 Waterloo - Bournemouth (W)	18.30 Weymouth - Waterloo (22.56)
N.Elms 34	WC 4-6-2	10.30 Waterloo - Weymouth	15.05 Bournemouth (W) - Waterloo (18.29)
EL 252	LN 4-6-0	11.30 Waterloo - Bournemouth (W)	07.03 S'ton Docks - Waterloo (09.01)
N.Elms 35	MN 4-6-2	12.30 Waterloo - Bournemouth (W)	16.34 Bournemouth (W) - Waterloo (18.50)
BM 381	WC 4-6-2	13.30 Waterloo - Weymouth	07.34 Weymouth - Waterloo (10.50)
BM 382	WC 4-6-2	15.20 Waterloo - Weymouth	08.35 Bournemouth (W) - Waterloo (11.55)
N.Elms 37	WC 4-6-2	15.30 Waterloo - Bournemouth (W)	07.20 Bournemouth (W) - Waterloo (Next day)
BM 383	WC 4-6-2	16.35 Waterloo - Weymouth	11.05 Bournemouth (W) - Waterloo (14.20)
BM 380	WC 4-6-2	17.30 Waterloo - Bournemouth (W)	13.33 Basingstoke - Waterloo (14.52)
BM 386	WC 4-6-2	18.30 Waterloo - Weymouth	11.30 Weymouth - Waterloo (14.59)
BM 385	WC 4-6-2	19.30 Waterloo - Bournemouth (W)	13.25 Weymouth - Waterloo (16.50)
N.Elms 31	LN 4-6-0	21.00 Waterloo - S'ton Docks	01.10 S'ton Term - Waterloo (03.53)
EL 253	LN 4-6-0	22.30 Waterloo - Dorchester	17.05 Bournemouth (W) - Waterloo (20.23)

WESSEX MAIN LINE : ENGINE WORKINGS

EL : Eastleigh. BM : Bournemouth

WORTING JUNCTION : SALISBURY (EAST). 05.45

05.30 Basingstoke to Bulford
700 0-6-0

Worting Jcn   Oakley   Overton   Whitchurch   Hurstbourne   To Romsey   **ANDOVER JCN**   Grateley   Idmiston   Porton   To Romsey   **SALISBURY**

17.21 Plymouth to Feltham.
King Arthur 4-6-0

To Cheltenham

21.30 Okehampton to Woking.
H15 4-6-0

To Bulford

To Waterloo

The major event during the last decade of steam was the rebuilding of the Bulleid Pacifics, the first Merchant Navy being dealt with in 1956 with the light Pacifics following a year later. The loss of the air-smoothed casing may have affected the engine aesthetically but it improved their availability to the extent that as soon as the light Pacific rebuilds started to appear in large quantities, older engines such as the King Arthur and Lord Nelsons were able to be withdrawn, the Pacifics and a number of BR standard 4-6-0's shouldering almost all mainline work from the early 1960's. A sight repeated every hour - more frequently in the summer - at Basingstoke was the arrival of two Pacific-hauled services simultaneously as in the case above where rebuilt West Country 34046 'Braunton' stands on the up through with the 11.16 Bournemouth (West) to York - which it will work as far as Oxford - whilst classmate 34055 'Fighter Pilot' waits on the up local with the 13.33 stopping train for Waterloo. Prior to rebuilding 34046 had long been a Brighton-based engine for working the through services to Plymouth and Cardiff as far as Salisbury.

As a class of 8P engines the Merchant Navy Pacifics were seen as something special and it was regarded as a little strange in the early 1950's that Bournemouth should be without an allocation of the class in order to provide a number of the class for the boat trains between Victoria and Dover. Once the rebuilding programme had got under way, the entire class was restored to the South Western with Bournemouth receiving an allocation of seven members of the class which considerably increased the number of Merchant Navies that could be seen at Basingstoke. 35005 'Canadian Pacific' rushes through Basingstoke with the 09.17 Weymouth - Waterloo express as the stock for the 12.12 stopping service to London is positioned in the up local.

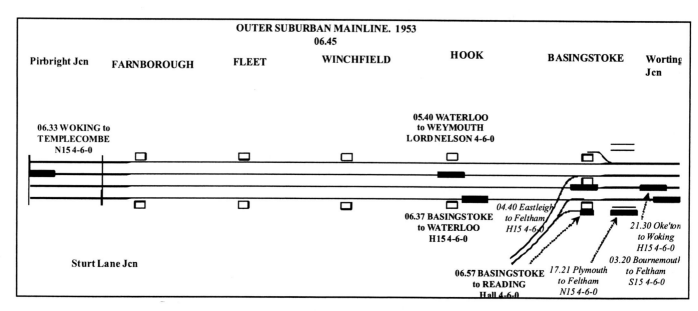

OUTER SUBURBAN MAINLINE. 1953
06.45

| Pirbright Jcn | FARNBOROUGH | FLEET | WINCHFIELD | HOOK | BASINGSTOKE | Worting Jcn |

05.40 WATERLOO to WEYMOUTH LORD NELSON 4-6-0

06.33 WOKING to TEMPLECOMBE N15 4-6-0

06.37 BASINGSTOKE to WATERLOO H15 4-6-0

04.40 Eastleigh to Feltham H15 4-6-0

21.30 Oke'ton to Woking H15 4-6-0

03.20 Bournemouth to Feltham S15 4-6-0

Sturt Lane Jcn

06.57 BASINGSTOKE to READING Hall 4-6-0

17.21 Plymouth to Feltham N15 4-6-0

DIESEL WORKINGS (1952/3)		
	Weekdays	
Arr	Station	Dep
	Waterloo	01.25
05.00	Exeter (C)	07.30
11.08	Waterloo	13.00
16.42	Exeter (C)	17.55
22.08	Waterloo	(01.25
	Sunday	
	Waterloo	01.35
05.31	Yeovil (T)	07.00
11.21	Waterloo	12.30
14.52	Bournemouth (W)	16.34
18.50	Waterloo	20.54
23.30	Southampton (T)	01.10
03.53	Waterloo	
	Monday	
	Maintenance	
	Tues - Saturday	
	Waterloo	05.40
10.07	Weymouth	11.30
14.49	Waterloo	16.35
19.55	Weymouth	21.55
03.53	Waterloo	(05.40
	Sunday	
	Maintenance	

The workings for diesel-electrics 10201 and 10202 covered both the West of England and Wessex mainlines, the idea being that each engine should spend a week on each route and change with the other at the week-end. Whether either engine ever succeeded in maintaining the fortnightly working is open to doubt.

London services without a change of engine and some trains enjoyed a rich variety of motive power for their journeys. The 08.30 from Waterloo was a case in point and started out behind a Nine Elms Merchant Navy Pacific which took the train as far as Bournemouth and returned to London with the 13.05 from Bournemouth West. The 08.30 divided into two portions at Bournemouth Central, the section to Bournemouth West being taken forward by an M7 0-4-4T whilst the main portion was worked through to Weymouth by a Dorchester-based U class 2-6-0.

The 10.30 from Waterloo was also worked by a Nine Elms Merchant Navy as far as Bournemouth, the engine uncoupling at the Central to run forward to allow the locomotive that had arrived with the 02.40 ex London to work forward the Weymouth section, after which it rejoined the train and continued forward to Bournemouth West.

Whilst the daily mileage covered by the through engines compared well with those of other regions - the return trip from London to Weymouth being similar to the distance from Kings Cross to Newcastle - the diagrams lacked the nicety of the Exeter workings so much so that one working, the 15.30 from Waterloo, had to be spread across a two day cycle - rather inexplicably since the working could have been based on Bournemouth without the resulting complications - with the engine staying overnight at Bournemouth and returning to London with the 07.20 from the West, the diagram concluding with the 15.54 stopping train from Waterloo to Basingstoke and the 19.40 return. Another curious working concerned the 06.35

stopping train from Bournemouth to Waterloo which was headed by a light Pacific as far as Basingstoke where it gave way to an N15x 'Remembrance' 4-6-0. The Pacific followed with a

DIESEL WORKINGS (1953)		
(LMS 10000/1)		
	Waterloo	02.40
05.54	Bournemouth C	
	Bournemouth W.	07.20
10.00	Waterloo	11.00
14.06	Exeter	16.30
20.25	Waterloo	(02.40
	Waterloo	08.30
12.24	Weymouth	13.25
16.50	Waterloo	18.00
22.00	Exeter	
	Exmouth Jcn	22.40
04.03	Nine Elms	
	Waterloo	(08.30

In May 1953 the two 1600hp LMS diesel-electric locomotives 10000 and 10001 were sent to the LSWR to augment the existing SR diesels by operating the diagrams shown above. It was a fortunate decision since their arrival coincided with the temporary withdrawal of the Bulleid Pacifics following an axle failure on a Merchant Navy locomotive. In actual fact the all the diesels were used on an ad hoc basis with little reference to the published diagrams. The failure rate of the locomotives was high and for several weeks during the summer season, when engines of any type were at a premium, it was unusual to have more than one of the diesels available at any given time.

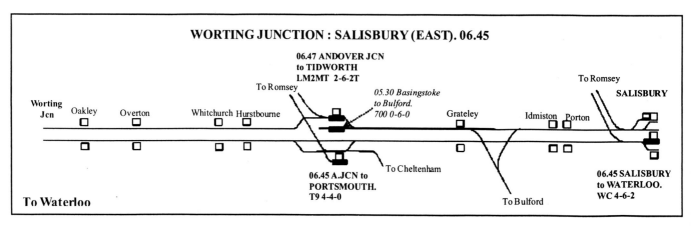

WORTING JUNCTION : SALISBURY (EAST). 06.45

06.47 ANDOVER JCN to TIDWORTH LM2MT 2-6-2T

To Romsey

To Romsey

SALISBURY

05.30 Basingstoke to Bulford. 700 0-6-0

| Worting Jcn | Oakley | Overton | Whitchurch | Hurstbourne | | Grateley | Idmiston | Porton |

06.45 A.JCN to PORTSMOUTH. T9 4-4-0

To Cheltenham

To Bulford

06.45 SALISBURY to WATERLOO. WC 4-6-2

To Waterloo

30

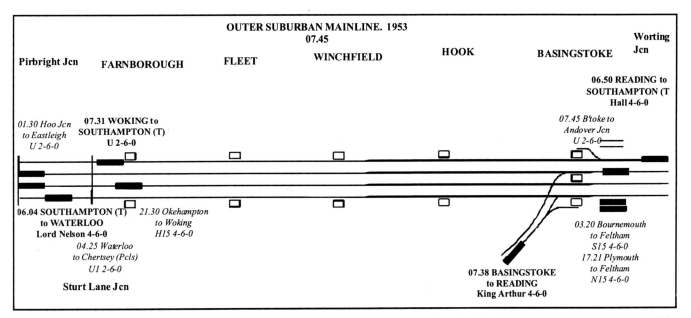

OUTER SUBURBAN MAINLINE. 1953
07.45

| Pirbright Jcn | FARNBOROUGH | FLEET | WINCHFIELD | HOOK | BASINGSTOKE | Worting Jcn |

01.30 Hoo Jcn to Eastleigh U 2-6-0

07.31 WOKING to SOUTHAMPTON (T) U 2-6-0

06.50 READING to SOUTHAMPTON (T Hall 4-6-0

07.45 B'toke to Andover Jcn U 2-6-0

06.04 SOUTHAMPTON (T) to WATERLOO Lord Nelson 4-6-0

21.30 Okehampton to Woking H15 4-6-0

04.25 Waterloo to Chertsey (Pcls) U1 2-6-0

03.20 Bournemouth to Feltham S15 4-6-0

17.21 Plymouth to Feltham N15 4-6-0

07.38 BASINGSTOKE to READING King Arthur 4-6-0

Sturt Lane Jcn

Apart from Merchant Navy Pacifics, the other speciality of the South Western was the Bournemouth Belle Pullman which was the crack train of the line. Enthusiasts liked it because it made a change from the humdrum green of other trains, passengers enjoyed it - advance bookings were necessary most of the time - because it allowed them an air of luxury at a very reasonable price and the staff at Waterloo - one assistant station master, at any rate - regarded the up working as the highlight of his shift since the chief steward made available (gratis) what were undoubtedly the best chips in the kingdom. The up train, paint and brass gleaming as usual, pulls away behind a rebuilt Merchant Navy 4-6-2 from Southampton Central.

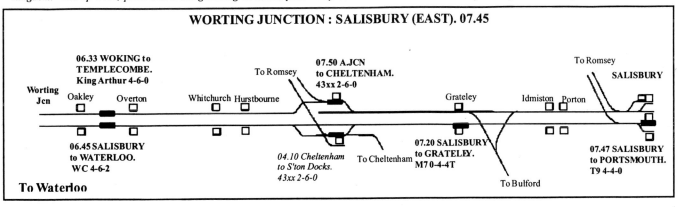

WORTING JUNCTION : SALISBURY (EAST). 07.45

| Worting Jcn | Oakley | Overton | Whitchurch | Hurstbourne | | Grateley | Idmiston | Porton | SALISBURY |

06.33 WOKING to TEMPLECOMBE. King Arthur 4-6-0

To Romsey

07.50 A.JCN to CHELTENHAM. 43xx 2-6-0

To Romsey

06.45 SALISBURY to WATERLOO. WC 4-6-2

04.10 Cheltenham to S'ton Docks. 43xx 2-6-0

To Cheltenham

07.20 SALISBURY to GRATELEY. M7 0-4-4T

To Bulford

07.47 SALISBURY to PORTSMOUTH. T9 4-4-0

To Waterloo

Although some drivers considered the rebuilt Merchant Navy's to be less free in their steaming than in their original form, general opinion favoured the reconstruction programme, not least amongst the maintenance staff who were spared the difficulties of internal oil-baths and air smoothed casing. The rebuilds also lost much of the mystique they had held for enthusiasts and from 1956 onwards had too much of a 'BR standard' appearance for many tastes. There was however no doubting their power and the way they could master a heavy express made the rebuilds the envy of many parts of BR. Rebuild 35009 'Shaw Savill' arrives at Salisbury from the Exeter direction with an up express for London.

Although many railwaymen might have opted for a more conventional type of locomotive, there can be no doubt that the Bulleid Pacifics put the Southern Railway firmly on the map from the enthusiasts perspective and many were a little saddened by the rebuilding programme of 1956 which stripped the Merchant Navy's and many West Country engines of their air-smoothed casing. Fortunately many light Pacifics escaped rebuilding and retained their impressive appearance and asthma-like exhaust until the last day of steam. 34057 'Biggin Hill' runs in to Salisbury with the 12.00 Ilfracombe to Waterloo on 16th May 1964.

Having no need for a six-coupled express tank on suburban work, the South Western did not employ the BR 4MT 2-6-4T and was one of the few parts of the BR system not to use the wheel arrangement. However a number of 2-6-2 tanks were taken into stock in an attempt to reduce the fleet of M7 0-4-4T's, the new engines being used in the Exeter and Eastleigh areas. These included fifteen of the BR standard 3MT locomotives, 82011-25, the first of which arrived in June 1952 and were allocated to Exmouth Junction. In later years the allocation was increased to take over ECS duties between Waterloo and Clapham Junction and the newcomers included 82027 which had earlier been a Kirkby Stephen (NER) locomotive.

later stopping train to London and returned to Bournemouth with the 17.30 down express.

For the benefit of the souls who tired of iron-clad Pacifics - and the Bulleid engines were by no means universally loved during the 1950's - there was always the 09.20 Weymouth - Waterloo which remained as a breath of fresh air for the enthusiast with traditionalist leanings since it was booked to be worked as far as Bournemouth by an Eastleigh King Arthur 4-6-0 and by the Lord Nelson off the 05.40 ex Waterloo for the remainder of the journey.

Whether or not the upheaval in workings to achieve through engine working between London and Weymouth was worthwhile is a matter for debate although the results were, to say the least, patchy with only two down services (13.30 and 15.30 ex Waterloo) being so worked whilst five engines (07.34, 11.30, 13.25, 17.35 and 18.30 departures from Weymouth) travelled through to London in the up direction. The remainder of the sixteen services all changed engines at Bournemouth Central.

The engines to be seen on services from Waterloo included all the larger SR classes with the notable exception of the Schools class whose post-war appearances on the South-Western

were rare and the result usually of an engine coming out of Eastleigh works and being used for the odd working before being returned to Kent. The SECR 4-4-0's were even rarer and apart from the routine exchange of Pacifics from time to time, express engines from the three constituent companies very largely kept to their own metals. This segregation remained in force until May 1958 when a number of Schools 4-4-0's, displaced by the introduction of multiple-units on the Charing Cross - Hastings route, were transferred to Nine Elms and Basingstoke.

Given the reputation of the Schools class and the feats they had performed between Waterloo and Bournemouth during the 1930s, it was expected that the transferred engines would write another interesting chapter of their lives. However the South-Western were in the throes of restocking with rebuilt Bulleid Pacifics and new standard 4-6-0's with the result that the redundant Schools engines were all but ignored, seeing service on the odd stopping trains between London and Basingstoke or Salisbury but only rarely, usually at times of peak holiday pressure, on long distance express duties.

A further tranche of émigrés, but on a much larger scale, arrived on the South Western a year

later following the electrification of the LCDR route from Victoria to Ramsgate and Dover, with the result that the overnight the South Western - principally Nine Elms - had so many engines, it not only had no idea what to use them for but had so little room to store them, that for weeks during the summer of 1959, redundant South Eastern engines were to be found parked out of the way in all sorts of nooks and crannies down the line.

It would be pleasant to record that the displaced engines - especially the Schools 4-4-0's - were given a new lease of life after leaving the South Eastern but, alas, for most of the year the South Western was more than adequately blessed with its native motive power with the result that the opportunities for seeing some of the strangers working regularly out of Waterloo was limited. From time to time some of the inside cylinder 4-4-0's found themselves booked to secondary passenger trains and parcels services but on the whole services to and from Waterloo remained in the hands of rebuilt Bulleid Pacifics and, after the demise of the N15 'King Arthurs', standard 5MT 4-6-0's.

| 11.22 p.m. ... ... | Nine Elms ... | Southampton Dks. | As many vacuum-fitted vehicles as possible to be attached next the engine (not less than twelve). Formation :— Engine, wagons for Gosport, Fareham, Cosham, Romsey to Andover road box, Eastleigh generals, mixed Northam wagons, Docks wagons, van. |

In an attempt to regularise traffic flows and to avoid some of the uncertainty endemic in goods working, specific instructions were issued for the loading and formation of the more important goods services. In the case of the example above - which might otherwise have been thought of as a service designed for shipping traffic - it allowed Fareham and the other points mentioned to know which service their traffic from London was likely to arrive in without having to be reminded every day. When traffic requirements dictated, however, altered arrangements could be made between the Inspectors at Nine Elms and Eastleigh to vary the order to vehicles.

LOCAL SERVICES

Amongst the most interesting large engines on the LSWR were the N15X 4-6-0's, all seven of which were allocated to Basingstoke until their withdrawal in the mid-1950's. The interest in the class stemmed from the fact that they were rebuilds of the celebrated LBSCR 4-6-4T express passenger engines, having been assimilated into the King Arthur class when made redundant by the 1933 Brighton line electrification. The rebuilds however were never the equal of the King Arthur 4-6-0's and were regarded as sluggish by comparison; a view that doubtless explained their exile to Basingstoke from where they worked stopping trains to Waterloo and Reading. 32332 'Stroudley' stands at Eastleigh after arriving with the 19.00 stopping train from Reading (General), part of a Basingstoke working which spent the daytime on the Reading branch and the night between Eastleigh and Waterloo, finishing with the 03.45 News from Waterloo to Farnborough.

Like the long distance and electric services, the steam-hauled outer suburban workings ran to fixed interval timings from London, leaving Waterloo at fifty-four minutes past most hours with additional trains during the rush hour. Up trains however, ran to no particular pattern and although they balanced the number of down trains they operated at irregular intervals, fitting themselves in between fast services from Exeter or Bournemouth.

It is probably true to state that no other element in the timetable, other than the electrified services, had seen so much change during the period of grouping and the pattern of services employed in the 1950's had very little in common with those of pre-1914 days when neither Basingstoke nor Salisbury were regarded as outer-suburban boundaries and stopping trains ran through to Exeter, Southampton and Bournemouth. The prize went to the 06.35 from Waterloo which not only called at most stations west of Clapham Junction but ran through to distant Torrington, where it arrived at 15.20. No doubt a through conveyance between Hook and South Molton Road was occasionally useful although it is doubtful if many availed of it.

By the 1950's the area covered by the outer-suburban trains had contracted considerably and most terminated at either Basingstoke or Salisbury with only a select handful being extended to serve local stations in Wiltshire and Hampshire.

LORD NELSON 4-6-0. 30865 'Sir John Hawkins'. 12 Pullmans : 462/495 tons. (1935)							
m.ch	Point	1 in	W.T.T.	Actual	mph	dbhp	pc
0.00	SOUTHAMPTON (C)	-	0.00	0.00	-	-	-
1.05	Northam Jcn	560999		3.23	20.0	437	1
3.42	Swaythling	865		7.20	40.5	1034	4
5.64	EASTLEIGH	570	9.00	10.22	48.0	990	4
9.49	Shawford	280		14.52	52.5	1286	6
12.60	Winchester	260		18.24	53.0	1283	7
17.39	Wallers Ash	265		23.53	54.0	1227	6
21.10	Micheldever	252		27.49	54.5	1381	7
22.77	Roundwood	265		29.51	55.5	1361	7
28.76	Worting Jcn	-757	37.00	35.56	67.0	748	5
31.39	BASINGSTOKE	-260	39.00	37.49	76.5	741	5
37.06	Hook	-689		42.21	72.0	331	2
42.61	Fleet	-790		46.54	76.0	864	6
46.02	Farnborough	-2852		49.35	74.0	663	4
48.19	MP.31	946		51.26	70.5	755	5
51.20	Brookwood	-306		53.52	75.0	483	4
54.72	WOKING	-318	60.00	56.46	75.5	144	1
57.45	West Byfleet	-367		58.54	75.5	213	2
60.07	Weybridge	-6128		60.59	68.0	-	-
67.16	Surbiton	-8960		66.56	67.5	846	6
72.00	Wimbledon	-20774		71.13	69.0	842	6
75.25	Clapham Jcn	-752	79.00	74.54	30.0	-	-
79.19	WATERLOO	3647	86.00	81.10	-	-	-

Eastleigh - Roundwood. 17.2 miles at 1/262 : 53 mph 1307 dbhp
Basingstoke : Brookwood. 19.8 miles at -1/823 : 74 mph 594 dbhp

In the right hands, the Lord Nelsons were capable of rousing performances as is shown above with a pre-war run on the Bournemouth Belle where over 1300 dbhp was sustained on the climb from Eastleigh followed by average speeds well into the 70's after Basingstoke. Such performances by the class were uncommon.

The most interesting aspect of the stopping trains was the range of motive power employed, which included just about every type of engine at the South Western's disposal except the Merchant Navy class. The standard engine - insofar as there was such an animal - for the workings was the N15 King Arthur 4-6-0 used by Nine Elms and Salisbury sheds for their share of the workings, the N15's working ten of the eighteen down services.

Strangely, given that it was a terminating point for many of the workings, Basingstoke played only a minor role in the working of the trains, three of the shed's N15 4-6-0's heading a trio of evening departures out of London whilst one of the 'Remembrance' class 4-6-0's was booked for the 13.54 ex Waterloo. This was not the only sighting to be had of an N15x at the intermediate stations since another of the class was diagrammed to an early morning newspaper train which terminated at Farnborough but ran forward empty to Basingstoke whilst a third example of the class worked the daily pick-up goods between Basingstoke and Farnborough.

Bulleid Pacifics were less in evidence than might have been supposed and only two departures from Waterloo, 11.54 and 15.54, were booked to the West Country class; one of which came from Salisbury and was return-

Train	arr	loco	Line	dep	Destination
17.18 Sidmouth Jcn (Milk)		*N15 4-6-0*	*L*	*00/30*	*Waterloo*
23.25 Nine Elms		*LN 4-6-0*	*T*	*00/35*	*Southampton Docks*
21.56 Bevois Park		*S15 4-6-0*	*L*	*00/40*	*Feltham*
00.23 Woking		*H15 4-6-0*	*L*	*00/45*	*Exmouth Jcn*
23.58 Feltham		*S15 4-6-0*	*T*	*01/20*	*Exmouth Jcn*
22.30 Southampton Docks		*U 2-6-0*	*L*	*01/20*	*Woking*
14.58 Gravesend		*N15 4-6-0*	*L*	*01/37*	*Yeovil Town*
12.45 Torrington		*N15 4-6-0*	*T*	*01/43*	*Nine Elms*
00.45 Nine Elms		*H15 4-6-0*	*L*	*02/02*	*Eastleigh*
01.25 WATERLOO		MN 4-6-2	T	02/09	PLYMOUTH
19.50 Dorchester		*H15 4-6-0*	*T*	*02/25*	*Nine Elms*
21.55 WEYMOUTH	02.38	LN 4-6-0	L	02.41	WATERLOO
02.10 Clapham Jcn		*N15 4-6-0*	*T*	*02/48*	*Fratton*
00.55 Feltham		*S15 4-6-0*	*L*	*02/55*	*Southampton Docks*
17.00 Torrington		*MN 4-6-2*	*T*	*03/05*	*Nine Elms*
02.40 WATERLOO		MN 4-6-2	T	03/29	BOURNEMOUTH
00.45 Eastleigh		*H15 4-6-0*	*L*	*03/30*	*Feltham*
00.50 Fratton		*S15 4-6-0*	*T*	*03/50*	*Feltham*
03.45 Waterloo	04.30	N15x 4-6-0	L	04.45	Basingstoke
13.55 Meldon		*H15 4-6-0*	*L*	*05/00*	*Woking*
04.07 Feltham		*S15 4-6-0*	*T*	*05/25*	*Southampton Docks*
03.10 Bevois Park		*S15 4-6-0*	*L*	*05/45*	*Woking*
05.32 Woking	05.57	*0395 0-6-0*	*T*	*05.57*	*Yard*
Engine & Brake		*0395 0-6-0*	*L*	*06.30*	*Woking*
05.40 WATERLOO		LN 4-6-0	T	06/32	WEYMOUTH
06.33 Woking	06.52	N15 4-6-0	L	06.54	Templecombe
06.37 Basingstoke	07.06	H15 4-6-0	L	07.07	Waterloo
04.40 Eastleigh		*H15 4-6-0*	*T*	*07/30*	*Feltham*
06.04 Southampton (T)	07.39	LN 4-6-0	L	07.40	Waterloo
07.31 Woking	07.47	U 2-6-0	L	07.48	Southampton (T)
01.30 Hoo Jcn		*U 2-6-0*	*T*	*07/55*	*Eastleigh*
21.30 Okehampton		*H15 4-6-0*	*T*	*08/00*	*Woking*
07.20 Waterloo	08.14	N15 4-6-0	L	08.15	Salisbury
07.03 SOUTHAMPTON (DOCKS)		LN 4-6-0	T	08/25	WATERLOO
06.45 Salisbury	08.30	WC 4-6-2	L	08.32	Waterloo
03.20 Bournemouth (C)		*S15 4-6-0*	*L*	*08/46*	*Feltham*
08.45 Woking	08.51	N15 4-6-0	L	08.52	Basingstoke
08.25 Basingstoke	08.53	N15 4-6-0	L	08.55	Waterloo
08.30 WATERLOO		MN 4-6-2	T	09/19	WEYMOUTH
07.40 Clapham Jcn	09.11	*H15 4-6-0*	*L*	*09/21*	*Eastleigh*
07.20 BOURNEMOUTH (W)		WC 4-6-2	T	09/24	WATERLOO
06.35 Bournemouth (C)	09.30	N15x 4-6-0	L	09.31	Waterloo
08.15 SALISBURY		MN 4-6-2	T	09/32	WATERLOO
09.00 WATERLOO		MN 4-6-2	T	09/47	PLYMOUTH
17.21 Plymouth		*N15 4-6-0*	*L*	*09/55*	*Feltham*

"/" = passing time

PASSING THE BOUNDARY AT FARNBOROUGH. Lest the traffic density of steam services become forgotten over the years, the sequence of trains and their booked engines that passed Farnborough in steam days on a normal weekday (1953) is illustrated in the accompanying tables. The average frequency was one train every ten minutes throughout the twenty-four hours, amounting to no less than 141 workings. Not shown are the un-advertised specials and boat trains - one good-sized liner could easily account for four or five trains - which at busy times could swell the total to over 200 trains. Even on normal days the variety of motive power was not only impressive but considerably more varied than on most of the other routes radiating from London. The engines - most of which passed more than once a day - ranged from the venerable 0395 0-6-0 goods engines which worked in from Woking twice a day to the lordly Merchant Navies - then three years away from rebuilding - which handled all the west of England expresses and some of the more important Wessex trains. Although numerically small - 30 only in number - no less than 28 Merchant Navy-hauled workings passed Farnborough each day, making them - by a considerable margin - the most frequently seen class on the line. Next in utility were the N15 'King Arthur' 4-6-0's of which eighteen were booked to appear whilst the S15 and H15 freight 4-6-0's ran a close third with sixteen and fourteen appearances respectively. Most surprising was the relatively small use made of the West Country Pacifics, given that there were 110 engines in the class, with only twenty trains - 14% - being diagrammed for them. Still at large were the Lord Nelsons - thirteen trains - whilst absences included all the once-familiar 4-4-0's although on summer Saturdays D15 and T9 engines would be drafted in to work the through service between Waterloo and Lymington Pier. Also well out of sight were the SR 2-6-0 types and only four of the U class - of which two passed within minutes of each other - were booked to be seen.

Train	Arr	Engine	Line	Dep	Destination
07.34 WEYMOUTH		WC 4-6-2	T	10.15	WATERLOO
09.52 Woking	*10.17*	*0395 0-6-0*	*L*	*10.17*	*Yard*
09.30 WATERLOO		WC 4-6-2	T	10.19	BOURNEMOUTH (W)
07.10 Yeovil Town	10.26	N15 4-6-0	L	10.27	Waterloo
07.30 EXETER		MN 4-6-2	T	10.33	WATERLOO
09.54 Waterloo	10.44	H15 4-6-0	L	10.45	Southampton (C)
10.35 Basingstoke	11.02	WC 4-6-2	L	11.03	Waterloo
10.30 WATERLOO		MN 4-6-2	T	11.09	WEYMOUTH
09.45 Feltham		*S15 4-6-0*	*L*	*11.10*	*Eastleigh*
08.35 BOURNEMOUTH (W)		WC 4-6-2	T	11.15	WATERLOO
11.00 WATERLOO		MN 4-6-2	T	11.37	PADSTOW
06.30 EXETER		MN 4-6-2	T	11.37	WATERLOO
10.54 Waterloo	11.44	LN 4-6-0	L	11.45	Salisbury
11.30 WATERLOO		LN 4-6-0	T	12.07	BOURNEMOUTH (W)
Light engine		*0395 0-6-0*	*L*	*12.08*	*Woking*
09.20 WEYMOUTH		LN 4-6-0	T	12.14	WATERLOO
10.45 Feltham		*S15 4-6-0*	*L*	*12.15*	*Exmouth Jcn*
12.02 Basingstoke	12.30	N15 4-6-0	L	12.31	Waterloo
11.54 Waterloo	12.44	WC 4-6-2	L	12.45	Salisbury
08.41 Basingstoke	12.48	N15x 4-6-0	L	12.48	Yard
03.20 Ashford		*S15 4-6-0*	*L*	*13.00*	*Eastleigh*
12.30 WATERLOO		MN 4-6-2	T	13.09	BOURNEMOUTH (W)
		N15x 4-6-0	L	13.33	Basingstoke
08.15 PLYMOUTH		MN 4-6-2	T	13.34	WATERLOO
11.05 BOURNEMOUTH (C)		WC 4-6-2	L	13.35	WATERLOO
13.00 WATERLOO		MN 4-6-2	T	13.42	PLYMOUTH
12.54 Waterloo	13.44	N15 4-6-0	L	13.45	Basingstoke
13.33 Basingstoke	14.01	N15 4-6-0	L	14.02	Waterloo
13.30 WATERLOO		WC 4-6-2	T	14.09	WEYMOUTH
11.30 WEYMOUTH		WC 4-6-2	T	14.13	WATERLOO
09.45 Tonbridge		*H15 4-6-0*	*T*	*14.20*	*Exmouth Jcn*
13.48 Basingstoke		*H15 4-6-0*	*L*	*14.25*	*Feltham*
13.00 Salisbury	14.41	S15 4-6-0	L	14.43	Waterloo
13.54 Waterloo	14.44	N15x 4-6-0	L	14.45	Basingstoke
10.30 ILFRACOMBE		MN 4-6-2	T	15.04	WATERLOO
14.45 Feltham		*S15 4-6-0*	*L*	*15.10*	*Southampton Docks*
13.05 Eastleigh (Pcls)	*15.10*	*H15 4-6-0*	*L*	*15.20*	*Clapham Jcn*
14.45 Basingstoke MPD (Light)	*15.23*	*S15 4-6-0*	*L*	*15.23*	*Yard*
11.36 Bournemouth (W)	15.30	H15 4-6-0	L	15.31	Woking
13.05 BOURNEMOUTH (W)		MN 4-6-2	T	15.33	WATERLOO
15.00 WATERLOO		MN 4-6-2	T	15.37	PLYMOUTH
14.54 Waterloo	15.44	N15 4-6-0	L	15.45	Basingstoke
15.20 WATERLOO		WC 4-6-2	T	15.47	WEYMOUTH

Variety on the Southern 1 : The BR4 2-6-0's were the first standard tender engines - apart from two Britannia Pacifics - to be allocated to the Southern, 76005/6 being sent to Eastleigh in December 1952: the first of 36 examples which eventually operated from Salisbury, Bournemouth, Eastleigh and Redhill sheds. Intended to replace D15 and T9 4-4-0's - a requirement they never wholly fulfilled - the class were more often to be seen on semi-fast cross country services than on main line workings although during the sixties some could be found working the London line in lieu of SR 2-6-0's. 76058 of Bournemouth runs into Winchester with the 07.31 Woking - Southampton Terminus.

Variety on the Southern 2 : When through trains from the Great Western operated with their own power over Southern metals, surprises could arise. Hall and 43xx engines were common enough but the sight of Grange 4-6-0 6845 'Paviland Grange' at Southampton Central on the 06.05 Birmingham (Snow Hill) to Bournemouth raised a few eyebrows. From its uncharacteristically grimy state it was probably a last-minute substitute for something larger.

Train	Arr	Engine	Line	Dep	Destination
13.20 Southampton Docks		*S15 4-6-0*	*L*	*16.00*	*Feltham*
15.30 WATERLOO		WC 4-6-2	T	16.12	BOURNEMOUTH (W)
13.25 WEYMOUTH		WC 4-6-2	T	16.14	WATERLOO
Yard		*S15 4-6-0*	*L*	*16.20*	*Woking*
15.15 Salisbury	16.41	N15 4-6-0	L	16.42	Waterloo
15.54 Waterloo	16.44	WC 4-6-2	L	16.45	Basingstoke
15.54 Clapham Jcn		*MN 4-6-2*	*L*	*16.57*	*Exeter (C)*
16.35 WATERLOO		WC 4-6-2	T	17.12	WEYMOUTH
17.00 WATERLOO		MN 4-6-2	T	17.45	EXETER
15.05 BOURNEMOUTH (W)		MN 4-6-2	T	17.45	WATERLOO
12.20 ILFRACOMBE		MN 4-6-2	T	17.52	WATERLOO
17.09 Waterloo	17.55	N15 4-6-0	L	17.56	Basingstoke
17.30 WATERLOO		WC 4-6-2	T	18.07	BOURNEMOUTH (W)
16.05 Salisbury	18.06	LN 4-6-0	L	18.07	Waterloo
16.34 BOURNEMOUTH (W)		MN 4-6-2	T	18.15	WATERLOO
17.39 Waterloo	18.28	N15 4-6-0	L	18.29	Salisbury
18.00 WATERLOO		MN 4-6-2	T	18.37	PLYMOUTH
17.35 SOUTHAMPTON DOCKS		LN 4-6-0	T	18.40	WATERLOO
18.09 Waterloo	18.55	N15 4-6-0	L	18.56	Basingstoke
17.15 Salisbury	19.05	N15 4-6-0	L	19.06	Waterloo
18.30 WATERLOO		WC 4-6-2	T	19.09	WEYMOUTH
16.20 Southampton Docks		*S15 4-6-0*	*L*	*19.23*	*Feltham*
17.05 BOURNEMOUTH (W)		LN 4-6-0	T	19.35	WATERLOO
14.20 ILFRACOMBE		MN 4-6-2	T	19.43	WATERLOO
18.54 Waterloo	19.44	S15 4-6-0	L	19.45	Yeovil Town
18.42 Waterloo (Pcls)		*H15 4-6-0*	*L*	*20.00*	*Eastleigh*
19.30 WATERLOO		WC 4-6-2	T	20.07	BOURNEMOUTH (W)
19.40 Basingstoke	20.12	WC 4-6-2	L	20.13	Waterloo
17.35 WEYMOUTH		MN 4-6-2	T	20.15	WATERLOO
15.50 PLYMOUTH		MN 4-6-2	T	20.21	WATERLOO
19.54 Waterloo	20.44	N15 4-6-0	L	20.45	Basingstoke
19.25 Nine Elms		*H15 4-6-0*	*T*	*20.55*	*Southampton Docks*
18.55 Southampton Docks		*N15 4-6-0*	*T*	*21.35*	*Nine Elms*
21.00 WATERLOO		LN 4-6-0	T	21.39	SOUTHAMPTON (DOCKS)
20.54 Waterloo	21.43	N15 4-6-0	L	21.44	Salisbury
21.15 Basingstoke	21.43	U 2-6-0	L	21.44	Woking
17.40 Yeovil Town		*N15 4-6-0*	*L*	*22.00*	*Gravesend*
18.20 WEYMOUTH		*WC 4-6-2*	*T*	*22.14*	*WATERLOO*
21.10 Nine Elms		*MN 4-6-2*	*T*	*22.15*	*Plymouth*
19.45 Eastleigh (Vans)		*H15 4-6-0*	*T*	*22.25*	*Waterloo*
21.05 Templecombe (Milk)		*MN 4-6-2*	*T*	*22.33*	*Clapham Jcn*
20.50 Salisbury	22.36	N15 4-6-0	L	22.37	Woking
19.35 Kensington (Pcls)		*H15 4-6-0*	*L*	*22.45*	*Poole*
22.25 Basingstoke		*S15 4-6-0*	*L*	*23.00*	*Feltham*
22.45 Woking		*S15 4-6-0*	*L*	*23.05*	*Eastleigh*
22.00 Nine Elms		*MN 4-6-2*	*T*	*23.05*	*Exmouth Jcn*
22.45 Feltham		*S15 46-0*	*L*	*23.15*	*Bournemouth (C)*
22.30 WATERLOO		LN 4-6-0	T	23.19	DORCHESTER (S)
21.15 Eastleigh		*S15 4-6-0*	*L*	*23.25*	*Feltham*
22.40 Waterloo	23.31	H15 4-6-0	L	23.32	Basingstoke
22.20 Feltham		*S15 4-6-0*	*T*	*23.40*	*Southampton Docks*
22.38 Nine Elms		*H15 4-6-0*	*T*	*23.50*	*Weymouth*
19.55 Eastleigh (Pcls)		*N15x 4-6-0*	*T*	*23.50*	*Waterloo*

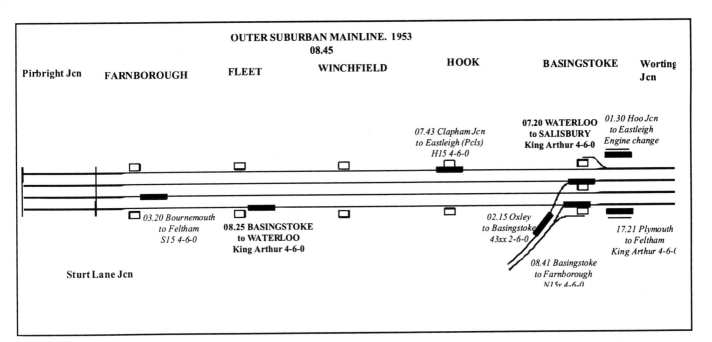

OUTER SUBURBAN MAINLINE. 1953
08.45

Pirbright Jcn   **FARNBOROUGH**   **FLEET**   **WINCHFIELD**   **HOOK**   **BASINGSTOKE**   Worting Jcn

07.43 Clapham Jcn to Eastleigh (Pcls) H15 4-6-0

07.20 WATERLOO to SALISBURY King Arthur 4-6-0

01.30 Hoo Jcn to Eastleigh Engine change

03.20 Bournemouth to Feltham S15 4-6-0

08.25 BASINGSTOKE to WATERLOO King Arthur 4-6-0

02.15 Oxley to Basingstoke 43xx 2-6-0

17.21 Plymouth to Feltham King Arthur 4-6-0

08.41 Basingstoke to Farnborough N15x 4-6-0

Sturt Lane Jcn

---

ing home after running up to London with the 06.45 slow from Salisbury whilst the other came from Nine Elms and returned home with the 19.40 ex Basingstoke. A third Pacific could also be seen on the 10.35 Basingstoke to London, the Bournemouth engine of which arrived in Basingstoke, where it gave way to an N15x 4-6-0, with the 06.35 stopping train from Bournemouth Central.

Although the Southern did not have, or need, a mixed traffic engine in the sense that the other regions did, the nearest to it was the H15 4-6-0 which, whilst mainly used on goods and parcels workings, could be seen on the 09.54 and 22.40 departures from Waterloo; both engines being based at Nine Elms. The first of the two had quite a varied day and after reaching Eastleigh, where it was replaced by a Lord Nelson 4-6-0 for the final few miles to Southampton, it retraced its steps as far as Basingstoke with an evening goods from Bevois Park, Southampton proceeding northwards to Reading with a late night stopping passenger.

OUTER-SUBURBAN SERVICE : 1910						
DOWN						
Train	F.boro	Fleet	W'field	Hook	B'stoke	Destination
06.35 Waterloo	7.40	7.47	7.55	8.01	8.10	Torrington 15.20
07.40 Waterloo	8.52	9.01	9.10	9.17	9.27	Southampton 10.32
09.44 Woking	10.00	10.07	10.14	10.20	10.29	Salisbury 12.01
09.32 Waterloo	11.01	11.08	11.15	11.21	11.30	
10.40 Waterloo	11.40	11.56	12.03		12.16	Swanage 15.44
11.23 Waterloo	12.40	12.47	12.55	13.01	13.10	Exeter 18.23
12.50 Waterloo	13.55	14.04	14.13	14.19	14.29	Southampton 15.37
15.00 Waterloo	16.01	16.09	16.17	16.23	16.33	Bournemouth W 19.25
15.50 Waterloo	17.00	17.09	17.18	17.24	17.34	Exeter 22.29
17.00 Waterloo	17.56	18.03	18.10	18.16	18.25	Salisbury 20.22
18.00 Waterloo	19.00	19.08	19.17	19.23	19.33	Southampton 20.40
18.45 Waterloo	19.41	19.49	19.57	20.03	20.13	
19.15 Waterloo	20.28	20.45	20.53	20.59	21.08	Salisbury 22.51
21.00 Waterloo	22.17	22.24	22.32	22.38	22.47	
UP						
Train	B'stoke	Hook	W'field	Fleet	F'boro	Destination
01.00 Southampton	2.11		2.23		2.33	Waterloo 3.35
06.03 Southampton	7.13	7.23	7.30	7.36	7.44	Waterloo 8.46
06.45 Southampton	8.17	8.27	8.35	8.42	8.50	Waterloo 9.47
06.00 Yeovil	8.59				9.19	Waterloo 10.11
	9.17	9.26	9.33	9.40	9.47	Waterloo 10.41
8.50 Southampton	9.58				10.18	Waterloo 11.04
	10.04	10.13	10.19	10.25	10.31	Woking 10.46
07.48 Yeovil	11.46	11.56	12.03	12.09	12.17	Waterloo 13.35
	13.00	13.10	13.17	13.25	13.33	Waterloo 14.42
13.38 Southampton	14.56	15.07	15.15	15.22	15.30	Waterloo 17.05
10.27 Exeter	15.28	15.37	15.43	15.49	15.55	Waterloo 17.15
12.05 Weymouth	16.29		16.41		16.52	Waterloo 17.52
12.25 Exeter	17.21	17.30	17.36	17.42	17.49	Waterloo 18.53
	18.45	18.55	19.02	19.09	19.17	Woking 19.31
	21.25	21.35	21.42	21.48	21.56	Waterloo 23.02
16.40 Exeter	22.25	22.35	22.42	22.48	22.56	Waterloo 00.35
19.35 Weymouth	22.49				23.09	Waterloo 00.02

After being released from the stock of its train, the H15 penetrated even further into the Great Western by running light to Moreton Sidings Yard, Didcot to work forward a goods service for Feltham.

The other H15 was playing a part in a two-day cycle which commenced with the previous day's 07.40 Clapham Junction to Eastleigh stock and parcels trains and, after running back to London with an early morning goods to Feltham, started the second part of the working with the last stopping train from Waterloo to Basingstoke, the duty being completed by taking over the 19.50 Dorchester - Nine Elms goods at Basingstoke from a another Nine Elms H15 which followed with the first up stopping train for Waterloo.

Even though the South Western had an amazing variety and quantity of passenger engines, one of the Salisbury-based workings was diagrammed for an S15 4-6-0 goods engine; a type more normally associated with heavy goods haulage from Feltham. The working was rather top heavy since the duty revolved around the 16.30 Wadebridge - Salisbury goods which the S15 worked from Yeovil Junction, reaching Salis-

---

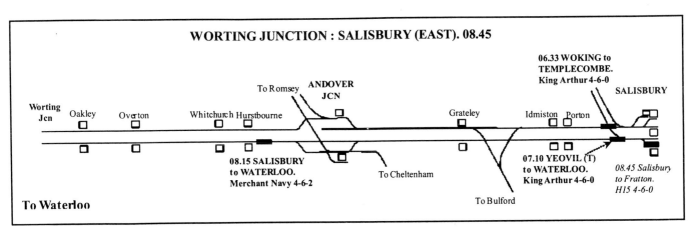

WORTING JUNCTION : SALISBURY (EAST). 08.45

Worting Jcn   Oakley   Overton   Whitchurch   Hurstbourne   To Romsey   **ANDOVER JCN**   Grateley   Idmiston   Porton   **SALISBURY**

06.33 WOKING to TEMPLECOMBE. King Arthur 4-6-0

08.15 SALISBURY to WATERLOO. Merchant Navy 4-6-2

To Cheltenham

To Bulford

07.10 YEOVIL (T) to WATERLOO. King Arthur 4-6-0

08.45 Salisbury to Fratton. H15 4-6-0

To Waterloo

39

| Schools Class 4-4-0 30932 'Radley'. 15: 473/510 tons (1939) | | | | | | |
m.ch Point	l/in	W.T.T.	Actual	mph	dbhp	pc
0.00 WATERLOO	-	0.00	0.00	-	-	-
7.19 Wimbledon	2176		13.07	47.0	625	2
24.27 WOKING	1966	29.00	30.22	59.0	853	5
27.79 Brookwood	318		34.18	53.0	921	5
31.00 MP 31	307		37.52	48.5	857	4
36.38 Fleet	-4581		43.34	65.5	1059	6
47.60 BASINGSTOKE	733	54.00	54.20	59.0	889	6
50.23 Worting Jcn	260	57.00	57.08	50.5	774	4
52.43 Wootton	278		59.55	47.5	891	4
58.09 Micheldever	-829		65.52	64.0	777	4
66.39 Winchester	-259		72.34	82.0	564	4
73.35 EASTLEIGH	-267	79.30	77.52	60.0	-	-
77.10 St Denys	-540		81.26	62.0	-	-
78.14 Northam Jcn	level	84.30	83.20	15.0	-	-
79.19 SOUTHAMPTON	-560999	87.30	86.32	-	-	-
Wimbledon - Worting Jcn. 43 miles 1/786. 59 mph 887 dbhp (pc 5)						

The Schools engine was a six-coupled engine in all but dimension and put up performances that would not have disgraced a Pacific. In the above run 30932 was called upon to work 15 coaches non-stop to Southampton and the 4-4-0 responded by not only averaging 64 mph between Fleet and St Denys but reached Southampton a minute early.

bury at 06.25. To get the engine to Yeovil, the rather roundabout expedient of routing the engine via London was resorted to, the S15 working up with the 13.00 stopping train from Salisbury and heading west with the 18.54 Waterloo - Yeovil.

The Lord Nelson 4-6-0's were not, after the introduction of the Merchant Navy and West Country Pacifics, seen in great numbers between Worting Junction and Salisbury and their only booked appearance over the route was with the 10.54 from Waterloo, returning with the 16.05 from Salisbury. Surprisingly, since Nine Elms had an allocation of the class, the engine was based at Eastleigh and worked to Salisbury as a filling-in turn between arriving in London with the 06.04 Southampton - Waterloo and returning home with the 23.25 express goods from Nine Elms. Apart from the boat trains, which were irregular runners, Lord Nelson workings were not great in number yet a visit to Waterloo just before the departure of the 10.54 usually rolled back the curtain of time a little, with one Lord Nelson getting ready to leave with the stopping train whilst another waited to follow with the 11.30 express to Bournemouth.

Two of the stopping trains were based upon Woking - a third was shown thus in the public timetable but actually started from Waterloo at 04.45 before forming the 06.33 Woking - Templecombe - and one used the services of a Guildford U class 2-6-0, a type normally uncommon on the main line. The engine, which worked the 07.31 Woking to Southampton Terminus, was one of a pair of Guildford moguls which wandered onto the main line and both spent a great deal of the day working in and around Basingstoke before returning to their home shed.

The first engine worked the Woking train as far as Eastleigh, where it was replaced by an Andover Junction 43xx 2-6-0, after which it was used on a pair of Southampton - Reading trains before working back to Woking on a night goods from Southampton Docks. Its place in the stopping train circuit was taken by the second Guildford U which took over the 01.30 Hoo Junction - Eastleigh goods as far as Basingstoke where it retired to the shed until the

evening when it emerged to work an evening trip to Reading before returning east with the 21.15 stopping train from Basingstoke to Woking.

In parenthesis it should be remembered that the 07.31 ex Woking was a dream for the enthusiast since the U class 2-6-0's moguls were uncommon power for scheduled trains within fifty miles of London whilst the train ambled down the local line to Basingstoke, being overtaken in the process by a host of early morning expresses from Waterloo. The writer has fond memories of arising betimes and travelling to Basingstoke on a combination of Southern multiple-unit and the 07.31. Traffic was heavy on the LSWR that day and as the 2-6-0 trickled westwards it was overtaken at frequent intervals by a rush of Southampton boat trains; a circumstance which gave the passengers the unusual experience of being able to see Bulleid Pacifics and Lord Nelson 4-6-0's at high speeds whilst the 2-6-0 did its best to keep up with them.

The terminating points of the down semi-fasts was as varied as the engines which worked them. Seven of the services ended at Basingstoke whilst six of the remainder continued on to Salisbury. (One of the latter - the 12.54 ex Waterloo - was advertised as terminating at Basingstoke but in fact shunted into the down bay platform and formed, after a wait of half an hour, a stopping train to Salisbury). Two of the trains, the 09.54 and 18.54, proceeded far beyond the normal limits of local trains and terminated at Southampton Central and Yeovil Town respectively.

In the up direction the service mirrored that of the down and consisted of fourteen trains of which half were in the hands of King Arthur 4-6-0's although there was no pretence at any sort of interval working; trains leaving Basingstoke at roughly hourly intervals but originating from a variety of locations which included Southampton, Salisbury (six trains), Bourne-

mouth (2) and Yeovil. Seven trains commenced their journeys at Basingstoke and three terminated at Woking.

One of the stopping trains lay apart from the status quo since it - the 11.36 ex Bournemouth - was essentially a parcels train to which passenger accommodation was added and called at all stations as far as Southampton (Central) from which point it ran without passengers to St Denys - spending over half an hour in Bevois Park to allow the 11.30 Weymouth - Waterloo to overtake - continuing forward at 13.48 and omitting only Swaythling before reaching Woking at 15.48. At Woking the passenger and parcels vehicles were uncoupled and the Nine Elms H15 4-6-0, which worked through from Bournemouth West, continued forward to Neasden with any fish vans that had been included in the train.

None of the intermediate stations between Basingstoke and Woking were served by anything other than the stopping trains except for Farnborough which, in the up direction, received a call from the night mail from Weymouth.

Mention has already been made of the diversity of motive power on the local trains and it would have been difficult to find another other

| LORD NELSON (Kylchap) 4-6-0 30865 'Sir John Hawkins'. 12:474/505 tons | | | | | | |
m.ch Point	l/in	W.T.T.	Actual	mph	dbhp	pc
0.00 WATERLOO		0.00	0.00	-	-	-
3.74 Clapham Jcn	-3642	7.00	7.11	46.0	843	3
7.19 Wimbledon	752		11.10	53.0	970	5
12.03 Surbiton	20774		16.00	64.5	1086	6
17.06 Walton	4242		20.23	71.0	1236	9
24.27 WOKING	998	29.00	26.37	65.5	941	7
31.00 MP 31	307		33.18	55.0	964	6
33.17 Farnborough	-946		35.32	62.5	1016	6
36.38 Fleet	2852		38.38	65.0	948	6
47.60 BASINGSTOKE	733	53.00	49.31	61.5	938	6
50.23 Worting Jcn	260	56.00	52.07	56.0	1066	6
52.43 Wootton	278		54.38	52.5	1003	5
56.22 Roundwood	6366		58.28	60.0	999	6
58.09 Micheldever	-265		60.13	67.0	589	4
66.39 Winchester	-259		67.00	80.5	358	3
73.35 EASTLEIGH	-267	78.30	74.31*	20.0	Signals	
77.10 St Denys	-540		78.51	60.0	1606	8
78.14 Northam Jcn	level	84.00	80.30	10.0	-	-
79.19 SOUTHAMPTON	-560999	87.00	83.47	-	-	-
Clapham Jcn - Roundwood. 52 miles 61 mph. 1/781 : 1011 dbhp (pc 6)						

A great deal of time and trouble was sent on the Lord Nelson 4-6-0's by both Maunsell and Bulleid with the result that, after over a decade, many of the early troubles were eradicated. Unfortunately by the time the improvements were completed, war and the end of high speed running was fast approaching. By 1945 the top place in the running sheds had been taken over by the Merchant Navy Pacifics leaving the Lord Nelson's very little express work. They did, however, survive into the 1960's; much of their later work being done on the Southampton Ocean Liner trains.

single flow of traffic in the country that could offer such a breadth of variety. For those who wished to sample as many engines as possible for the price of one ticket and had the time to spare, they could do worse than to book from London to Basingstoke, leaving Waterloo on the 09.54 as far as Farnborough and thereafter alight at each station to pick up the following train. Five services were used in all, each with a different engine starting with an H15 (09.54), a Lord Nelson (10.54), a West Country (11.54), an N15 4-6-0 (12.54) and, finally, an N15x rebuilt Remembrance on the 13.54. To crown matters a quick turn-round at Basingstoke, re-

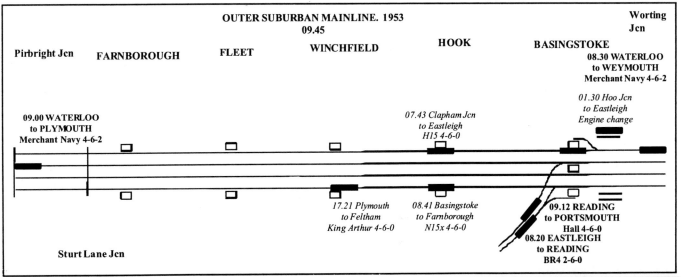

OUTER SUBURBAN MAINLINE. 1953
09.45

Worting Jcn

Pirbright Jcn   FARNBOROUGH   FLEET   WINCHFIELD   HOOK   BASINGSTOKE

08.30 WATERLOO
to WEYMOUTH
Merchant Navy 4-6-2

01.30 Hoo Jcn
to Eastleigh
Engine change

09.00 WATERLOO
to PLYMOUTH
Merchant Navy 4-6-2

07.43 Clapham Jcn
to Eastleigh
H15 4-6-0

17.21 Plymouth
to Feltham
King Arthur 4-6-0

08.41 Basingstoke
to Farnborough
N15x 4-6-0

09.12 READING
to PORTSMOUTH
Hall 4-6-0
08.20 EASTLEIGH
to READING
BR4 2-6-0

Sturt Lane Jcn

Thanks to the large number of six-coupled classes allocated to the South Western, the chances of getting a trip on the main line behind a 4-4-0 in the 1950's were slim. Nine Elms retained a handful of T9 and D15 4-4-0's until the mid-1950's but apart from the 04.15 Waterloo - Kingston newspaper train - a T9 duty - and the summer Saturday Lymington boat trains, there was no booked mainline work for them and it was only at the most straightened of times that a 4-4-0 could be found on a train from Waterloo. One either had to wait until the Basingstoke T9 pilot was called to rescue an ailing Pacific or resort to the secondary lines of Hampshire where the T9's could be found in respectable numbers. 4-4-0 30729 of Fratton attacks Fullerton bank in style. The driver, having set the lever and regulator as far forward as they will go, waits nonchalantly for the results.

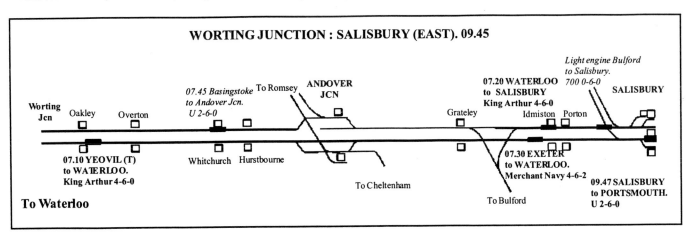

WORTING JUNCTION : SALISBURY (EAST). 09.45

Light engine Bulford
to Salisbury.
700 0-6-0

SALISBURY

07.20 WATERLOO
to SALISBURY
King Arthur 4-6-0

Worting Jcn   Oakley   Overton

07.45 Basingstoke
to Andover Jcn.
U 2-6-0

To Romsey   ANDOVER JCN

Grateley   Idmiston   Porton

07.10 YEOVIL (T)
to WATERLOO.
King Arthur 4-6-0

Whitchurch   Hurstbourne

To Cheltenham

07.30 EXETER
to WATERLOO.
Merchant Navy 4-6-2

To Bulford

09.47 SALISBURY
to PORTSMOUTH.
U 2-6-0

To Waterloo

Given the Southern's penchant for publicity and the wide use made of the N15 4-6-0's, it is surprising that their nameplates were such miserable affairs; requiring good eyesight to be identified from any distance. During the early 1960's some of the names were transferred to BR 5MT 4-6-0's although it made no impact with the public. 30454 'Queen Guinevere' was a regular engine on the stopping trains to and from Waterloo and was based at Salisbury throughout the nationalisation period until its withdrawal in March 1959.

turning on the 13.05 ex Bournemouth West, added a Merchant Navy to the list.

The one type of modern engine rarely seen on the South Western after the war was the Schools 4-4-0, the class being exclusively employed between Charing Cross and Hastings, Ramsgate and Margate. From time to time, however, odd members of the class, displaced off special workings or following a visit to Eastleigh, found their way onto LSWR workings before being returned to the Eastern section. On these rather rare occasions the 4-4-0's were treated with no degree of inferiority, two of the class, 30924 and 30928, being seen on the 06.45 Salisbury and 06.30 Exeter expresses respectively during January 1953; both trains being booked to Merchant Navy engines. In later years, after 1958, some of the class re-

turned to the South Western but were surplus to requirements. Rebuilding had greatly improved the availability of the Bulleid Pacifics whilst new Standard 4-6-0's were being drafted in to manage the stopping trains; factors which left very little for the Schools engines to do and they were rarely, if ever, stretched in South Western service, much of their time being out of traffic at Nine Elms and Basingstoke.

Variety of engines was not always the only attraction of the stopping trains and on Saturdays, for a short period in the summer of 1952, the 14.54 from Waterloo was formed from the stock of an up P&O boat train; a formation which included a pair of Pullman cars.

Generally however the off-peak outer suburban trains ran to a more sober make-up and very often did not exceed three or four vehicles

which in some cases made them almost the same weight as the engine hauling them. The blessing was that they ran at all since BR was not normally generous with its services to out of the way stations in the home counties and passengers from Kings Cross to the Great Northern equals of Whitchurch and Porton (Yaxley and Connington) could count their trains on the fingers of one hand. Oakleigh on the Midland - coincidentally the same distance from London as its LSWR namesake - was treated almost as thought it didn't exist. The Southern however had the clerical force of an interval timetable which to the orderly mind of the timing clerks meant that the pattern of trains had to operate according to the scheme of things, demand or no; something for which we, who worked on them or watched them for recreation (or both), were grateful.

BASINGSTOKE : READING

Six of the Reading - Basingstoke services were 'extended' south to Portsmouth, three of the trains being worked by GWR Hall class 4-6-0's: two from Reading shed and one from far-off Oxley. The balance were worked by an assortment of SR locomotives made up of an N15x, a U class 2-6-0 and a BR 4MT 4-6-0. The incidence of Great Western power beyond Basingstoke increased considerably on summer Saturdays when large numbers of excursions, specials and summer-only services operated between the Black Country and Bournemouth. Thanks to the Great Western's liking for complex cyclic engine diagrams, engines from a number of strange locations could be seen on South-Western metals, such as Hall 4-6-0 'Dodington Hall' of Bristol (Bath Road) which was seen at Worting Junction on Saturday 2nd August 1958 at the head of a Wolverhampton - Portsmouth special.

The Great Western line from Basingstoke to Reading opened as a broad gauge connection to the north in 1848, nine years after the LSWR main line, and although converted to mixed gauge eight years later, when running connections were installed between the two companies, it remained very much a self-contained unit so far as the LSWR was concerned; the GWR maintaining its own facilities until 1932 when, under the rigours of the great depression, the passenger facilities were absorbed by the Southern Railway at Basingstoke.

Although the line retained a distinct Great Western flavour, the years following the erosion of boundaries in 1932 saw a gradual extension of Southern influence by the joint working of trains between Portsmouth or Southampton and Reading; with each company being responsible for exactly half the service.

Altogether there were six such trains from Reading, three of which were worked by the Southern who diagrammed them (in 1953) to a BR4 2-6-0, a U class 2-6-0 and an N15X 4-6-0. The GWR trio were rather less colourful with each service being headed by a Hall 4-6-0 al-

though one of the engines, that of the 13.48 Reading - Portsmouth, came from Oxley and was likely to be an unusual representative of the class.

In addition there were two expresses over the route - the 09.30 Birkenhead - Bournemouth West and the 10.23 York - Bournemouth West - both of which were Southern workings, diagrammed to a King Arthur and a Lord Nelson respectively.

The local trains, on the other hand, were dominated by the Great Western who worked five of the seven services, using 61xx 2-6-2 tanks for most of the trains with one being given a 43xx 2-6-0, leaving two trains to the Southern who made up for their smaller share by the added interest of a King Arthur and a 'Remembrance' 4-6-0.

The joint arrangements extended only to the passenger workings and the Western had exclusive dominion over the goods workings, a good proportion of which were long distance in nature running to Wolverhampton, Oxford and Crewe with one service taking traffic to the North

Eastern via Woodford Halse on the Great Central.

Of the eight daily departures from Basingstoke, four were diagrammed to Hall class 4-6-0's - three of which were allocated to far-off Oxley MPD, Wolverhampton - and three to 61xx 2-6-2T's. The balance was made up by a Reading-based 28xx 2-8-0 which was booked to work the daily pick-up goods.

Parcels traffic, of which there was one train in each direction, was also a Great Western province although there was only one service in each direction. The down train was the 21.45 Eastleigh to Crewe which was notable in that it was worked into Basingstoke by an Oxley-based Hall 4-6-0 which gave way in the station to another of the same class - an Oxford engine which ran light from Reading. The Oxley 4-6-0, which had come south with the 13.48 Reading - Portsmouth, returned to its own area later in the night with the 02.10 Wolverhampton goods. The southbound equivalent - the 16.55 Worcester to Eastleigh - was an afternoon train, reaching Basingstoke in the late evening behind an Oxford Hall 4-6-0 and giving way to an

The insularity of the companies and regions continued well into the 1960's and the locations where locomotives of more than one undertaking could be seen were far from numerous. The Southern was as self-contained as the others although some thawing of boundaries existed south of Basingstoke with a limited number of GW engines working through from Reading to Southampton (Terminus) or Portsmouth & Southsea as a reciprocation for the Southern working the Birkenhead and Newcastle services north to Oxford. In the majority of cases however engines changed at Basingstoke which in the summer resulted in a large number of SR engines being specially diagrammed simply to run the 50-odd miles to Bournemouth. The engine changing did at least provide some additional activity whilst the sight of GW engines in a Southern stronghold lent a cosmopolitan air to the station. In the above picture Banbury Hall 6976 'Graythwaite Hall' arrives in the SR section of Basingstoke with a relief service from Newcastle to Bournemouth whilst in the lower view Grange 4-6-0 6848 'Toddington Grange' of Oxford prepares to restart a through service to Birmingham.

By 1964 the dieselisation of the Great Western was all but complete and one needed a very good knowledge of workings to get a run behind a steam engine. Reading shed was still in operation and although most of its steam functions were directed towards local goods trips, the passenger pilot remained a steam working until the shed closed in early 1965. The engine concerned was usually a rather disreputable 4-6-0 and it appears to have been called to duty on the 4th July when Modified Hall 6980 'Llanrumney Hall' worked into basingstoke from the WR with a cross country express. Seen here about to set off on the return working, the state of the engine, filthy and lacking a nameplate, is enough to bring tears to the eyes of anyone familiar with the Western of a year or two earlier. The fireman is putting his back into the task of raising steam and prompts one to recall how reluctant many GW drivers were to allow the blower to be used as a fast means of rallying the boiler. Below - a reminder of how frequent and varied the services (and locomotives) were on the Reading branch.

TRAIN WORKING : MORTIMER (1953)					
Train	arr	Engine	Shed & Diagram	Dep	Destination
19.48 Weymouth		Hall 4-6-0	Reading 66	00/10	Reading
00.30 Basingstoke (Gds)		*Hall 4-6-0*	*Oxley 9*	*00/44*	*Oxford*
19.10 Victoria Basin		*Hall 4-6-0*	*Oxley 208*	*03/05*	*Basingstoke*
03.15 Reading (Pcls)		*61xx 2-6-2T*	*Reading 47*	*03/29*	*Basingstoke*
04.30 Basingstoke (Gds)		*Hall 4-6-0*	*Reading 201*	*04/41*	*Crewe*
05.10 Basingstoke (Gds)		*61xx 2-6-2T*	*Reading 47*	*05/29*	*Woodford*
06.50 Reading	07.06	Hall 4-6-0	Reading 66	07.07	S'ton Terminus
06.57 Basingstoke	07.14	Hall 4-6-0	Oxley 208	07.15	Reading
07.38 Basingstoke	07.53	N15 4-6-0	Eastleigh 264	07.54	Reading
07.58 Reading	08.09	61xx 2-6-2T	Reading 70	08.12	Basingstoke
02.15 Oxley		*43xx 2-6-0*	*Oxley 207*	*08/26*	*Basingstoke*
08.24 Reading	08.39	N15X 4-6-0	B'stoke 236	08.40	Reading
09.12 Reading	09.24	Hall 4-6-0	Reading 50	09.27	Portsmouth
08.20 Eastleigh	09.55	BR4 2-6-0	Eastleigh 273	09.56	Reading
09.15 Reading (Gds)	*10.06*	*28xx 2-8-0*	*Reading 202*	*10.15*	*Basingstoke*
09.50 Basingstoke (Gds)		*61xx 2-6-2T*	*Reading 70*	*10/13*	*Reading*
10.17 Reading	10.30	N15X 4-6-0	B'stoke 236	10.32	Basingstoke
09.40 Moreton Cutting		*N15 4-6-0*	*Eastleigh 264*	*10/49*	*Basingstoke*
10.13 S'ton Terminus	11.38	Hall 4-6-0	Reading 66	11.39	Reading
09.20 BOURNEMOUTH		N15 4-6-0	Bournemouth 399	11/53	BIRKENHEAD
12.15 Reading	12.29	BR4 2-6-0	Eastleigh 273	12.30	Portsmouth
11.16 BOURNEMOUTH		LN 4-6-0	Bournemouth 395	13/46	NEWCASTLE
12.31 S'ton Terminus	14.00	U 2-6-0	Guildford 181	14.01	Reading
13.48 Reading	14.01	Hall 4-6-0	Oxley 208	14.03	Portsmouth
13.05 Basingstoke (Gds)	*14.15*	*28xx 2-8-0*	*Reading 202*	*14.25*	*Reading*
09.30 BIRKENHEAD		N15 4-6-0	Bournemouth 399	15/10	BOURNEMOUTH
15.10 Reading	15.22	61xx 2-6-2T	Reading 71A	15.23	Basingstoke
15.55 Basingstoke	16.11	N15X 4-6-0	B'stoke 236	16.12	Reading
08.37 NEWCASTLE		LN 4-6-0	Bournemouth 395	16/28	BOURNEMOUTH
14.45 Portsmouth	17.01	Hall 4-6-0	Reading 50	17.02	Reading
17.10 Bramley	17.15	61xx 2-6-2T	Reading 71A	17.16	Reading
17.10 Reading	17.23	U 2-6-0	Guildford 181	17.24	S'ton Terminus
17.50 Reading	18.02	61xx 2-6-2T	Reading 69	18.04	Basingstoke
18.05 Basingstoke	18.21	U 2-6-0	Guildford 182	18.23	Reading
19.00 Reading	19.13	N15X 4-6-0	B'stoke 236	19.14	S'ton Terminus
19.12 Reading (Light)		*U 2-6-0*	*Guildford 182*	*19/34*	*Basingstoke*
17.17 Portsmouth	19.55	BR4 2-6-0	Eastleigh 273	19.56	Reading
19.55 Basingstoke (Gds)		*61xx 2-6-2T*	*Reading 69*	*20/13*	*Scours Lane Jcn*
20.38 Reading	20.51	61xx 2-6-2T	Reading 74	20.52	Basingstoke
21.17 Reading	21.30	Hall 4-6-0	Reading 66	21.31	Basingstoke
18.35 Bournemouth	21.35	H15 4-6-0	Nine Elms 68	21.36	Reading
21.25 Reading (light)		*Hall 4-6-0*	*Oxley 7*	*21/48*	*Basingstoke*
21.45 Basingstoke (Gds)		*43xx 2-6-0*	*Oxley 207*	*21/55*	*Oxley*
16.55 Worcester (Pcls)		*Hall 4-6-0*	*Oxley 9*	*22/07*	*Eastleigh*
22.05 Reading (Gds)		*Hall 4-6-0*	*Reading 201*	*22/28*	*Basingstoke*
22.35 Basingstoke	22.50	61xx 2-6-2T	Reading 74	22.51	Reading
23.00 Reading	23.12	BR4 2-6-0	Eastleigh 273	23.13	Basingstoke
21.45 Eastleigh (Pcls)		*Hall 4-6-0*	*Oxley 7*	*23/58*	*Crewe*
Goods/Parcels trains in italics. Passing time : "/"					

Eastleigh 4-6-0 for the last leg of the journey. Residual overnight parcels vans for the Southern were not moved en block but brought onto the Southern by the 03.15 ex Reading - a Reading 2-6-2T working- where they were remarshalled and attached to forwarding services as circumstances required.

The two intermediate stations, Bramley and Mortimer, were well served by the passenger service; the only trains not to call at either being the York and Birkenhead expresses and the midnight from Basingstoke (19.48 ex Weymouth) which called at Bramley but not Mortimer.

In addition to the booked service, Bramley also had an unadvertised train each afternoon, empty stock from Basingstoke to form the 17.10 to Reading, for the benefit of employees at the nearby Ordnance Works whose extensive sidings were one of the reasons for the provision of a 2-8-0 on the pick-up goods.

The conventional view of the line as being a sleepy backwater lies at odds with the number of trains - over 50 a day - which plied between Reading and Basingstoke. It was unfortunate that popular judgements of lines were usually based on the timetable and consisting largely of Reading - Basingstoke locals, the line was often written down as just another rural line. (The same could be said for the Midland & South Western which operated quite a heavy goods service between the West Midlands and Southampton yet, because of the paucity of passenger trains, had the reputation of being of far less importance than was actually the case).

To visiting enthusiasts trying to get a quart into a pint pot, the branch was a Godsend since, with a knowledge of the train timings of the Great Western and the South Western plus enough change for the requisite number of day-returns, one could flit more or less at will between Basingstoke and Reading General viewing the best that both main lines had to offer.

GOODS SERVICES

Improvisation at Basingstoke. S15 4-6-0 30829 was the booked engine for the 19.04 express goods from Basingstoke to Plymouth, having arrived earlier in the day with the 10.42 ex Salisbury. The engine had a four hour turn-round at Basingstoke but has been 'utilised' to work a special freight to Southampton Docks which is seen at Worting Junction. There will be some fairly feverish activity going on Behind the scenes as Basingstoke cast around for a substitute for the Plymouth and make arrangements for 30829 to get back to Salisbury when it reaches Southampton.

Although the volume of freight traffic was far from insignificant, the amount of traffic moved by the South Western was minimal in comparison to what was moved on the other regions, the reason being that - Southampton Docks apart - there were no major industrial locations served by the system and most of the regular traffic consisted of wagon loads to and from the hundred and one goods stations on the line; much of which included industrial and household coal en route from the north country collieries which came onto the South Western via Feltham. Traffic which originated in London tended to start from Nine Elms goods depot which ran a daily series of seven express services to Wessex and the west of England.

In the down direction there was a basic service of nineteen express goods trains of which eleven went to the Southampton/Eastleigh area, six to the West Country and one each for Bournemouth and Weymouth. Of these one was an internal service which returned ballast wagons to Exmouth junction for Meldon quarry - where most of the region's track ballast was obtained - whilst another started from Bas-

ingstoke conveying traffic which had been collected locally together with West of England traffic that arrived from the WR via Reading.

BASINGSTOKE : GOODS TRAFFIC (1)					
Train	Arrive	Yard	Engine	Depart	Destination
22.30 S'ton Docks	00.11	Up	U 2-6-0 (Guildford 181)		(Fwd at 00.45)
		North	Hall 4-6-0 (Oxford 9)	00.30	Oxford
23.15 Eastleigh	00.30	North	H15 4-6-0 (Eastleigh 310)		
22.50 Salisbury	00.41	Up	S15 4-6-0 (Salisbury 439)		
(22.30 S'ton Docks)			U 2-6-0 (Guildford 181)	00.45	Feltham
(22.45 Woking)			S15 4-6-0 (Feltham 110)	00.47	Eastleigh
22.45 Feltham	01.22	West	S15 4-6-0 (Feltham 112)		(Fwd at 01.56)
19.50 Dorchester	01.33	Up	H15 4-6-0 (N. Elms 74)*		(Fwd at 01.55)
(19.50 Dorchester)			H15 4-6-0 (N. Elms 66)*	01.55	Nine Elms
(22.45 Feltham)			S15 4-6-0 (Feltham 112)	01.56	Bournemouth
00.45 Eastleigh	02.00	Up	H15 4-6-0 (N. Elms 64)		(Fwd at 02.50)
23.58 Feltham	02.09	West	S15 4-6-0 (Feltham 115)		(Fwd at 02.44)
		North	Hall 4-6-0 (Oxley 208)	02.10	Oxley
(23.58 Feltham)			S15 4-6-0 (Feltham 115)	02.44	Exmouth Jcn
(00.45 Eastleigh)			H15 4-6-0 (N. Elms 64)	02.50	Feltham
00.45 Nine Elms	02.49	West	H15 4-6-0 (N.Elms 79)	03.14	Eastleigh
19.10 Victoria Basin (GW)	03.22	West	Hall 4-6-0 (Oxley 208)		
		West	S15 4-6-0 (Salisbury 439)	03.30	Salisbury
00.55 Feltham	03.37	West	S15 4-6-0 (Feltham 102)		(Fwd at 04.40)
		North	Hall 4-6-0 (Reading 201)	04.30	Crewe
03.10 Bevois Park	04.32	Up	S15 4-6-0 (Feltham 108)		(Fwd at 05.02)
(00.55 Feltham)			S15 4-6-0 (Feltham 102)	04.40	S'ton Docks
(03.10 Bevois Park)			S15 4-6-0 (Feltham 108)	05.02	Woking
		West	61xx 2-6-2T (Reading 47)	05.10	Woodford (GC)
		West	700 0-6-0 (B'stoke 242)	05.30	Bulford
04.40 Eastleigh	06.07	Up	H15 4-6-0 (N. Elms 66)	06.43	Feltham
17.21 Plymouth	06.36	Up	N15 4-6-0 (Salisbury 436)		(Fwd at 09.18)
03.20 Bournemouth	06.50	Up	S15 4-6-0 (Feltham 110)		(Fwd at 08.12)
		West	U 2-6-0 (B'toke 239)	07.45	Andover Jcn
(03.20 Bournemouth)			S15 4-6-0 (Feltham 110)	08.12	Feltham
01.30 Hoo Junction	08.37	West	U 2-6-0 (Guildford 182)*		(Fwd at 10.48)
		Down	N15X 4-6-0 (B'stoke 241)	08.41	Farnborough

*: Engine change. Through trains in bold type

(The last - the 19.04 ex Basingstoke - was quite a sight during the winter months since it was booked to be worked as far as Salisbury by a King Arthur 4-6-0 with an S15 4-6-0 as pilot. Contrary to popular belief there was no prohibition on double-heading by the Southern although it was uncommon, especially on the main line with two large engines. During the summer the S15 handled the train unaided).

The most urgent down traffic was that from Nine Elms and this was reflected in the motive power allocated to the seven services, since the trains were integrated so far as it was possible with the express engine diagrams and included haulage by two Merchant Navy Pacifics and a Lord Nelson 4-6-0. Mixed traffic H15 4-6-0's worked the balance of trains except for one which was given over to a 6F S15 4-6-0. (One service, introduced in late 1954, had a rather curious engine working. The train - the 19.36 meat from Exeter Central to Nine Elms - was initially worked by the new 10203 diesel locomotive which, lacking train heating equipment at the time, could not be used for passenger traffic. On reaching London the diesel returned light

Due to its exceptionally heavy passenger interests the SR did its best to keep goods and passenger traffic well apart and most of the latter moved during the night when passenger activities were at a low ebb. The segregation was not complete and a number of freight trains operated during the day, the most important of which was the 10.45 Feltham - Exmouth Junction; a service which cleared any traffic that arrived in London from the other regions too late to be dealt with by the night trains. The train ran fast to Basingstoke where it removed the Salisbury section to make room for any West of England traffic that had arrived via Reading, vehicles displaced thus being forwarded on the 19.04 departure from Basingstoke. From Salisbury the train conveyed only vehicles for Exeter and beyond. S15 4-6-0 30836 picks its way through Salisbury station to recess the train in the West Yard where it will be re-engined by another of the same class for the run to Exmouth Junction. The crew on the engine have worked the train from Basingstoke, arriving there after working the 06.30 Exeter - Waterloo, a Merchant Navy turn, from Salisbury.

to Exeter - probably the most extravagant instance of a light engine movement on record - since the 19.36 had no return working).

S15 4-6-0's were more in evidence on the marginally less important workings based upon Feltham - which tended to include large quantities of coal from the North of England - and were allocated to all eight originating main line departures from the yard, made up of five trains to Eastleigh/Southampton, two for the West of England and a single service to Bournemouth.

Not all inter-regional traffic came via Feltham and the Great Western's Basingstoke branch allowed some relief to the very congested cross-London route. Five inward trains per day (including a service each from Birmingham and Didcot) used the route bringing to Basingstoke four Great Western engines: three Hall 4-6-0's, and a 28xx 2-8-0. The fifth train was worked by a Southern engine - the only goods on the line not to be GWR worked - and was the King Arthur 4-6-0 which had worked north with the 07.38 Basingstoke -Reading passenger. In the northbound direction there were two additional services for which two GWR 61xx 2-6-2 tanks were employed.

The flow of goods traffic in and out of Basingstoke was significant in that it amounted to twenty eight services a day - thirteen arrivals and

fifteen departures - the bulk of which came in either from the Reading branch or from the Salisbury direction.

A particularly useful service was the 05.10 ex Basingstoke - also a Reading 61xx 2-6-2T - which ran to Woodford Halse on the Great Central and saved traffic several days in transit by enabling the cross London route to be avoided.

Local goods traffic on the London side of Basingstoke was light with the intermediate stations as far as Farnborough being served by a single pick-up goods which left Basingstoke at 08.41 and returned at 15.41. Traffic for these stations from the east was brought in to Farnborough by the 09.52 trip from Woking - a working worth looking out for since it was worked by an 0395 0-6-0 from Guildford shed. The 0-6-0 returned light to Woking at midday, return traffic being worked from Farnborough at 16.20 by an S15 4-6-0 which came light from Basingstoke after being re-engined on the 03.30 Ashford (Kent) - Eastleigh.

In addition to the pick-up, Basingstoke ran two trains for Feltham, each clearing exchange traffic which had arrived in the yards during the early and late shifts. Curiously there was very little activity in the direction of Southampton, two trains ran into Basingstoke from Winchester and Eastleigh respectively with nothing booked to leave Basingstoke in the opposite direction. Traffic for Southampton was dealt with by being attached to through trains whilst they called en route from Feltham.

BASINGSTOKE : GOODS TRAFFIC (2)					
Train	Arrive	Yard	Engine	Depart	Destination
02.15 Oxley	08.56	West	43xx 2-6-0 (Oxley 207)		
(17.21 Plymouth)			N15 4-6-0 (Salisbury 436)	09.18	Feltham
		West	61xx 2-6-2T (Reading 70)	09.50	Reading
(01.30 Hoo Junction)			H15 4-6-0 (E'leigh 310)*	10.48	Eastleigh
09.15 Reading	11.16	West	28xx 2-8-0 (Reading 202)		
09.40 Didcot	11.30	West	N15 4-6-0 (Eastleigh 264)		
09.45 Feltham	**11.5**	**West**	**S15 4-6-0 (Fltham 105)**	**13.03**	**Eastleigh**
		North	28xx 2-8-0 (Reading 202)	13.05	Reading
10.45 Feltham	13.1	West	S15 4-6-0 (Feltham 101)	(Fwd at 14.14)	
03.20 Ashford	13.4	West	S15 4-6-0 (Feltham 112)*	(Fwd at 14.45)	
		Up	H15 4-6-0 (Nine Elms 76)	13.48	Feltham
(10.45 Feltham)			S15 4-6-0 (Feltham 101)	14.14	Plymouth
10.42 Salisbury	14.41	Up	S15 4-6-0 (Salisbury 438)		
(03.20 Ashford)			N15 4-6-0 (E'leigh 264)*	14.45	Eastleigh
13.20 Ston Docks	14.5	Up	S15 4-6-0 (Feltham 104)	15.23	Feltham
13.33 Farnborough	15.41	West	N15X 4-6-0 (B'stoke 241)		
14.25 Salisbury	16.00	Up	S15 4-6-0 (Feltham 106)		
14.45 Feltham	**17**	**West**	**S15 4-6-0 (Feltham 107)**	(Fwd at 17.46)	
16.33 Overton	17.08	Up	U 2-6-0 (B'toke 239)		
(14.45 Feltham)			S15 4-6-0 (Feltham 107)	17.46	S'ton Docks
16.20 S'ton Docks	**17.5**	**Up**	**S15 4-6-0 (Feltham 102)**	(Fwd at 18.45)	
17.18 Winchester	18.38	Up	S15 4-6-0 (Feltham 103)		
(16.20 S'ton Docks)			S15 4-6-0 (Feltham 102)	18.45	Feltham
16.35 Amesbury	18.53	Up	700 C 6-0 (B'stoke 242)		
		West	S15 4-6-0 (Salisbury 438)	19.04	Plymouth
17.50 Bevois Park	19.43	Up	H15 4-6-0 (N. Elms 68)		
		North	61xx 2-6-2T (Reading 69)	19.55	Reading
18.55 S'ton Docks	**20.4**	**Up**	**N15 4-6-0 (Eastleigh 264)**	**21.00**	**Nine Elms**
		North	43xx 2-6-0 (Oxley 207)	21.45	Oxley
		Up	S15 4-6-0 (Feltham 103)	22.25	Feltham
22.05 Reading	22.58	West	Hall 4-6-0 (Reading 201)		
22.45 Woking	**23.5**	**West**	**S15 4-6-0 (Feltham 110)**	(Fwd at 00.47)	

* : Engine change. Through trains in bold type

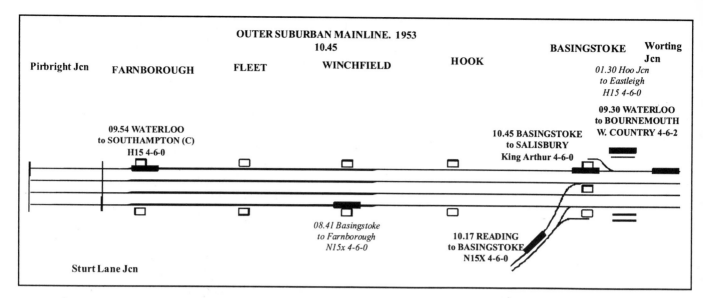

OUTER SUBURBAN MAINLINE. 1953
10.45

Pirbright Jcn   FARNBOROUGH   FLEET   WINCHFIELD   HOOK   BASINGSTOKE   Worting Jcn

01.30 Hoo Jcn to Eastleigh H15 4-6-0

09.30 WATERLOO to BOURNEMOUTH W. COUNTRY 4-6-2

09.54 WATERLOO to SOUTHAMPTON (C) H15 4-6-0

10.45 BASINGSTOKE to SALISBURY King Arthur 4-6-0

08.41 Basingstoke to Farnborough N15x 4-6-0

10.17 READING to BASINGSTOKE N15X 4-6-0

Sturt Lane Jcn

Local traffic on the Great Western line was catered for by the 09.15 pick-up from Reading which arrived in Basingstoke at 11.16 and returned, serving all stations, at 13.05.

Four groups of sidings were provided at Basingstoke to deal with the remarshalling of traffic, the West and North yards being prima-

2T - on continuous turns of duty with the U class 2-6-0 assisting for four hours each evening after arriving back with the goods from Overton. A second E5 shunted the North Yard on late and night turns, movements outside these hours being dealt with by train engines.

The method by which traffic in and between the yards was arranged was not especially sophisticated and much depended on the wits and experience of the Inspectors and their staff who managed chiefly by trying to anticipate the nature of traffic which was approaching and by being prepared for surprises when they occurred. The train supervision office - the SR equivalent of the control organisation - gave advice in very general terms of the loads that approaching trains were conveying whilst details of each wagon was transmitted by telegraph from sending points; a system which combined to give too little information on the one hand and too much to be properly digested on the other.

The usual modus operandi was to dedicate a number of sidings in each yard for the destinations that starting trains served - the West yard, for example, reserved two sidings each for GW

and Salisbury traffic and as each arrival was broken up, the wagons would be placed in the appropriate siding until a complete train was made up. Generally the Inspectors had a free hand in making up trains although in a limited number of cases attention had to be given to headquarters instructions in respect of trains which conveyed multiple portions such as the 19.04 Basingstoke to Plymouth which had to be restricted to 50 wagons in order to ensure that capacity was available to make up to a full load at Andover Junction. The service also had to be strictly marshalled with vehicles for Exeter and beyond next to the engine with those for stations between Yeovil and Broad Clyst running next to the brake-van. The 19.04 was

PRINCIPAL GOODS SERVICES (DOWN)				
Nine Elms	Feltham	Other	Destination	Engine
00.45			Eastleigh	H15 4-6-0
	00.55		Southampton	S15 4-6-0
	04.07		Southampton	S15 4-6-0
		01.30 Hoo Jcn	Eastleigh	U 2-6-0
	09.45		Eastleigh	S15 4-6-0
	10.45		Exmouth Jcn	S15 4-6-0
		03.20 Ashford	Eastleigh	S15 4-6-0
		09.45 Tonbridge	Exmouth Jcn	H15 4-6-0
	14.45		Southampton	S15 4-6-0
		19.04 Basingstoke	Plymouth	S15 4-6-0
19.25			Southampton	H15 4-6-0
21.10			Plymouth	MN 4-6-2
		22.45 Woking	Eastleigh	S15 4-6-0
22.00			Exmouth Jcn	MN 4-6-2
	22.20		Southampton	S15 4-6-0
22.38			Weymouth	H15 4-6-0
	22.45		Bournemouth	S15 4-6-0
23.25			Southampton	LN 4-6-0
	23.58		Exmouth Jcn	S15 4-6-0

PRINCIPAL GOODS SERVICES (UP)			
West	Wessex	Destination	Engine
12.45 Torrington		Nine Elms 03.00	N15 4-6-0
	19.50 Dorchester	Nine Elms 03.26	H15 4-6-0
	22.30 S. Docks	Feltham 04.30	U 2-6-0
	00.45 Eastleigh	Feltham 04.47	H15 4-6-0
17.00 Torrington		Nine Elms 04.03	MN 4-6-2
	00.50 Fratton	Feltham 05.03	S15 4-6-0
13.55 Meldon		Woking 05.20	H15 4-6-0
	03.10 Bevois Park	Woking 06.02	S15 4-6-0
21.30 Okehampton		Woking 08.27	H15 4-6-0
	04.40 Eastleigh	Feltham 10.19	H15 4-6-0
	03.20 Bournemouth	Feltham 10.49	S15 4-6-0
17.21 Plymouth		Feltham 11.49	N15 4-6-0
	13.20 S. Docks	Feltham 17.42	S15 4-6-0
	16.20 S. Docks	Feltham 20.49	S15 4-6-0
	18.55 S. Docks	Nine Elms 22.40	N15 4-6-0
	21.15 Eastleigh	Feltham 01.19	S15 4-6-0
	21.56 Bevois Park	Feltham 02.21	S15 4-6-0

rily devoted to workings to and from the Great Western whilst traffic travelling from West to East was normally dealt with in the Up yard. Trains to the West - the traffic for which more often than not arrived from the Reading direction - tended to be based on the West Yard which was the busiest of the sidings and employed two pilot engines - a G6 0-6-0T and an E5 0-6-

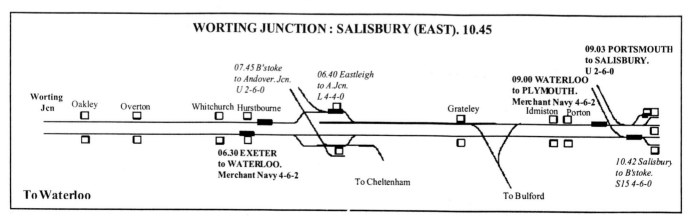

WORTING JUNCTION : SALISBURY (EAST). 10.45

Worting Jcn   Oakley   Overton   Whitchurch   Hurstbourne   Grateley   Idmiston   Porton

07.45 B'stoke to Andover. Jcn. U 2-6-0

06.40 Eastleigh to A.Jcn. L 4-4-0

09.03 PORTSMOUTH to SALISBURY. U 2-6-0

09.00 WATERLOO to PLYMOUTH. Merchant Navy 4-6-2

06.30 EXETER to WATERLOO. Merchant Navy 4-6-2

10.42 Salisbury to B'stoke. S15 4-6-0

To Cheltenham   To Bulford

To Waterloo

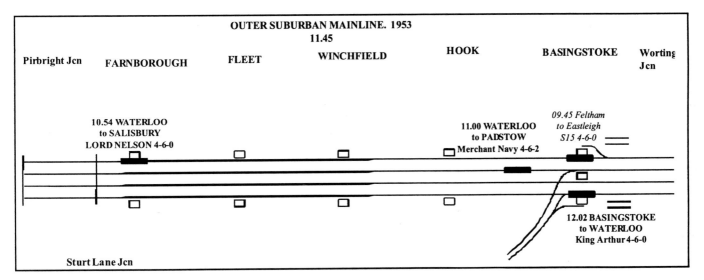

OUTER SUBURBAN MAINLINE. 1953
11.45

| Pirbright Jcn | FARNBOROUGH | FLEET | WINCHFIELD | HOOK | BASINGSTOKE | Worting Jcn |

10.54 WATERLOO
to **SALISBURY**
LORD NELSON 4-6-0

11.00 WATERLOO
to **PADSTOW**
Merchant Navy 4-6-2

09.45 Feltham
to Eastleigh
S15 4-6-0

12.02 BASINGSTOKE
to **WATERLOO**
King Arthur 4-6-0

Sturt Lane Jcn

30836 creeps up to the signal with the 10.45 ex Feltham, waiting for the 13.00 Waterloo - Plymouth to clear the section so that it can draw into Salisbury West Yard to remarshal and change engines. In the middle-distance one of the new 0-6-0 diesel shunters can be seen; the LBSCR E4 0-6-2T's having been replaced in 1959 and 1961 respectively.

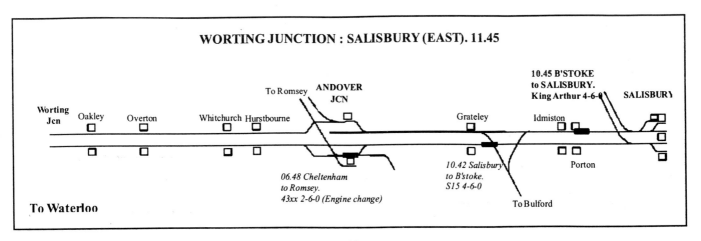

WORTING JUNCTION : SALISBURY (EAST). 11.45

| Worting Jcn | Oakley | Overton | Whitchurch | Hurstbourne | To Romsey ANDOVER JCN | Grateley | Idmiston | 10.45 B'STOKE to SALISBURY. King Arthur 4-6-0 | SALISBURY |

06.48 Cheltenham
to Romsey.
43xx 2-6-0 (Engine change)

10.42 Salisbury
to B'stoke.
S15 4-6-0

Porton

To Bulford

To Waterloo

49

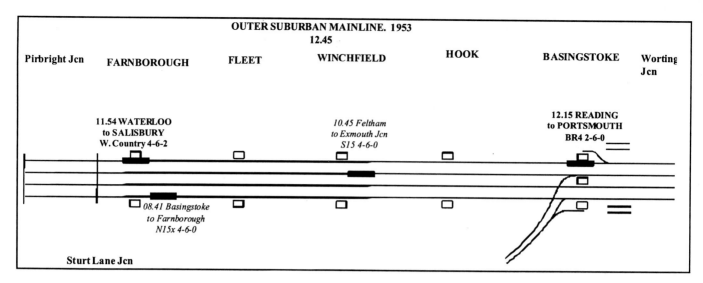

OUTER SUBURBAN MAINLINE. 1953
12.45

Pirbright Jcn | FARNBOROUGH | FLEET | WINCHFIELD | HOOK | BASINGSTOKE | Worting Jcn

11.54 WATERLOO to **SALISBURY** W. Country 4-6-2

10.45 Feltham to Exmouth Jcn S15 4-6-0

12.15 READING to **PORTSMOUTH** BR4 2-6-0

08.41 Basingstoke to Farnborough N15x 4-6-0

Sturt Lane Jcn

the only SR train from Basingstoke to be regulated thus although several of the Great Western services were subject to printed instructions which related to the organisation of traffic in the Reading complex; matters on which the Basingstoke staff could not automatically be expected to know.

For example the 19.55 Basingstoke to Reading terminated at Scours Lane Yard in order to connect with down mainline workings to Gloucester and South Wales and Basingstoke had a standing instruction to forward all perishable traffic for those part of the country on the service although the train could be made up - provided the 2-6-2T which worked the service had the capacity - with traffic for stations between Twyford and Paddington.

In addition to supervising the preparation of trains the inspectors also spend a great deal of time 'chasing' engines, making sure that locomotives due to work trains out were on time and that they were of the correct type. For engines that started their working at Basingstoke it was sufficient to keep in touch with the MPD who would quote the engine number or class for each working and confirm that it would (or should) come into the yard on time. More problematic were foreign engines which were half way through their workings and were arriving in the area on goods trains which were liable to be delayed and it was necessary to maintain a close liaison with the train supervision office and local signalboxes in order to ascer-

tain the extent of any delays on the line and to estimate their effect on the yard's working.

An especially irritating difficulty was that of the wrong type of engine being put into a

diagram when, for example, a 700 0-6-0 would turn up for a train that was booked for an S15.

The one great variable factor of South Western freight traffic was Southampton Docks

m.ch	Point	1/in	W.T.T.	Actual	mph	dbhp	pc
0.00	WATERLOO	-	0.00	0.00	-	-	-
3.74	Clapham Jcn	-3642	7.00	7.30	42	785	2
5.46	Earlesfield	664		9.44	56	1554	7
7.19	Wimbledon	866		11.44	64	1355	7
9.62	New Malden	-29773		14.18	68	964	6
12.03	Surbiton	7153		16.21	66	666	4
14.31	Esher	-1428		18.22	75	1783	13
17.06	Walton	948		20.29	77	1701	13
19.12	Weybridge	-5242		22.09	72	303	2
21.54	West Byfleet	6116		24.11	77	1743	13
24.27	WOKING	367		Signal check to 28 mph			
27.79	Brookwood	318		31.29	48	1449	7
31.00	MP 31	307		35.00	54	1449	7
33.17	Farnborough	-946		37.16	64	1257	7
36.38	Fleet	2852		40.18	68	1167	7
39.66	Winchfield	674		43.00	69	1616	12
42.13	Hook	1046		45.00	75	1912	13
47.60	BASINGSTOKE	688	51.00	49.31	64	927	7
50.23	Worting Jcn	260	54.00	52.03	46	-	-
58.09	Micheldever	12596		60.00	76	1414	8
66.39	Winchester	-259		66.45	74	118	1
73.35	EASTLEIGH	-267	75.30	72.30	70	-	-
77.10	St Denys	-540		75.44	65	-	-
79.19	SOUTHAMPTON	level	83.00	79.31	24	-	-
82.43	Totton	level		84.29	42	784	3
85.34	Lyndhurst Road	526		88.30	52	1033	4
88.06	Beaulieu Road	583		91.31	54	996	5
93.60	LYMINGTON JCN	1842	100.00	97.16	42	384	2
95.45	Sway	246		99.32	55	2112	10
98.44	New Milton	-1324		102.30	64	1117	7
101.1	Hinton Admiral	-266		104.3	76	1567	12
104.3	Christchurch	-330		107.3	56	-	-
108	BOURNEMOUTH (C)	227	116.00	112.5	-	-	-

MERCHANT NAVY 4-6-2 35001 'Union Castle'. 17:517/520 tons (1945)

Clapham Jcn - West Byfleet. 18 miles 64 mph 1/3039 : 1303 dbhp (pc 8)
Brookwood - Basingstoke. 20 miles 66 mph 1/823 : 1337 dbhp (pc 9)

In prewar days the best timing between London and Bournemouth had been 116 minutes using a Schools Class 4-4-0 on a load of eleven bogies and with reinstatement in mind, a trial was held immediately after the war to ascertain the practicability of resumption. The load of seventeen vehicles on an express timing was probably unprecedented yet the Merchant Navy Pacific demonstrated that not only could they improve upon what was considered a very fast timing but could do so with over 500 tons behind the tender. The commercial potential of the trial was the demonstration that relief sections could be combined with the parent train but unfortunately the length of platforms inhibited the operating department from using the new engines to their greatest advantage. Neither were regular non-stop schedules ever reintroduced between London and Bournemouth and although considerable criticism originated from the council chambers of Dorset during the 1950's, Waterloo steadfastly maintained that Southampton was too important a station to overlook.

WORTING JUNCTION : SALISBURY (EAST). 12.45

Worting Jcn | Oakley | Overton | Whitchurch | **10.54 WATERLOO** to **SALISBURY.** Lord Nelson 4-6-0 | **ANDOVER JCN** | Grateley | Idmiston | Porton | **SALISBURY**

10.23 Bevois Pk to Rogerstone. H15 4-6-0

Hurstbourne

light engine Overton. U 2-6-0

10.42 Salisbury to B'stoke. S15 4-6-0

08.15 PLYMOUTH to **WATERLOO.** Merchant Navy 4-6-2

10.27 BRISTOL to **P'MOUTH.** U 2-6-0

To Waterloo

To Bulford

With no coalfields to serve the Southern had no need for a large eight-coupled mineral engine and the nearest they came to it was the S15 4-6-0 which was used on most of the long distance workings from Feltham. In common with other Maunsell standard types, the S15's included a number of variants within the class, the original Urie engines of 1920 being added to by Maunsell in 1927 and 1936. 30503, above, was recognisable from the raised footplating over the cylinders as being one of the original batch whilst 30829, lower, is one of the 1927 series.

where the incidence of shipping had an enormous effect on the railway. It was impossible to estimate realistically what calls were going to be made on operations and the timetable generally reflected the minimum with special trains being run as notice was given to the railway by the shipping companies. Few cargo vessels operated to any sort of a meaningful schedule and an entire department at Waterloo was employed to assess forthcoming shipping arrivals and the cargoes that were to be unloaded, details of which would have to be translated into terms of wagons; the necessary numbers being culled from other parts of BR who would work them as far as Feltham, the SR arranging special trains - often at very short notice - to convey the empties to the docks and to work out the loaded vehicles as soon as they were released for movement.

The servicing of Southampton Docks with empty wagons - vans and vanfits were the norm - was one of the gems of transport organisation and it is curious that the Southern's well deserved reputation for excellence of passenger services was not paralleled with a corresponding respect for its abilities in other directions.

Typically the docks and stations assessed their requirements in advance and telephoned their individual requirements to the District Manager's Office who would aggregate the needs of the entire district into categories of wagons and then communicate with the Regional HQ at Waterloo to estimate the extent to which needs could be met from within the Southern region. (The London area, for example, unloaded considerable numbers of vehicles each day and these would be available within hours of arrival for returning to Southampton, or wherever they were needed, for reloading).

The shortfall, which was often considerable, was then forwarded by Waterloo to the wagon control office at the Railway Executive whose task it was to liaise with the other regions - a knowledge of locations where empty wagons of one sort or another were liable to be was useful - and issue them with quota's of empty wagons to be sent within twenty-four hours to Feltham or Basingstoke. Thus Liverpool Street - who supervised the former LNER south of York - might at any time have an instruction to forward two thousand vans to the

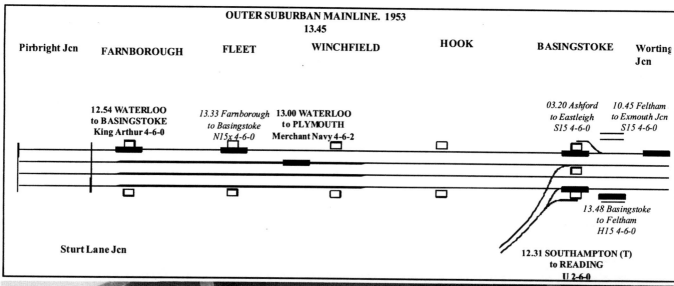

OUTER SUBURBAN MAINLINE. 1953
13.45

Pirbright Jcn   **FARNBOROUGH**   **FLEET**   **WINCHFIELD**   **HOOK**   **BASINGSTOKE**   Worting Jcn

12.54 WATERLOO
to BASINGSTOKE
King Arthur 4-6-0

13.33 Farnborough
to Basingstoke
N15x 4-6-0

13.00 WATERLOO
to PLYMOUTH
Merchant Navy 4-6-2

03.20 Ashford
to Eastleigh
S15 4-6-0

10.45 Feltham
to Exmouth Jcn
S15 4-6-0

13.48 Basingstoke
to Feltham
H15 4-6-0

Sturt Lane Jcn

12.31 SOUTHAMPTON (T)
to READING
U 2-6-0

The business end of S15 30830. One can see from the position of the regulator why these engines were driven on the reversing wheel - changing the regulator setting meant risking either the firemans blade or the heat from the firebox.

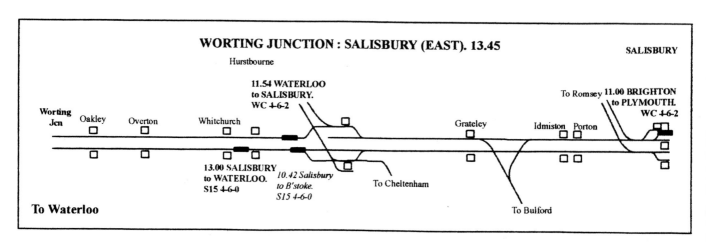

WORTING JUNCTION : SALISBURY (EAST). 13.45

            Hurstbourne   **SALISBURY**

11.54 WATERLOO
to SALISBURY.
WC 4-6-2

To Romsey **11.00 BRIGHTON**
to PLYMOUTH.
WC 4-6-2

Worting Jcn   Oakley   Overton   Whitchurch   Grateley   Idmiston   Porton

13.00 SALISBURY
to WATERLOO.
S15 4-6-0

10.42 Salisbury
to B'stoke.
S15 4-6-0

To Cheltenham

To Bulford

To Waterloo

The H15 4-6-0's were a mixed traffic version of the N15 King Arthur class and consisted of five variations appearing from 1914 until 1927. They handled much of the fast goods traffic between Nine Elms and Southampton Docks and could often be found on local passenger services south of Eastleigh whilst a Nine Elms-based member of the class put in a daily appearance at Waterloo, working the 09.54 to Southampton Central as far as Eastleigh. The upper view shows one of the original Urie 1914 locomotives, 30483, preparing to leave Eastleigh with the 17.27 stopping train for Portsmouth & Southsea in 1949. The differing appearance of engines within the class can be seen in the lower view of 30331, one of the 1924 series rebuilt from the Drummond F13 4-cylinder 4-6-0's.

Southern, a thousand of which were to combed from the North Eastern through its HQ at York.

Each station routinely had to declare - more or less honestly - the number and type of empty wagons it had on hand each morning; figures that were aggregated by each District and forwarded to the regional headquarters so that each region was in a position to determine whether or not it could meet the requirements of the Railway Executive.

General user wagons such as vans - which always seemed to be in short supply - were almost a unit of currency since each of the unloading districts had their own needs which they had to balance against demands from outside interests.

Once, however, it had been established that the wagons needed could be supplied from various parts of the country, it fell to each district to ensure that they were worked away without delay and, at times of heavy demand, it was uncommon for booked service to have the ca-

pability to cope and a district finding itself having to despatch - at the drop of a hat - two hundred and fifty empty vans to, say, New England for Feltham would find itself having to organise three or four special workings; one of which might be arranged with an unbalanced engine and men, another by cancelling a booked service and using the engine and men for the vans and the remainder with spare engines and men wherever they could be found.

Such hurried arrangements were not confined to the originating district alone since specials of vans from Nottingham (GC) to Feltham, for example, would require relief and a change of engines at Peterborough and Ferme Park (or Woodford, Banbury and Reading if it was more convenient to direct them via the Great Central: a decision that would be taken on the basis of crewing availability and congestion in the London area).

The extraordinary thing was that, as a matter of daily routine, a single telephone call from

a clerk in the Southampton district could put all this machinery into motion with dozens of people the length of the country being involved but with such little fuss that few people, even within the railway industry, were ever aware of the organisation that lay behind the receipt of the empties that were required.

Needless to say a single ship alone could tie up extraordinary numbers of engines, men and vehicles, none of which were allowed for in the timetables. A similar form of working applied to passenger traffic to and from Southampton and even though the larger shipping lines operated to a timetable of sorts, variable passenger loadings and the vagaries of the weather militated against trains being included in the working and public timetables.

From the spectators point of view the daytime was not the best time to see the South Western long distance freight working at its best and there was nothing comparable with the intermingling of goods, mineral and passenger

WC. 4-6-2 34044 'Woolacombe'. 11 : 362/390 tons (1					
m.ch point	1/in	WTT	Actual mph	dbhp	pc
0.00 SALISBURY		0.00	0 -	-	-
5.24 Porton	216		8.55 48.5	1189	4
7.69 Amesbury Jcn	237		12.08 52.5	1080	5
17.24 ANDOVER JCN	-3932	2.00	19.44 83.5	976	7
			pwc		
24.35 Whitchurch	369		29.00 47.0	-	-
28.01 Overton	549		32.50 60.0	1220	7
31.12 Oakley	2937		35.44 69.0	1154	7
33.20 Worting Jcn	-7344	0.00	37.34 70.0	447	3
35.63 BASINGSTOKE	-2604	2.30	39.28 81.0	1145	9
41.30 Hook	-684		43.33 79.0	476	4
43.57 Winchfield	-1046		45.20 80.0	744	6
47.05 Fleet	-674		47.47 79.0	487	4
50.26 Farnborough	-2852		50.18 78.0	677	5
52.43 MP.31	946		51.59 76.0	884	7
55.44 Brookwood	-307		54.16 84.0	794	6
59.16 WOKING	-3186	3.00	56.45 68.0	-	-
61.69 W. Byfleet	-367		59.16 81.0	851	5
64.31 Weybridge	-6116		61.14 74.5	-	-
70.16 Hampton Ct Jcn	-23487	2.00	65.40 78.0	920	7
			signals		
83.43 WATERLOO	-71138	9.00	82.31 -	-	-

Worting Jcn to Brookwood. 22.3 miles -1/646. . 80mph : 690 dbhp

Occasionally Exmouth Junction, who provided power for the up Atlantic Coast Express, substituted a light Pacific for the booked Merchant Navy as happened when 34044 was turned out to work the train. Thanks to a very light load, the 89-minute schedule from Salisbury to Waterloo was no great challenge for the West Country Pacific which succeeded in gaining six and a half minutes in spite of two slacks en route. The extraordinary thing is that the engine was worked almost casually after passing Oakley with occasional short bursts of power being applied to keep the speed at around the 80 mph mark.

SR DIESEL 10203 (2000 bhp). 11:366/390 tons (1955)						
m.ch Point	1/in	WTT	m.s	mph	dbhp	pc
0.00 WATERLOO		0.00	0.00	-	-	-
			Fog			
14.31 Esher	7529		21.5	60.0	518	2
19.12 Weybridge	1952		26	66.0	973	7
24.27 WOKING	676	28.00	30.20	70.0	1228	9
27.79 Brookwood	318		33.3	67.5	1214	8
31.00 MP.31	307		36.10	66.5	1230	8
33.17 Farnborough	-946		38.00	73.0	1157	8
42.13 Hook	1072		45.1	77.0	1106	8
50.23 WORTING JCN	435	51.00	51.4	67.0	1010	8
55.42 Overton	2923		56.1	75.0	1111	8
			pwc : 15 mph			
61.07 Hurstbourne	-429		62.5	62.5	-	-
66.19 ANDOVER JCN	-401		67.1	80.0	8245	6
72.49 Grateley	275		72.4	66.0	1026	7
			Signals			
83.43 SALISBURY	-317	83.00	85.4	-	-	-

Esher-Overton. 41 miles, 1/719. 72 mph. 1106 dbhp (pc 8)

From late 1951 until mid-1955 all BR's main line diesels were allocated to Nine Elms working turn and turn about with Merchant Navy 4-6-2's. In the above log 10203, the most powerful of the quintet, is seen on the down Atlantic Coast Express on a day when the load was rather lighter than the norm. With a clear run the engine could have handled the train without difficulty but, hampered in the early sages by fog and latterly by permanent way and signal delays, it had insufficient reserve to achieve an on-time arrival at Salisbury. In fairness it has to be pointed out that the schedule was the tightest on the system whilst the engine's rating was barely the equal of a 7P light Pacific and fell considerably short of the much more powerful Merchant Navy engines.

V2 2-6-2 60893 12:488/510 Pullmans. (1953)					
m.ch Point	1/in	WTT	Actual mph	dbhp	pc
0.00 WATERLOO		0.00	0.00 -	-	-
3.74 Clapham Jcn	-3642	7.00	7.38 38.0	655	2
7.19 Wimbledon	752		12.03 48.0	931	4
12.03 Surbiton	20774		17.25 56.0	784	4
19.12 Weybridge	8963		24.37 56.0	655	4
24.27 WOKING	676	30.00	29.40 60.0	1199	7
27.79 Brookwood	318		33.37 58.0	1138	6
31.00 MP.31	307		37.00 53.0	931	5
33.17 Farnborough	-946		39.20 62.5	1099	6
36.38 Fleet	2852		42.35 61.0	642	4
			pwc		
42.13 Hook	789		51.20 42.0	196	1
47.60 BASINGSTOKE	684		57.55 55.0	1082	6
50.23 Worting Jcn	260	56.00	61.05 45.0	640	3
58.09 Micheldever	12596		69.25 70.0	1136	6
61.60 Wallers Ash	-252		72.21 78.0	534	4
66.39 WINCHESTER	-265	73.30	75.55 82.0	314	3
69.50 Shawford	-260		78.07 86.0	632	5
73.35 EASTLEIGH	-281	80.00	80.53 80.0	-	-
			Signal delays		
79.19 SOUTHAMPTON	-894	88.00	90.03 -	-	-

Weybridge to Farnborough. 14.1 miles 1/527.
57 mph. 1095 dbhp (pc 6)

For a short period in 1953 the Bulleid Pacifics were withdrawn for emergency axle examinations and a number of V2 2-6-2's and B1 4-6-0's were borrowed from the ER to make good the shortage. Most of the visitors were in a pretty disreputable condition - or so it was claimed - and not all Southern men were overjoyed with the substitutes. On a number of occasions a Green Arrow was turned out to work the Bournemouth Belle and a recording was secured of 60893 (New England) which might, had it not been for adverse signals, have reached Southampton on time. Making allowances for the pwc at Winchfield it was not a bad effort although the drivers were by no means certain how to get the best from an LNER engine and on one run a GN inspector had to use some persuasion to get the driver to fully open the regulator during the early stages of the run. The driver didn't think the engine 'would take it' and was quite surprised when it did. On the above run it can be taken that the driver had got used to the V2 by the time the train had got to Shawford.

Southampton or the tourist season was in full bloom, and in order to avoid conflict and congestion most goods services were run during the night hours.

This segregation was taken even further in the suburban area where, prior to 1922, considerable difficulties had arisen with goods traffic from other companies which arrived on the LSWR at a variety of border points. The solution had been to open a central focal point, well clear of the busiest sections of line, for all incoming freight traffic so that it could be marshalled at leisure and despatched to stations on the LSWR system in an organised manner. The location selected was Feltham which was situated on the relatively quiet loop line serving the Houslow area with its good connections to the northern main lines.

Some goods trains could always be seen on the main line during the daylight hours although in the main they were rather secondary affairs, many of which tended to spend long periods waiting at Basingstoke until the rush of passenger traffic had died down in the London area.

Apart from the main line and the Reading branch, there were two other important freight arteries within the district, one being the Salisbury to Eastleigh route which conveyed a respectable volume of traffic between the Bristol and South Wales districts to Southampton, Portsmouth and the LBSCR area and the other being the MSWR over which three through services per day ran between Cheltenham and Southampton. The latter was a very useful connection since it reduced, by a considerable margin, the time taken for wagon-load traffic to move from the North Avon area to Southampton docks by avoiding the shunting and trip working that would otherwise have been called for in the Bristol and Salisbury area's. Over 150 through wagons per day were moved from Cheltenham to Southampton via the MSWR - a fact that reflects its importance in a way its passenger workings never could - with a normal transit taking no more than about seven hours for the one hundred-odd mile distance.

Wherever you worked on the railway, sooner or later the fates were likely to land you in a yard Inspectors Office (sometimes as the Inspector if some-

trains that could be found at any time of day on, for example, the Great Northern. The passenger lines between Waterloo and Worting Junction were fully occupied with passenger services, especially when shipping was heavy at

one at Waterloo thought you had promise). It was as rewarding an environment as anyone could wish for with complex alterations to the working - effecting many hundreds of miles and the destinations of several souls - being made absolutely routinely.

"Charlie.." the Inspector would blare into one telephone whilst waving another in the air, "there's fifty expedite Northam vans leaving Reading. Have yer got an engine and men for them?" He looks at the ceiling and tells it that 'he'll not have an engine this time of night'. He never has one any time. A tinny voice comes to life on one of the handsets. "God almighty Charlie. You've got a yard full of bloody engines. What about the Andover loco?" Another pause and then more crackling from the phone. "Of course it can piddle down to Eastleigh and back light. Good grief Charlie the thing'll be back before the Andover men sign on. Get it ready and send it to the down side for forty five. OK Charlie well done". He switches phones. "Rightho matey, we'll handle them. Wheel 'em in and, what, Oh aye, Oxley engine back light to Reading." The telephones bang onto their cradles and the Inspector stands and stretches. "Good man, Charles, you know. Damn fine railwayman - never lets you down when you need an engine in a hurry......"

BASINGSTOKE

Engine with a past... At first glance just 'another' SR mogul yet the number reveals it as the locomotive which altered the direction of early SR motive power. The short distances run by many SECR and LBSCR expresses prompted thoughts as to the practicability of operating them with large 2-6-4 tank locomotives and following an experiment commenced in 1917 twenty-one such locomotives were in operation by the end of 1926. 31800 started life as A800 'River Cray', one of the 2-6-4T fleet in July 1926, operating initially from Redhill on the Reading workings but, after a few weeks of service, from Dover on the main line to Charing Cross via Ashford. The 2-6-4T locomotives quickly gained a reputation for instability but before any lasting measures could be taken A800 left the road near Sevenoaks on August 21st 1927 whilst working the 17.00 Cannon Street - Ramsgate express. The incident claimed no less than thirteen lives and although the chief culprit was the permanent way, the 2-6-4T engines were summarily withdrawn from traffic and rebuilt as 2-6-0 tender locomotives. In their rebuilt form the class saw little regular express passenger work - other than during the peak periods - and tended to be confined to the secondary routes of the system. Thirty years after its conversion U class 2-6-0 31800 is seen arriving on Basingstoke loco after working the daily goods to Andover Junction.

Occupying a strategic position at the divergence of the Wessex route from the west of England main line, together with the Reading branch, and being at the periphery of the London suburban area, Basingstoke MPD might have been expected to have been of critical importance to the main line; playing a major role in the supply of locomotives for the many trains which originated in the area.

In fact its operational contribution was much less than is generally believed and, having an allocation of only nineteen engines, was used more as a servicing point for visiting engines which called to turn and water in the middle of their workings.

Much of this was due to the fact that prominent amongst the services from Basingstoke were workings over the Reading line whose engines were primarily Great Western and based, after the closure of the GWR shed at Basingstoke, either at Oxford, Wolverhampton (Oxley) or Reading; six daily visitors appearing from the last mentioned, the highest number from any shed other than Basingstoke itself.

In addition to visiting GW locomotives - Oxford and Oxley sent one and three respectively - fourteen engines from LSWR sheds were booked to make daily appearances: four each from Nine Elms and Eastleigh, three from Feltham, two from Salisbury and a single representative from Guildford. Against this total of twenty-four visitors, Basingstoke shed despatched a mere twelve engines a day, only eight of which were for main line workings.

35005 ' Canadian Pacific'. 363/390 tons. (1956)					
m.ch Point	1/in WTT	Actual	mph	dbhp	pc
0.00 WATERLOO	0.00	0.00	-	-	-
3.74 Clapham Jcn	-3642 7.00	7.17	47.0	675	2
7.19 Wimbledon	752	11.14	55.0	818	4
12.03 Surbiton	20774	15.48	66.0	945	6
21.54 W. Byfleet	7988	23.42	75.0	987	7
24.27 WOKING	367 28.00	25.51	72.0	1130	8
27.79 Brookwood	318	28.58	68.0	1136	8
31.00 MP.31	307	31.41	65.5	1124	7
33.17 Farnborough	-946	33.35	71.5	1015	7
36.38 Fleet	2852	36.20	73.0	875	6
39.66 Winchfield	674	39.06	70.0	858	6
47.60 BASINGSTOKE	761	45.41	69.5	1002	7
50.23 Worting Jcn	260 51.00	48.00	63.0	896	6
52.31 Oakley	734	49.56	69.0	1390	9
55.42 Overton	-2937	52.36	75.0	1025	7
59.08 Whitchurch	-549	55.20	82.0	940	7
66.19 ANDOVER JCN	-369	60.19	93.0	823	7
72.49 Grateley	275	65.45	57.0	252	2
78.19 Porton	-571	70.56	82.0	1041	7
Signal delays					
83.43 SALISBURY	-216 83.00	82.04	-	-	-
Wimbledon - Andover Jcn 59 miles 1/1969.					
72 mph, 977 dbhp (pc 7)					

Designed with trains of fifteen and more vehicles in mind, the Merchant Navy Pacifics were wasted on light-weight services especially as the maximum speed permitted was (nominally) 85 m.p.h. 35005 could, had the road been clear, have reached Salisbury in 77 minutes even though the engine had been reigned in for much of the journey. It is clear that the reduction in boiler pressure from 280 to 250lb, effected in 1955/6, had no effect on performance.

One of the reasons for the relatively small proportion of 'home' engines coming off shed arose from the fact that very little traffic originated at Basingstoke and much of the exchange with the Great Western, for example, was arranged by Paddington who determined the level of inward goods trains to Basingstoke which in turn dictated the number of outward departures with the Southern playing no part in the workings.

Similarly on the LSWR, traffic was limited to a trio of goods trains, one each to Farnborough, Bulford and Andover Junction; everything else being worked by 'foreign' engines off inward workings.

Thus although Basingstoke shed saw a continual procession of engines arriving and departing, relatively few of them were locally based and even rural branch working had become a thing of the past with the closure of the Alton branch in 1932.

Originating LSW passenger traffic was only marginally greater than the freight and dense though the steam morning peak service was, many of the stopping trains started from Salisbury or the Wessex districts, obviating the need for Basingstoke to play a prominent part in their working. (In fact the only 'true' season ticket train to start from Basingstoke - the 06.37 to Waterloo - was

It was unusual to see a Great Western passenger engine that was not clean and Modified Hall 4-6-0 7923 'Speke Hall' sports an uncharacteristic covering of grime as it waits for its next working in the GW section of Basingstoke station. It was also unusual to see anything as large as a Castle at Basingstoke - Hall 4-6-0's were the staple fare for passenger trains to and from Reading - and doubtless the sight of 5018 'St. Mawes Castle' when it paid its visit in 1961 gave local enthusiasts something to talk about. The 4-6-0 is backing onto the loco in order to turn before returning in the Reading direction. Also on shed is H15 4-6-0 30523.

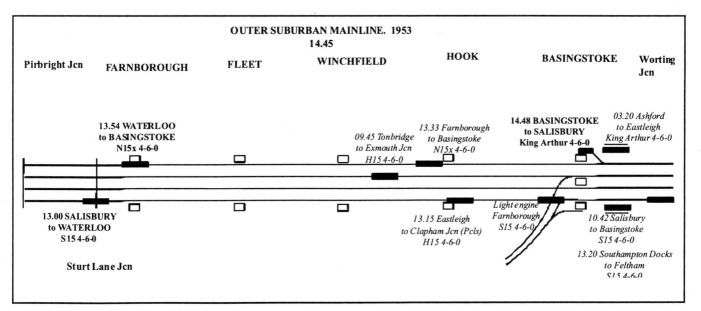

OUTER SUBURBAN MAINLINE. 1953
14.45

| Pirbright Jcn | FARNBOROUGH | FLEET | WINCHFIELD | HOOK | BASINGSTOKE | Worting Jcn |

13.54 WATERLOO
to BASINGSTOKE
N15x 4-6-0

09.45 Tonbridge
to Exmouth Jcn
H15 4-6-0

13.33 Farnborough
to Basingstoke
N15x 4-6-0

14.48 BASINGSTOKE
to SALISBURY
King Arthur 4-6-0

03.20 Ashford
to Eastleigh
King Arthur 4-6-0

13.00 SALISBURY
to WATERLOO
S15 4-6-0

13.15 Eastleigh
to Clapham Jcn (Pcls)
H15 4-6-0

Light engine
Farnborough
S15 4-6-0

10.42 Salisbury
to Basingstoke
S15 4-6-0

13.20 Southampton Docks
to Feltham
S15 4-6-0

Sturt Lane Jcn

In addition to its N15X 4-6-0's, Basingstoke provided further interest by having an allocation of two 700 class 'Black Pig' 0-6-0's, one of which worked the morning goods to Bullford. Introduced in 1897 and superheated just before the grouping, the 700's had a wider route availability than many successive types and almost thirty examples survived the 1950's. 30368 stands on Basingstoke loco in 1961 in company with a 'stopped' Bulleid Pacific and H15 30523.

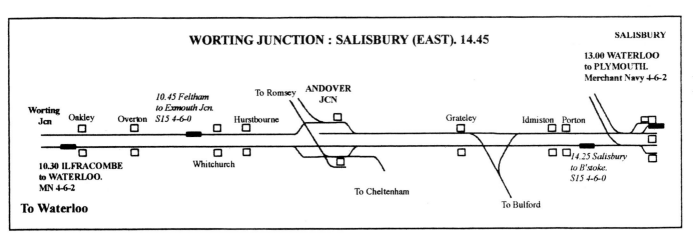

WORTING JUNCTION : SALISBURY (EAST). 14.45

SALISBURY

13.00 WATERLOO
to PLYMOUTH.
Merchant Navy 4-6-2

| Worting Jcn | Oakley | Overton | | Hurstbourne | ANDOVER JCN | | Grateley | Idmiston | Porton | |
To Romsey

10.45 Feltham
to Exmouth Jcn.
S15 4-6-0

10.30 ILFRACOMBE
to WATERLOO.
MN 4-6-2

Whitchurch

To Cheltenham

To Bulford

14.25 Salisbury
to B'stoke.
S15 4-6-0

To Waterloo

booked to the Nine Elms H15 4-6-0 which had arrived with an overnight goods from Brockenhurst earlier in the morning).

Other visitors which stole some of the Basingstoke limelight were West Country Pacifics from Bournemouth and Nine Elms which worked the 10.35 and 19.40 Waterloo trains, and a Guildford 2-6-0 which powered an evening service to Reading and back before disappearing home with the 21.15 Basingstoke - Woking.

This incursion left only three starting services for Basingstoke engines to work although the position was alleviated by the 'gift' of an additional train, the 06.35 Bournemouth - Waterloo changing engines at Basingstoke; its Pacific standing as main line pilot for an hour and a half before continuing east with the 10.35 to Waterloo.

These four workings were covered by three N15 and an N15x from Basingstoke; each engine doing little more than running up to Waterloo and returning again after servicing on Nine Elms.

Although in 1953 the entire N15x class was intact and allocated to Basingstoke, it is significant that the greater part of the London workings - and especially those that included the 17.09 and 18.09 business trains from Waterloo - were entrusted to the King Arthur 4-6-0's - of which Basingstoke had three - rather than the Remembrance rebuilds, which were considered rather sluggish engines and not the equal of an N15,

Whilst the Remembrance class had enjoyed a high reputation on the LBSCR, where they had been the pride of the line, their rebuilding had not been especially successful - the Southern seem to have made a sows ear from a silk purse - and so far as their everyday workings from Basingstoke was concerned, little might have been lost had they been transferred in their original form. This however would have restricted their availability for the excursion work from London to Bournemouth for which they were often borrowed; the original 4-6-4 design having a very limited water capacity.

Ousted to a considerable degree from the London trains by the King Arthur 4-6-0's, one of the N15x diagrams called for the highest daily mileage of any Basingstoke engine - 204 miles - by working two trips from Basingstoke to Reading and a parcels train from Eastleigh to Waterloo, concluding with the early morning newspaper train from London. It was just possible to keep one engine on this working, as it was with the other Basingstoke diagrams, although - given that the engine was in steam for twenty-two hours and there was an adequate reserve of 4-6-0's - more often than not a change of engines was made each day.

Of the other N15x duties, one engine relieved the Bournemouth West Country 4-6-0 with the 06.35 Bournemouth -Waterloo stopping train and the other was relegated to the daily pick-up goods to Farnborough; a curious duty for a named passenger 4-6-0 and a sight that suggested, not inaccurately, that by the early 1950's the days of the class were numbered.

The fact that the N15x 4-6-0's were earmarked for early withdrawal did not prevent their use on long distance trains at the height of the season and in August 1953 - a period when all four of the diesel-electric locomotives were out of action - two engines of the class worked the 13.05 relief from Waterloo to Exeter on separate occasions (one being as a substitute for a failed Lord Nelson at Basingstoke) whilst a third was seen at the head of a Southampton - Waterloo Ocean Liner Express. Another member of the class broke new ground in the same month by being allocated by Basingstoke shed to a Reading South - Brighton special which the engine worked as far as Redhill.

In spite of their reputation for sluggishness, occasionally the N15x's could rise to the challenge as happened on 25th June 1955 when West Country 34063 '229 Squadron' came to grief at Basingstoke with the 15.05 Bournemouth West - Waterloo. 32332 'Stroudley' took the place of the ailing Pacific and after a forty-five minute delay, succeeded in getting its twelve vehicles to London without further loss of time.

Although it was generally accepted that the Remembrance rebuilds were destined for the scrap heap as soon as an excuse could be found for their disposal, the fact a King Arthur 4-6-0, 30754 of Basingstoke, preceded them in December 1952 came as something of a surprise and although 30754 had had a good innings, it was nevertheless understood that the larger engines would outlive the Brighton imports. In the event the demise of 30754 proved to be an

BASINGSTOKE MPD : ENGINES OFF SHED					
Inward Working	Arr	Engine	Depot	Dep	Train
16.44 Worcester	23.00	Hall 4-6-0	Oxford 9	00.00	00.30 Hinksey
Carriage shunt	00.10	U 2-6-0	239 (stale)		
22.40 Waterloo	00.15	H15 4-6-0	Nine Elms 66	01.25	01.55 Nine Elms
21.45 Eastleigh	22.45	Hall 4-6-0	Oxley 208	01.40	02.10 Oxley
22.50 Salisbury	01.00	H15 4-6-0	Salisbury 439	03.00	03.30 Salisbury
22.05 Reading	23.10	Hall 4-6-0	Reading 201	04.00	04.30 Crewe
03.15 Reading	04.00	61xx 2-6-2T	Reading 47	04.40	05.10 Reading
		700 0-6-0	242	05.00	05.30 Bulford goods
03.45 Waterloo	05.20	N15X 4-6-0	236 (stale)		
23.20 Brockenhurst	**01.50**	**H15 4-6-0**	**Nine Elms 74**	**05.30**	**06.37 Waterloo**
19.10 Victoria Basin	**03.40**	**Hall 4-6-0**	**Oxley 208A**	**06.05**	**06.57 Reading**
North Yard Pilot	06.10	E5 0-6-2T	243 (stale)		
		N15 4-6-0	**231**	**06.50**	**12.02 Waterloo**
21.22 Bournemouth	**23.45**	**N15 4-6-0**	**Eastleigh 264**	**07.08**	**07.38 Reading**
		U 2-6-0	239	07.15	07.45 Andover Jcn goods
West Yard Pilot	07.20	E5 0-6-2T	245 (stale)		
		N15 4-6-0	**232**	**07.25**	**08.25 Waterloo**
		N15X 4-6-0	**236/1**	**07.54**	**08.24 Reading**
		N15X 4-6-0	241	08.20	08.41 Farnborough goods
		N15X 4-6-0	**233**	**08.30**	**09.02 Waterloo**
		E5 0-6-2T	245	08.30	West Yard pilot
		G6 0-6-0T	244	09.00	West Yard pilot
West Yard Pilot	09.10	G6 0-6-0T	244 (stale)		
Carriage shunt	09.30	T9 4-4-0	240 (stale)		
23.15 Eastleigh	00.55	H15 4-6-0	Eastleigh 310	10.15	10.48 Eastleigh
		T9 4-4-0	240	10.30	Carriage pilot
09.15 Reading	11.30	28xx 2-8-0	Reading 202	12.35	13.05 Reading
		N15 4-6-0	**234**	**13.00**	**13.33 Waterloo**
21.02 Clapham Jcn	23.20	H15 4-6-0	Nine Elms 76	13.20	13.48 Feltham
10.17 Reading	**11.00**	**N15X 4-6-0**	**236/2**	**13.45**	**15.55 Reading**
		E5 0-6-2T	243	13.45	North Yard pilot
09.40 Moreton C.	11.50	N15 4-6-0	Eastleigh 264	14.15	14.45 Eastleigh
12.33 Woking	14.00	S15 4-6-0	Feltham 112	14.45	L/E Farnborough
13.54 Waterloo	15.30	N15X 4-6-0	233 (stale)		
13.33 Farnborough	15.50	N15X 4-6-0	241 (stale)		
15.10 Reading	**16.00**	**61xx 2-6-2T**	**Reading 71**	**16.30**	**16.55 Bramley**
07.34 Woking	**10.40**	**U 2-6-0**	**Guildford 182**	**17.35**	**18.05 Reading**
14.25 Salisbury	16.15	S15 4-6-0	Feltham 106	18.30	19.00 Eastleigh
10.42 Salisbury	14.55	S15 4-6-0	Salisbury 438	18.35	19.04 Salisbury
17.09 Waterloo	18.35	N15 4-6-0	234 (stale)		
16.30 Amesbury	19.00	700 0-6-0	242 (stale)		
15.54 Waterloo	**17.30**	**WC 4-6-2**	**Nine Elms 38**	**19.10**	**19.40 Waterloo**
18.09 Waterloo	19.35	N15 4-6-0	231 (stale)		
West Yard Pilot	20.16	E5 0-6-2T	245 (stale)		
Light from Reading	**19.54**	**U 2-6-0**	**Guildford 182**	**20.45**	**21.15 Woking**
02.15 Oxley	09.10	43xx 2-6-0	Oxley 207	21.15	21.45 Oxley
		E5 0-6-2T	245/2	21.30	West Yard pilot
19.54 Waterloo	21.30	N15 4-6-0	232 (stale)		
17.18 Winchester	19.00	S15 4-6-0	Feltham 103	22.00	22.25 Feltham
20.38 Reading	**21.30**	**61xx 2-6-2T**	**Reading 74**	**22.20**	**22.35 Reading**
18.35 Bournemouth	21.20	N15 4-6-0	Eastleigh 266	22.40	23.10 Eastleigh
21.17 Reading	**22.00**	**Hall 4-6-0**	**Reading 66**	**23.25**	**23.55 Reading**

Passenger workings in bold type. Stale refers to an engine finishing a diagram

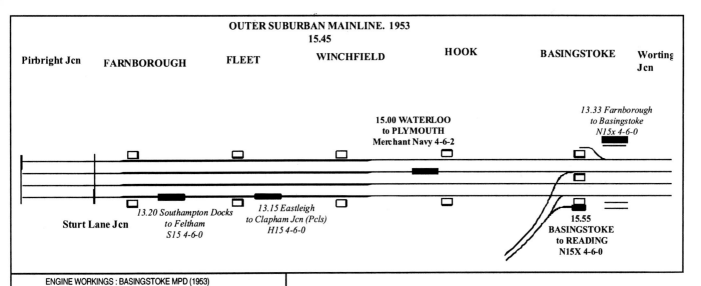

OUTER SUBURBAN MAINLINE. 1953
15.45

Pirbright Jcn FARNBOROUGH FLEET WINCHFIELD HOOK BASINGSTOKE Worting Jcn

13.33 Farnborough
to Basingstoke
N15x 4-6-0

15.00 WATERLOO
to PLYMOUTH
Merchant Navy 4-6-2

Sturt Lane Jcn

13.20 Southampton Docks
to Feltham
S15 4-6-0

13.15 Eastleigh
to Clapham Jcn (Pcls)
H15 4-6-0

15.55
BASINGSTOKE
to READING
N15X 4-6-0

ENGINE WORKINGS : BASINGSTOKE MPD (1953)

Dia	Class	Time	Train	To Shed	Rev Miles
231	N15 4-6-0	06.50	Carriage shunting		
			12.02 Basingstoke : Waterloo		
			16.59 C. Jcn : Waterloo ECS		
			18.09 Waterloo : Basingstoke	19.30	96
232	N15 4-6-0	07.25	ECS Barton Mill : Basingstoke		
			08.25 Basingstoke : Waterloo		
			10.23 Waterloo : Clapham Jcn ECS		
			Nine Elms MPD		
			19.54 Waterloo : Basingstoke	21.20	96
234	N15 4-6-0	13.00	**13.33 Basingstoke : Waterloo**		
			Nine Elms MPD		
			17.09 Waterloo : Basingstoke	18.30	96
236	N15X 4-6-0	07.54	**08.24 Basingstoke : Reading**		
			10.17 Reading : Basingstoke		
			Carriage shunting		
			15.55 Basingstoke : Reading		
			19.00 Reading : Eastleigh		
			22.15 (Pcls) Eastleigh : Waterloo		
			Nine Elms MPD		
			03.45 (News) Waterloo : Basingstoke	05.15	209
241	N15X 4-6-0	08.20	08.41 Basingstoke : Farnborough		
			13.33 Farnborough : Basingstoke	15.50	29
233	N15X 4-6-0	08.30	**09.02 Basingstoke : Waterloo**		
			Nine Elms MPD		
			13.54 Waterloo : Basingstoke	15.20	96
239	U 2-6-0	07.15	07.45 Basingstoke : Andover Jcn		
			13.08 light to Overton (shunt)		
			16.33 Overton : Basingstoke		
			West Yard Pilot	00.10	26
242	700 0-6-0	05.00	05.30 Basingstoke : Bulford		
			Shunt and light engine to Amesbury		
			16.30 Amesbury : Basingstoke	19.00	67
240	T9 4-4-0	09.15	Carriage shunting	09.15	
265	E5 0-6-2T	08.30	West Yard Pilot	07.20	
243	E5 0-6-2T	13.5	North Yard Pilot	06.05	
244	G6 0-6-0T	09.00	West Yard Pilot	09.00	

Passenger workings in bold type. Rev Miles indicates main line revenue mileage

isolated case and the remainder of the N15's remained at work for several years more.

Apart from the ten 4-6-0's, the only other large engines allocated to Basingstoke were a pair of U class 2-6-0's for which there was one diagram: the morning goods to Andover Junction, returning in the afternoon with a freight from Overton.

To the regret of many the T9 4-4-0's were a scarcity on main line workings, relegated from the front line by the various 4-6-0 classes that had been introduced since the grouping, yet almost seventy of the class survived into the mid-1950s; many of them continuing to see regular employment on secondary trains between Wessex and Salisbury and in the far west of England. There was little call for their services in the London area but two survived at Basingstoke, one of the pair being used on continuous carriage shunting duties and, as such, a candidate ready to assist any main line failures which, when it happened, was liable to take the 4-4-0 into uncharted waters, as was the case in August 1953 when a Bulleid Pacific failed at Basingstoke with the Bournemouth - Birkenhead express and 30724 was used to take the service as far as Oxford. Perhaps the highpoint in the engine's post-war career came on Saturday 14th August when it had

to rescue the 10.48 Torrington - Waterloo (a section of the Atlantic Coast Express). Three weeks later the same engine was selected to work a 100-minute BTC special from Portsmouth Harbour to Waterloo; the choice of engine being made by the Chairman of the Commission who had a soft spot for elderly locomotives.

Another Drummond survivor at Basingstoke was 700 class 0-6-0 30368 - the only example of the class on the shed's books - which was the regular engine for the daily goods service to and from Bulford, a working which serviced most of the intermediate stations between Basingstoke and Salisbury.

The Remembrance Baltic tanks were not the only steam engines made redundant by the 1933 Victoria - Brighton electrification and the mass introduction of multiple-unit electric units had made a considerable number of relatively modern shunting engines surplus to LBSCR requirements. A number of these displaced engines found their way to the LSWR, two of which were to be found shunting the West and North yards at Basingstoke. The type of engine varied over the years and included E1 0-6-0T's in addition to E4 and E5 0-6-2T's, the latter remaining at Basingstoke until deposed by diesel shunting engines in 1957.

Shunting engines - yard pilots as they were more normally referred to - were often surprisingly difficult to locate and although they generally remained local to an area, they were usually hidden by a sea on wagons in a yard where the presence of visitors was not normally encouraged. More often than not, the trouble was not worth the effort as the engines to be seen were of a predictable and humdrum nature although Basingstoke was an exception in this respect since not only were most of its shunt-

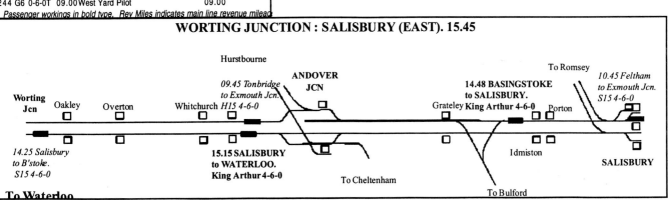

WORTING JUNCTION : SALISBURY (EAST). 15.45

Hurstbourne To Romsey

09.45 Tonbridge
to Exmouth Jcn.
H15 4-6-0

ANDOVER JCN

14.48 BASINGSTOKE
to SALISBURY.

10.45 Feltham
to Exmouth Jcn.
S15 4-6-0

Worting Jcn Oakley Overton Whitchurch Grateley King Arthur 4-6-0 Porton SALISBURY

14.25 Salisbury
to B'stoke.
S15 4-6-0

15.15 SALISBURY
to WATERLOO.
King Arthur 4-6-0

To Cheltenham

Idmiston

To Bulford

To Waterloo

Life on the mainline was not all Bulleid Pacifics and 4-6-0's since pregrouping classes could be seen quite regularly almost until the end of steam. The 700 class of 0-6-0's lasted well with a number being allocated to Salisbury for workings across to Bulford and Bournemouth in addition to miscellaneous duties such as the ballast train seen in the charge of 30317 as it gets to grips with Grateley bank circa 1955.

ing engines foreign in origin, but an examination of the West Yard could run to ground one of the Adams G6 0-6-0 tanks, of which less than a dozen could be found by the mid-50's. The class had been long lived and one of the Basingstoke examples, 30258, was one of the 1894 batch. It survived in traffic until the early 1960's.

The one type of engine very largely absent from the scene - curiously, in view of the number owned - was the Maunsell 2-6-0. Basingstoke used only one per day on the Andover goods and the only other example booked to the shed was a U class from Guildford which arrived with the 07.34 local from Woking and departed, after spending the greater part of the day on the shed, with the 18.05 passenger to Reading. (The engine later came back, briefly, to Basingstoke, returning light from Reading and turning before working the 21.15 stopping train to Woking).

Freight 4-6-0's of both types appeared with regularity but one had to be patient to see a Bullied Pacific at rest in the shed, the only booked visitor being the Nine Elms Pacific which turned between arriving with the 15.54 ex Waterloo and returning to London with the 19.40 departure. This was actually part of a two-day diagram, the Pacific starting from London with the 15.30 Waterloo - Bournemouth (Central) and returning the next morning with the up Royal Wessex, reaching Waterloo at 10.00 after which it 'filled in' with the stopping duty from and to Basingstoke.

The attraction of Basingstoke shed was the Southern Railway atmosphere which it

retained until the early 1960's. Even visiting SR engines, which formed the greater part of the locomotive establishment, were pedigree Urie and Maunsell products with very little evidence that much had changed since 1939. The high proportion of foreign engines always to be found on the shed was a boon to visiting enthusiasts who could be guaranteed to see something different on each visit.

The same could be said of the GWR visitors which, in many cases, coming from distant parts of the Midlands and working on complex cyclic diagrams produced not a few strangers to the area.

Altogether, ten Great Western engines from three sheds were booked to come onto Basingstoke loco during the course of a day; half of

BR5 4-6-0 73110. 366/395 tons (1956)				
m.ch Point	1/in WTT	Actual	mph	dbhp pc
0.00 WATERLOO	-	0.00	0.00	- -
3.74 Clapham Jcn	-3642		7.37 45	592 2
7.19 Wimbledon	752		11.41 52	745 4
9.62 New Malden	-29773		14.26 60	826 5
12.03 Surbiton	7153		16.35 64	874 5
19.12 Weybridge	8963		22.50 66	719 5
21.54 W. Byfleet	6116		25.02 72	1177 8
24.27 WOKING	36731.00		27.48 -	- -
Clapham Jcn : West Byfleet. 17.75 Miles 1/3039.				
61 mph:815 dbhp (pc 5)				

When the BR standard 5MT 4-6-0's arrived at Nine Elms in November 1955 the Feltham men who worked the 17.39 Waterloo to Basingstoke rose to the occasion of having a 'new' engine - probably the first they had handled in living memory - and set their sights at matching the 27-minute timing of the Portsmouth electrics as far as Woking.

their number being Hall 4-6-0's. The rarest of these was one an Oxford engine which arrived in the station at 22.36 with the evening Worcester - Eastleigh parcels which it handed over to an Eastleigh N15 4-6-0 before turning on the shed and returning northwards with the 00.30 goods to Hinksey. Given that the 4-6-0 spent less than an hour and a half - if it was on time - in Basingstoke, it was a difficult one to run to earth.

An equally interesting working - and one more easy to witness - was that of two Wolverhampton (Oxley) Hall's which alternated on a cyclic working, running into Basingstoke in the small hours with the 19.10 goods from Wolverhampton (Victoria Basin) and, after turning, departing with the 06.57 local to Reading. The engine reappeared in the early afternoon with the 13.48 Reading to Portsmouth, which it worked through, returning with the 19.17 passenger to Eastleigh and the 21.45 parcels train to Basingstoke. The engine was then serviced before being turned out for the 02.10 goods to Oxley, passing its opposite number on the Reading branch. The Great Western were very fond of such complicated workings, as was the LMS, and whilst they provided the enthusiast with a satisfyingly variable diet - sometimes engines from two or more sheds alternated on the same trains - a failure in traffic was the very devil to put right in terms of balancing engines.

Another cyclic diagram from Wolverhampton involved a pair of 43xx 2-6-0's which worked the 02.15 Oxley to Basingstoke and the 21.45 return, each engine be-

It was not until late 1955 that BR standard locomotives started to appear in large numbers when a batch of new BR 5MT 4-6-0's were sent to Nine Elms to take over the duties formerly worked by N15 4-6-0's. In 1950 the original ten engines were joined by a further ten which had been made redundant at Stewarts Lane following the electrification of the LCDR route to Ramsgate and in a halfhearted attempt to draw attention to them they were allocated names from withdrawn King Arthur locomotives. 73087 'Linette', one of the former Stewarts Lane engines, waits to leave Basingstoke with a stopping train for Waterloo on the 4th July 1964 whilst on the same day, below, 73111 'King Uther' approaches the up local platform with a stopping train from Southampton Terminus to Waterloo.

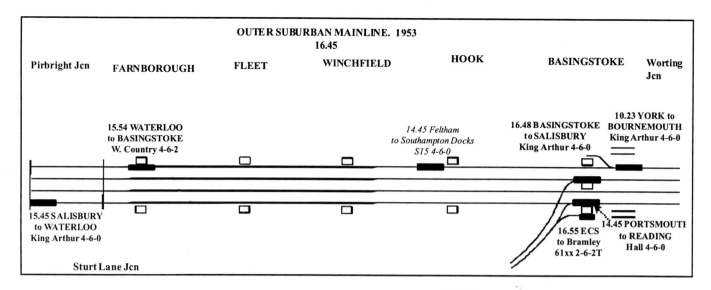

OUTER SUBURBAN MAINLINE. 1953
16.45

ing away from its home depot for exactly twenty-four hours, necessitating thus a second locomotive in the working. On arrival at Basingstoke each engine spent some twelve hours on the shed where they acted as a stand-by for the Oxley Hall workings.

As might be expected the greatest incidence of GWR motive power on Basingstoke shed

WC. 4-6-2 34041 'Wilton'. 12 : 379/400 tons (1958)						
m.ch point	1/in	WTT	Actual	mph	dbhp	pc
0.00 SOUTHAMPTON		0.00	0	-	-	-
5.64 Eastleigh	849	10.00	10.20	58.0	790	3
2.60 Winchester	267		17.24	61.0	1247	7
21.10 Micheldever	259		25.57	59.0	1159	7
22.77 Roundwood	252		27.52	56.5	981	6
28.76 WORTING JCN	-756	37.00	33.12	57.0	376	3
36.86 Hook	-435		39.33	81.0	1063	8
39.33 Winchfield	-1046		41.24	79.5	441	3
42.61 Fleet	-674		43.52	82.0	815	7
46.02 Farnborough	-2852		46.15	82.0	906	7
48.19 MP 31	946		47.58	77.0	534	4
51.20 Brookwood	-307		50.11	81.0	531	4
54.72 WOKING	-318	58.00	52.50	85.0	520	4
57.45 West Byfleet	-367		54.48	80.0	-	-
65.72 Hampton Ct Jcn	-2887	67.00	61.17	78.0	718	6
				pwc		
75.25 Clapham Jcn	-3188	77.00	72.46	45.0	-	-
79.19 WATERLOO	3642	84.00	79.45	-	-	-

Eastleigh to Roundwood. 17.1 miles 1/261.
59 mph. 1176 dbhp (pc 7)

There is no doubt that the Southern could have had more mile-a-minute schedules than the solitary Atlantic Coast Express had it wished. 34041 managed to bring up a moderately heavy service from Southampton in under eighty minutes - a gain of more than four minutes - in spite of the long - 24 mile - climb from Eastleigh to Roundwood and a permanent way check at Surbiton.

came from Reading and included two Hall 4-6-0's, three 61xx 2-6-2T's and a 28xx 2-8-0.

One of the Reading Hall workings - which employed two engines alternating - was almost as elusive as that of Oxford; the engine arriving with the 22.05 goods from Reading and, after turning, returning with the 04.30 goods to Crewe. The other Reading Hall was much easier to find and although it did not arrive on Basingstoke shed until late at night, it spent the day on through workings between Reading and Southampton (Terminus), its visit to the shed being on its third arrival of the day at Basingstoke - with the 21.17 passenger ex Reading - after which it returned home with the midnight local from Basingstoke.

Although the 61xx 2-6-2T's were common currency between Reading and Paddington, where they had a monopoly of the suburban services, their several appearances at Basingstoke struck an incongruous note since not only did they appear to be well away from their beaten track but were involved in a number of goods workings, which seemed a strange use for a suburban passenger engine.

Three of the class were booked to use Basingstoke MPD - a number

BR5 4-6-0 73111. 365/400 tons (1956)					
m.ch Point	1/in	WTT	Actual	mph	dbhp	pc
0 WATERLOO	-	0.00	0	-	-	-
3.74 Clapham Jcn	-3642		7.33	46	618	2
7.19 Wimbledon	752		11.26	54	844	4
9.62 New Malden	-29773		13.57	64	1121	7
12.03 Surbiton	7153		16.00	67	881	6
19.12 Weybridge	8963		21.53	69	817	6
21.54 W. Byfleet	6116		23.59	75	1300	9
24.27 WOKING		367	31.00	27.01	-	-	-

Clapham Jcn : West Byfleet. 17.75 Miles 1/3039.
65 mph:938 dbhp (pc 6)

It took a good engine and a determined crew to match the 27-minute timing of the Portsmouth electrics between Waterloo and Woking but it was done on occasions. What was surprising was that the service was worked by men who spent most of their days trundling up and down the main line at pedestrian speeds on S15 4-6-0's from Feltham.

of others arrived and departed from the station without coming on shed - and departed from the shed to work the 16.55 and 22.35 locals to Reading and the 05.10 goods.

Reading shed also provided the only regular example of a 2-8-0 to visit Basingstoke, a 28xx being diagrammed to work the daily pickup between Reading and Basingstoke; a working which, because of the volume of traffic at the intermediate stations, called for a more powerful locomotive than one would normally expect to find on a local goods service.

As the accompanying table illustrates, there was no shortage of motive power variety on Basingstoke shed and the visiting enthusiast who eschewed a visit ran the risk of missing something interesting. From the railway's point of view however, the depot was rather a secondary affair and did not, until the closure of the

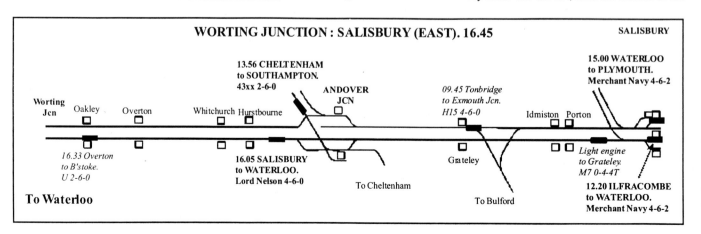

WORTING JUNCTION : SALISBURY (EAST). 16.45

62

TRAFFIC MOVEMENTS : BASINGSTOKE 1953 (NIGHTS)					
Train	Arr	Engine	Shed	Dep	Destination
(19.45 Eastleigh)		H15 4-6-0	Nine Elms 72	22.01	Waterloo
Light engine Reading	22	Hall 4-6-0	Oxley 7		
20.50 Salisbury	22.03	N15 4-6-0	Salisbury 432	22.08	Woking
20.54 Waterloo	22.13	N15 4-6-0	Salisbury 436	22.17	Salisbury
22.25 Basingstoke		S15 4-6-0	Feltham 103	22/27	Feltham
21.10 Nine Elms		MN 4-6-2	Exmouth 497	22/34	Plymouth
21.45 Eastleigh	22.3	49xx 4-6-0	Oxley 208		(Fwd at 23.40)
		61xx 2-6-2T	Reading 74	22.35	Reading
21.15 Eastleigh	22.30	S15 4-6-0	Feltham 111	22.36	Feltham
22.05 Reading (Gds)		49xx 4-6-0	Reading 201	22/50	Basingstoke
19.35 Kensington (Pcls)	23.2	H15 4-6-0	Nine Elms 75		(Fwd at 00.37)
16.55 Worcester (Pcls)	22.4	Hall 4-6-0	Oxley 9		(Fwd at 23.10)
(16.55 Worcester)		N15 4-6-0	Eastleigh 285	23.10	Eastleigh
21.05 Templecombe (Milk)	23.1	MN 4-6-2	Nine Elms 5	23.12	Clapham Jcn
19.55 Bournemouth (Pcls)	23.1	N15X 4-6-0	B'stoke 256	23.26	Waterloo
22.00 Nine Elms		MN 4-6-2	Salisbury 461	23/26	Exmouth Jcn
23.00 Reading	23.29	BR4 2-6-0	Eastleigh 273		
19.48 Weymouth	23.39	N15 4-6-0	Eastleigh 283		(Fwd at 23.55)
(21.45 Eastleigh)		Hall 4-6-0	Oxley 7	23.40	Crewe (Pcls)
22.45 Woking		S15 4-6-0	Feltham 110	23/48	Eastleigh
22.30 WATERLOO	23.42	LN 4-6-0	Eastleigh 253	23.53	DORCHESTER
(19.48 Weymouth)		49xx 4-6-0	Reading 66	23.55	Reading
22.40 Waterloo	00.01	H15 4-6-0	Nine Elms 66		
17.18 Sidmouth Jcn (Milk)	23.5	N15 4-6-0	Nine Elms 11	00.02	Waterloo
22.20 Feltham		S15 4-6-0	Feltham 109	00/06	S'ton Docks
21.56 Bevois Park	00.01	S15 4-6-0	Feltham 106	00.08	Feltham
22.38 Nine Elms		H15 4-6-0	Nine Elms 73	00/20	Weymouth
		Hall 4-6-0	Oxley 9	00/30	Hinksey
(19.35 Kensington)		BR4 2-6-0	Eastleigh 289	00/37	Poole
23.15 Eastleigh		H15 4-6-0	Eastleigh 310	00/38	Basingstoke
22.50 Salisbury	00.41	S15 4-6-0	Salisbury 439		
22.30 S'ton Docks		U2-6-0	Guildford 181	00/47	Feltham
22.45 Feltham		S15 4-6-0	Feltham 112	00/57	Bournemouth
23.25 Nine Elms	01.08	LN 4-6-0	Eastleigh 251	01.16	S'ton Docks
12.45 Torrington		N15 4-6-0	Nine Elms 10	01/24	Nine Elms
00.23 Woking	01.25	H15 4-6-0	Salisbury 441	01/33	Exmouth Jcn
19.50 Dorchester		H15 4-6-0	Nine Elms 66	01/57	Nine Elms
23.58 Feltham		S15 4-6-0	Feltham 115	02/04	Exmouth Jcn
		Hall 4-6-0	Oxley 208	02.10	Oxley (Wolves)
21.55 WEYMOUTH	02.15	LN 4-6-0	Nine Elms 31	02.02	WATERLOO
14.58 Gravesend (Milk)	02.00	N15 4-6-0	Salisbury 432	02.25	Yeovil Town
00.45 Nine Elms	02.37	H15 4-6-0	Nine Elms 79	02.44	Eastleigh
17.00 Torrington		MN 4-6-2	Nine Elms 7	02/47	Nine Elms
00.45 Eastleigh		H15 4-6-0	Nine Elms 64	02/52	Feltham
02.10 Clapham Jcn (Fish)	03.01	N15 4-6-0	Eastleigh 265	03.11	Fratton
19.10 Victoria Basin		49xx 4-6-0	Oxley 208	03/15	Basingstoke
00.50 Fratton		S15 4-6-0	Feltham 101	03/22	Feltham
		S15 4-6-0	Salisbury 439	03.30	Salisbury
00.55 Feltham		S15 4-6-0	Feltham 102	03/32	S'ton Docks
03.15 (Pcls) Reading	03.04	61xx 2-6-2T	Reading 47		
02.40 WATERLOO	03.47	MN 4-6-2	Nine Elms 30	03.51	B'MOUTH (C)
13.55 Meldon	04.08	H15 4-6-0	Salisbury 440	04.16	Woking
		49xx 4-6-0	Reading 201	04.30	Crewe
03.10 Bevois Park		S15 4-6-0	Feltham 108	05/04	Woking
03.45 Waterloo (News)	05.10	N15X 4-6-0	B'stoke 236		
05.10 Basingstoke		61xx 2-6-2T	Reading 47	05/15	Woodford
		700 0-6-0	B'stoke 242	05.30	Bulford
04.07 Feltham	06.13	S15 4-6-0	Feltham 103	06.21	S'ton Docks
		H15 4-6-0	Nine Elms 74	06.37	Waterloo
04.40 Eastleigh		H15 4-6-0	Nine Elms 66	06/45	Feltham
05.40 WATERLOO	06.50	LN 4-6-0	Nine Elms 31	06.53	WEYMOUTH
		49xx 4-6-0	Oxley 208	06.57	Reading
21.30 Okehampton	06.50	H15 4-6-0	Salisbury 441	07.01	Woking
06.04 S'ton Terminus	07.09	LN 4-6-0	Eastleigh 271	07.11	Waterloo

TRAFFIC MOVEMENTS : BASINGSTOKE 1953 (MORNING)					
Train	Arr	Engine	Shed	Dep	Destination
06.33 Woking	07.28	N15 4-6-0	Nine Elms 2	07.33	Templecombe
06.50 Reading	07.27	49xx 4-6-0	Reading 66	07.36	S'ton Terminus
		N15 4-6-0	Eastleigh 264	07.38	Reading
		U2-6-0	B'stoke 239	07.45	Andover Jcn
06.45 Salisbury	07.59	WC 4-6-2	Salisbury 430	08.02	Waterloo
07.22 Eastleigh	08.09	LN 4-6-0	Eastleigh 272	08.10	Waterloo
03.20 Bournemouth		S15 4-6-0	Feltham 110	08/14	Feltham
07.31 Woking	08.16	U2-6-0	Guildford 181	08.19	S'ton Terminus
		N15X 4-6-0	B'stoke 230	08.24	Reading
		N15 4-6-0	B'stoke 232	08.25	Waterloo
07.58 Reading	08.30	61xx 2-6-2T	Reading 70		
01.30 Hoo Jcn		U2-6-0	Guildford 182	08/32	Eastleigh
08.41 Basingstoke		N15X 4-6-0	B'stoke 241	08/43	Farnborough
07.20 Waterloo	08.44	N15 4-6-0	Nine Elms 3	08.50	Salisbury
02.15 Oxley		43xx 2-6-0	Oxley 207	08/50	Basingstoke
06.35 Bournemouth	08.55	WC 4-6-2	B'mouth 380		(Fwd at 09.02)
(06.35 Bournemouth)		N15X 4-6-0	B'stoke 233	09.02	Waterloo
08.15 SALISBURY	09.01	MN 4-6-2	Salisbury 431	09.15	WATERLOO
07.20 BOURNEMOUTH		WC 4-6-2	Nine Elms 38	09/15	WATERLOO
17.21 Plymouth		N15 4-6-0	Salisbury 436	09/20	Feltham
08.45 Woking	09.28	N 15 4-6-0	Nine Elms 1		
08.20 Eastleigh	09.28	BR4 2-6-0	Eastleigh 273	09.40	Reading
08.30 WATERLOO	09.37	MN 4-6-2	Nine Elms 32	09.40	WEYMOUTH
09.12 Reading	09.47	Hall 4-6-0	Reading 50	09.55	Portsmouth
09.50 Basingstoke		61xx 2-6-2T	Reading 70	09/55	Reading
07.10 Yeovil Jcn	09.56	N15 4-6-0	Salisbury 432	10.00	Waterloo
07.34 WEYMOUTH		WC 4-6-2	B'mouth 381	10/05	WATERLOO
09.00 WATERLOO	10.04	MN 4-6-2	Nine Elms 4	10.06	PLYMOUTH
23.55 Okehampton		H15 4-6-0	Salisbury 441	10/07	Woking
07.43 Clapham Jcn (Pcls)	09.51	H15 4-6-0	Nine Elms 65	10.19	Eastleigh
07.30 EXETER		MN 4-6-2	Exmouth 495	10/22	WATERLOO
		WC 4-6-2	B'mouth 380	10.35	Waterloo
09.30 WATERLOO	10.39	WC 4-6-2	Nine Elms 33	10.41	BOURNEMOUTH
		N15 4-6-0	Nine Elms 1	10.45	Salisbury
10.17 Reading	10.51	N15X 4-6-0	B'toke 236		
08.35 BOURNEMOUTH	10.57	WC 4-6-2	B'mouth 382	10.59	WATERLOO
09.15 Reading		28xx 2-8-0	Reading 202	11/08	Basingstoke
09.54 Waterloo	11.14	H15 4-6-0	Nine Elms 68		(Fwd at 11.36)
06.30 EXETER	11.15	MN 4-6-2	Exmouth 494	11.21	WATERLOO
10.12 S'ton Terminus	11.17	49xx 4-6-0	Reading 66	11.22	Reading
10.30 WATERLOO		MN 4-6-2	Nine Elms 34	11/24	WEYMOUTH
09.40 Didcot		N15 4-6-0	Eastleigh 284	11/25	Basingstoke
09.20 BOURNEMOUTH	11.26	N15 4-6-0	B'mouth 399	11.35	BIRKENHEAD
(09.54 Waterloo)		H15 4-6-0	Nine Elms 68	11.36	Southampton
09.45 Feltham		S15 4-6-0	Feltham 105	11/45	Eastleigh
11.00 WATERLOO		MN 4-6-2	Nine Elms 5	11/47	PADSTOW
		N15 4-6-0	B'stoke 231	12.02	Waterloo
09.20 WEYMOUTH		LN 4-6-0	Nine Elms 31	12/03	WATERLOO
10.54 Waterloo	12.14	LN 4-6-0	Eastleigh 251	12.17	Salisbury
11.30 WATERLOO	12.27	LN 4-6-0	Eastleigh 252	12.30	BOURNEMOUTH
12.15 Reading	12.46	BR4 2-6-0	Eastleigh 273	12.53	Portsmouth
10.45 Feltham	12.6	S15 4-6-0	Feltham 101	13.04	Exmouth Jcn
13.05 Basingstoke		28xx 2-8-0	Reading 202	13.05	Reading
11.54 Waterloo	13.11	WC 4-6-2	Salisbury 430	13.13	Salisbury
11.05 BOURNEMOUTH	13.17	WC 4-6-2	B'mouth 383	13.20	WATERLOO
08.15 PLYMOUTH		MN 4-6-2	Exmouth 496	13/22	WATERLOO
12.30 WATERLOO		MN 4-6-2	Nine Elms 35	13/26	BOURNEMOUTH
11.16 BOURNEMOUTH	13.23	LN 4-6-0	B'mouth 395	13.27	NEWCASTLE
		N15 4-6-0	B'stoke 234	13.33	Waterloo
03.20 Ashford		S15 4-6-0	Feltham 112	13/37	Eastleigh
12.31 S'ton Terminus	13.37	U2-6-0	Guildford 181	13.45	Reading
13.48 Basingstoke		H15 4-6-0	Nine Elms 76	13/50	Feltham
13.00 WATERLOO		MN 4-6-2	Salisbury 431	13/56	PLYMOUTH

adjacent Great Western shed, even warrant a running foreman.

The reason for this was that a shed's standing depended almost wholly on the size of its complement of drivers and firemen together with the number of engine workings, which normally excluded visiting locomotives. Thus the man in charge would be held fully responsible for his starting turns - thirteen workings - but would get little credit for the other twenty engines, most of which were expected to turn, coal and water without any - or very much - local supervision. To add to the frustrations of local staff

who, like everyone else, scanned local workings closely to see if they held any grounds for an increase in grade (and salary), almost all Basingstoke's 'home' diagrams came off the shed during the early turn, leaving - on paper- very little for the other two shifts to do.

The best that can said for the shed was that it was a useful training ground for an aspiring manager to cut his teeth on. All the ingredients of shed working were present - the politics of list workings - the way in which drivers were allocated to turns of duty - and a steady succession of engines to turn round and get ready for

service. It was an excellent depot at which to acquire a sense of urgency in getting engines off shed at the right time and to see that they lost no time whilst they were in traffic whilst at the same time the volume of work was such that one had time to draw a breath between moves.

Apart from the very last months of steam when Bulleid Pacifics and BR 5MT 4-6-0's handled just about every train on the line, the allocation of engines at Basingstoke did not change a great deal and the most significant sign of the times came in May 1956 when an allocation of BR standard 4MT 4-6-0's was received

In spite of the arrival of redundant engines from the SECR between 1959 and 1962 - the period in which the Kent electrification was completed - motive power variety tended to wane during the 1960's with most trains being worked either by rebuilt Bulleid Pacifics or standard 5MT 4-6-0's, thirty-four of the latter being at work on the South Western by the beginning of 1961. Inevitable the more interesting engines on the cross-country services eventually had to give way to the new order and one of the first to change was the 10.30 Cardiff (General) - Portsmouth & Southsea which, ten years earlier, had been worked by an Eastleigh D15 4-4-0 between Salisbury and Portsmouth. (It had also been worked into Salisbury by nothing less than a GWR Castle 4-6-0). In 1963 the train pulls out of Southampton Central behind 5MT 4-6-0 73081, an exile from Stewarts Lane and a casualty of the 1959 Kent Coast electrification. The destination board is an interesting reminder of the trouble the railways took to ensure that trains could be identified by the travelling public.

Whilst not the most outstanding express passenger engine ever produced, the Lord Nelson 4-6-0's were arguable one of the best looking locomotives to operate south of the Thames. They were certainly impressive in terms of size - one can speculate on how the proposed Pacific version might have appeared - and it is a matter for regret that their regular postwar workings were so limited in number. 30859 'Lord Hood' stands on Eastleigh MPD in 1954.

TRAFFIC MOVEMENTS : BASINGSTOKE (LATE) 1953

Train	Arr	Engine	Shed	Dep	Destination
11.30 WEYMOUTH		WC 4-6-2	B'mouth 386	14/03	WATERLOO
12.54 Salisbury	14.10	S15 4-6-0	Salisbury 435	14.14	Waterloo
12.54 Salisbury	14.14	N15 4-6-0	Nine Elms 11		
13.30 WATERLOO	14.27	WC 4-6-2	B'mouth 381	14.30	WEYMOUTH
13.48 Reading	14.22	49xx 4-6-0	Oxley 208	14.35	Portsmouth
13.15 Eastleigh (Pcls)	14.3	H15 4-6-0	Eastleigh 311	14.40	Clapham Jcn
10.42 Salisbury (Goods)	14.4	S15 4-6-0	Salisbury 438		
		S15 4-6-0	Feltham 112	14.45	Farnborough (light)
		N15 4-6-0	Nine Elms 11	14.48	Salisbury
10.30 ILFRACOMBE		MN 4-6-2	Exmouth 497	14/55	WATERLOO
09.45 Tonbridge	14.5	H15 4-6-0	Salisbury 440	15.00	Exmouth Jcn
11.36 Bournemouth	14.55	H15 4-6-0	Nine Elms 79	15.01	Woking/Neasden
13.54 Waterloo	15.14	N15X 4-6-0	B'stoke 253		
13.05 BOURNEMOUTH	15.14	MN 4-6-2	Nine Elms 32	15.17	WATERLOO
13.20 S'ton Docks		S15 4-6-0	Feltham 104	15/25	Feltham
09.30 BIRKENHEAD	15.24	N15 4-6-0	B'mouth 399	15.29	BOURNEMOUTH
13.33 Farnborough		N15X 4-6-0	B'stoke 241	15/36	Basingstoke
15.10 Reading	15.40	61xx 2-6-2T	Reading 71a		
		N15X 4-6-0	B'stoke 236	15.55	Reading
15.00 WATERLOO	15.55	MN 4-6-2	Nine Elms 7	15.57	PLYMOUTH
14.25 Salisbury (Goods)	16.00	S15 4-6-0	Feltham 106		
13.25 WEYMOUTH		WC 4-6-2	B'mouth 385	16/03	WATERLOO
15.20 WATERLOO		WC 4-6-2	B'mouth 382	16/10	WEYMOUTH
14.54 Waterloo	16.14	N15 4-6-0	Salisbury 432		
15.15 Salisbury	16.08	N15 4-6-0	Nine Elms 1	16.15	Waterloo
14.45 Portsmouth	16.28	H15 4-6-0	Reading 50		(Fwd at 16.45)
15.30 WATERLOO	16.30	WC 4-6-2	Nine Elms 37	16.33	BOURNEMOUTH
10.00 YORK	16.38	LN 4-6-0	B'mouth 395	16.44	BOURNEMOUTH
(14.45 Portsmouth)		H15 4-6-0	Reading 50	16.45	Reading
		N15 4-6-0	Salisbury 432	16.48	Salisbury
		61xx 2-6-2T	Reading 71a	16.55	Bramley BCS
14.45 Feltham		S15 4-6-0	Feltham 107	16/59	S'ton Docks
16.33 Overton (Goods)	17.10	U 2-6-0	B'stoke 233		
15.54 Waterloo	17.14	WC 4-6-2	Nine Elms 38		
16.05 Salisbury	17.21	LN 4-6-0	Eastleigh 251		(Fwd at 17.37)
16.35 WATERLOO		WC 4-6-2	B'mouth 383	17/27	WEYMOUTH
15.05 BOURNEMOUTH	17.25	MN 4-6-2	Nine Elms 34	17.29	WATERLOO
15.54 Clapham Jcn (Milk)	17.3	MN 4-6-2	Exmouth 494	17.30	Exeter
(16.05 Salisbury)		LN 4-6-0	Eastleigh 271	17.37	Waterloo
12.20 ILFRACOMBE		MN 4-6-2	Salisbury 461	17/40	WATERLOO
17.10 Reading	17.43	U 2-6-0	Guildford 181	17.46	S'ton Terminus
16.34 BOURNEMOUTH		MN 4-6-2	Nine Elms 35	18/05	WATERLOO
		U 2-6-0	Guildford 182	18.05	Reading
17.00 WATERLOO	18.04	MN 4-6-2	Exmouth 496	18.08	EXETER
17.50 Reading	18.21	61xx 2-6-2T	Reading 69		
17.30 S'TON DOCKS	18.21	LN 4-6-0	Eastleigh 274	18.23	WATERLOO
17.09 Waterloo	18.25	N15 4-6-0	B'stoke 234		
17.30 WATERLOO	18.25	WC 4-6-2	B'mouth 380	18.29	BOURNEMOUTH
17.15 Salisbury	18.31	N15 4-6-0	Nine Elms 2	18.37	Waterloo
17.18 Winchester (Goods)	18.4	S15 4-6-0	Feltham 103		
16.35 Amesbury (Goods)	18.5	700 0-6-0	B'stoke 242		
16.20 S'ton Docks		S15 4-6-0	Feltham 102	18/47	Feltham
18.00 WATERLOO	18.55	MN 4-6-2	Exmouth 495	18.57	PLYMOUTH
		S15 4-6-0	Feltham 106	19.00	S'ton Docks
		S15 4-6-0	Salisbury 438	19.04	Plymouth
17.17 Portsmouth	19.05	BR4 2-6-0	Eastleigh 289		
17.39 Waterloo	19.00	N15 4-6-0	Nine Elms 10	19.06	Salisbury
17.05 BOURNEMOUTH	19.15	LN 4-6-0	Eastleigh 273	19.19	WATERLOO
18.30 WATERLOO		WC 4-6-2	B'mouth 386	19/22	WEYMOUTH
18.09 Waterloo	19.25	N15 4-6-0	B'stoke 231		
14.20 ILFRACOMBE	19.24	N15 4-6-0	Nine Elms 4	19.27	WATERLOO
19.00 Reading	19.30	N15X 4-6-0	B'stoke 236	19.35	S'ton Terminus
		WC 4-6-2	Nine Elms 38	19.40	Waterloo
		BR4 2-6-0	Eastleigh 273	19.40	Reading
19.12 Reading (Light)	19.5	U 2-6-0	Guildford 182		
		61xx 2-6-2T	Reading 69	19.55	Scours Lane
17.35 WEYMOUTH		MN 4-6-2	Nine Elms 30	20/04	WATERLOO
18.54 Waterloo	20.14	S15 4-6-0	Salisbury 435		(Fwd at 20.35)
17.50 Bevois Park		H15 4-6-0	Nine Elms 68	20/14	Basingstoke (North)
19.30 WATERLOO	20.25	WC 4-6-2	B'mouth 385	20.28	BOURNEMOUTH
(18.54 Waterloo)		N15 4-6-0	Salisbury 415	20.35	Yeovil Town
18.42 Waterloo (Pcls)	20.4	H15 4-6-0	Nine Elms 64		(Fwd at 21.07)
19.45 Eastleigh (BCS)	20.5	H15 4-6-0	Nine Elms 72		(Fwd at 22.01)
15.50 PLYMOUTH	21.00	MN 4-6-2	Exmouth 498	21.02	WATERLOO
(18.42 Waterloo (Pcls))		H15 4-6-0	Nine Elms 64	21.07	Eastleigh
18.55 S'ton Docks	21	N15 4-6-0	Eastleigh 264	21.08	Nine Elms
20.38 Reading	21.10	61xx 2-6-2T	Reading 74		
18.35 Bournemouth	21.12	N15 4-6-0	Eastleigh 285		(Fwd at 21.20)
19.54 Waterloo	21.14	N15 4-6-0	B'stoke 232		
		U 2-6-0	Guildford 204	21.15	Woking
(18.35 Bournemouth)		H15 4-6-0	Nine Elms 68	21.20	Reading
17.40 Yeovil (Milk)	21.4	N15 4-6-0	Nine Elms 3	21.42	Gravesend
		43xx 2-6-0	Oxley 207	21.45	Oxley
21.17 Reading	21.47	H15 4-6-0	Reading 66		
19.25 Nine Elms	21.40	H15 4-6-0	Eastleigh 311	21.56	S'ton Docks
18.30 WEYMOUTH	21.53	WC 4-6-2	Nine Elms 33	21.58	WATERLOO
21.00 WATERLOO	21.56	LN 4-6-0	Nine Elms 31	21.59	S'TON DOCKS

BASINGSTOKE ALLOCATION : 1949-1960

Feb-49	Apr-50	Mar-53	Mar-54	Nov-55	Jan-57	Mar-59	Feb-60
G6 0-6-0T (1894)							
30265	30258	30258	30258	30258	30160	30160	30160
	30272	30266	30266		30258	30258	30258
E1 0-6-0T (1874)							
32160	32160						
32162							
E4 0-6-2T (1897)							
32490				32502			
E5 0-6-2T (1902)							
32568		32591	32591	32583			
		32592					
L12 4-4-0 (1904)							
30418	30418						
30426	30426						
700 0-6-0 (1897)							
30368	30368	30368	30368	30368	30368	30368	30368
30693	30693						
T9 4-4-0 (1899)							
30307	30302	30705	30705	30705	30724		
30706	30712	30724	30724	30724			
U 2-6-0 (R/B 2-6-4T) 1928							
			31806	31806	31806	31806	
U 2-6-0 (1928)							
31627	31633	31633	31633	31611	31611	31611	31611
31629		31634	31634	31633	31633		
31632							
31633							
V 4-4-0 (1930)							
						30904	30904
						30905	30905
						30923	30908
N15X 4-6-0 (1914/34)							
32327	32327	32327	32327	32327	32331		
32328	32328	32328	32328	32329			
32329	32329	32329	32329	32331			
32330	32330	32330	32330	32332			
32331	32331	32331	32331	32333			
32332	32332	32332	32332				
32333	32333	32333	32333				
N15 4-6-0 (1918)							
30741		30744	30745	30744	30749		
		30745	30749	30745	30751		
		30753	30753	30753	30753		
					30755		
N15 4-6-0 (1925)							
30457	30451	30451	30451	30451	30451	30451	30451
	30456			30763		30455	30455
				30770		30456	30456
				30771		30765	30765
						30773	30773
						30794	30794
BR4 4-6-0 (1951)							
					75075	75076	75076
					75076	75077	75077
					75077	75078	75078
					75078	75079	75079
					75079		

The tables on this and the facing page recall the volume of traffic - and variety of motive power - that passed through Basingstoke on an ordinary weekday during the 1950's. Also shown are the engines allocated to Basingstoke at various times between 1949 and 1960.

in replacement for the N15x 4-6-0's. A year later the five standard engines were supplemented by a trio of Schools 4-4-0's made redundant from St Leonards after the introduction of diesel multiple-units on the Hastings - Charing Cross services. The 4-4-0's had initially gone to Nine Elms but, with little of a regular nature for them to do, they were eventually transferred to Basingstoke where they remained until the shed's closure in 1963. It seemed a terrible waste of a good engine which might have had a far more productive final five years of life than was actually the case. One looked towards the lines in Devon and thought it strange that T9's - fine engines though they were - were still hard at work in 1961 whilst the Schools' languished away. Alas the absolute limit of westward penetration for the Schools class was Exeter St Davids.

ANDOVER JUNCTION

The chief attraction of Andover Junction was derived from the activities of the ancient and modern that could be seen at all times of day from its platforms. T9 4-4-0's and GWR 43xx 2-6-0's rubbed shoulders on the MSW line to Cheltenham and the extension to Romsey whilst ultramodern Bulleid Pacifics passed through at hourly intervals with West of England expresses to and from Waterloo. Not everything that the Merchant Navy class worked was an express passenger, several goods services were booked to the class including the 15.54 Clapham Junction to Exeter milk empties, seen here passing the station at speed. The engine, 35011 'General Steam Navigation' had worked towards London earlier in the day with the 06.30 Exeter (Central) to Waterloo stopping train.

The section of line between Worting Junction and Salisbury was very different from that between Basingstoke and London with the volume of traffic consisting largely of the two-hourly West of England service plus the occasional stopping train which called at all stations between Woking and Salisbury. There were a handful of freight services, although not very many during daylight hours, and as a result a spell at one of the smaller stations on the route was rarely a time of sustained excitement.

The exception was Andover Junction which served both the LSWR main line and the MSWR route to Cheltenham; the conjunction of the two producing some interesting moments with a surprisingly varied diversity of trains and locomotives which could produce engines from every constituent part of British Railways apart from the LNER.

The variety of motive power which had been built up by the Southern Railway over the years had been extended further by nationalisation following the arrival during the early 1950's of a handful of BR standard types at Eastleigh in the form of 3MT 2-6-2 tank engines and a small number of 4MT moguls, both types being introduced to the area with the aim of elimi-

nating the T9 and D15 4-4-0's which worked in large numbers between Salisbury and Portsmouth and from Southampton to Andover Junction. These post-nationalisation designs were accompanied by a trio of LMS Ivatt 2-6-2 tanks which had been sent to Eastleigh to dilute the the M7 0-4-4's which worked many of the local services in and around Southampton, some of which were extended to the fringes of the Salisbury area.

Other BR types were rare on the West of England route - the 5MT 4-6-0's which latterly became a familiar sight did not arrive until the mid 1950's although in 1953 an occasional glimpse of a Britannia Pacific could be obtained thanks to the loan of 70009 ' Alfred the Great' to ease the loss, for a few weeks in 1953, of the Bulleid Pacifics.

Greater evidence of modernisation could be seen in the five diesel-electrics which for a time were all allocated to the LSWR; an episode speckled with the engine failures and general unreliability that became the hall-mark of diesel traction a decade later. It was rather ironic that the greatest concentration of early diesels should be on the same line that was destined to

become an outpost of steam several years after diesels were a commonplace sight elsewhere in the country. Perhaps the experiences of the early diesels had something to do with the longevity of steam at Waterloo.

One of the attractions of watching trains between Worting and Salisbury was the possibility of seeing a Southern locomotive that had somehow got through the iron curtain of Salisbury which tended to keep London-based engines apart from those of the West Country. This separation had become diluted a little with the introduction of through workings between London and Exeter in 1950 but all trains apart from the expresses and a handful of Yeovil trains continued to change engines at Salisbury with the result that engines from Exmouth Junction and sheds to the west were rarely seen in normal circumstances. Generally the most distant engines to be seen were the Exmouth Junction Merchant Navy Pacifics which took a share in the working of the West of England expresses although now and again a light Pacific would turn up as a substitute and give local observers something to talk about for a day or two. (The best time for getting a glimpse of rarities came

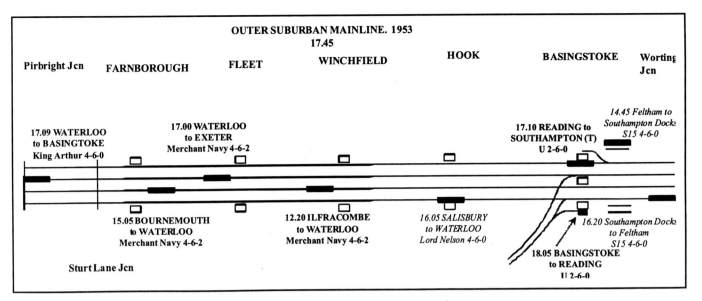

OUTER SUBURBAN MAINLINE. 1953
17.45

Pirbright Jcn   FARNBOROUGH   FLEET   WINCHFIELD   HOOK   BASINGSTOKE   Worting Jcn

17.09 WATERLOO to BASINGTOKE King Arthur 4-6-0

17.00 WATERLOO to EXETER Merchant Navy 4-6-2

17.10 READING to SOUTHAMPTON (T) U 2-6-0

14.45 Feltham to Southampton Docks S15 4-6-0

15.05 BOURNEMOUTH to WATERLOO Merchant Navy 4-6-2

12.20 ILFRACOMBE to WATERLOO Merchant Navy 4-6-2

16.05 SALISBURY to WATERLOO Lord Nelson 4-6-0

16.20 Southampton Docks to Feltham S15 4-6-0

18.05 BASINGSTOKE to READING U 2-6-0

Sturt Lane Jcn

on summer Saturdays when anything that could turn a wheel was likely to make an appearance. One light Pacific based on Exmouth Junction actually encompassed the entire distance from Padstow to Waterloo on Saturdays at the height of the season. It was not, however, done on the same train and the engine spent several hours at Exeter before proceeding forward).

There were eight intermediate stations in the thirty-six miles between Basingstoke and Salisbury - one for every four and a half miles of route which, surprisingly, was about the same as the Woking to Basingstoke section - for which a series of ten stopping and one express service was given per weekday. These were for the most part extensions of the fifty-four minute departures from Waterloo although two were advertised to start from Basingstoke - both actually ran through from London - and one started from Woking.

To the relief of conservative observers - and it is well to recollect that in the 1950's critics of the Bulleid regime on aesthetic grounds were legion - almost all the stopping trains between Basingstoke and Salisbury were diagrammed to a link of five Nine Elms King Arthur N15 4-6-0's with only one - the 11.54 ex Waterloo - booked to be worked by a light Pacific. The comments made about the Bulleid Pacifics, and the West Country class in particular, raise a smile nowadays but were said at the time between clenched teeth with a degree of conviction that could only be paralleled by those who

had to maintain them. The Spam Cans - and the phrase was not born of affection - were ugly, they sounded as though they had a bad attack of asthma and were so unstable that they couldn't move three coaches without grinding half an inch off the track surface. (Not everyone, the author included, agreed wholeheartedly since there was another side to the coin. The engines could steam like nothing on earth and when they did go, it could take your breath away).

Interestingly most of these moans focused on the light Pacifics - perhaps the majesty of 8P insulated the Merchant Navy class from inexpert comment - but few were upset to find that the King Arthurs held dominion on the stopping trains. They were a link with the past, had an honourable history and - most of all - looked like a steam engine.

In the down direction seven of the ten services were booked to King Arthurs (five from Nine Elms and the balance from Salisbury) with other trains being worked by a West Country, a Lord Nelson and an S15 goods engine.

The working arrangements for some of the engines, especially the Nine Elms King Arthur 4-6-0's, was rather intricate since only one of

ANDOVER JUNCTION MPD. ENGINE MOVEMENTS (1953)					
Inward working	Arr	Engine	Diagram	Dep	Working
		T9 4-4-0	246		05.00 Shunt/09.37 goods
		T9 4-4-0	248		06.20 06.45 Southampton (T)
		2MT 2-6-2T	247		06.30 06.47 Tidworth
		45xx 2-6-2T	Swindon 77		06.45 07.00 Marlborough
		43xx 2-6-0	249		07.15 07.30 Romsey
		43xx 2-6-0	250		07.20 07.50 Cheltenham
		43xx 2-6-0	Swindon 78		08.00 08.15 Swindon
08.33 Southampton (T)	10.20	T9 4-4-0	248		11.00 11.25 Eastleigh
05.42 Cheltenham	10.30	43xx 2-6-0	Cheltenham 24		11.40 Light/as required Ch'ham
07.05 Swindon Jcn	09.15	45xx 2-6-2T	Swindon 74		11.45 12.00 Romsey
07.45 Basingstoke	11.00	U 2-6-0	Basingstoke 239		13.10 Light to Overton
06.48 Cheltenham	11.50	43xx 2-6-0	Cheltenham 23		14.20 14.35 Swindon Town
11.19 Portsmouth	13.30	2MT 2-6-2T	Eastleigh 306		15.10 Yard Pilot
14.00 Ludgershall	14.15	2MT 2-6-2T	247		15.45 16.12 Romsey
14.02 Romsey	15.20	45xx 2-6-2T	Swindon 74 (stale)		(Works Swindon 77)
06.40 Eastleigh/Shunt	17.15	L1 4-4-0	Eastleigh 309		18.20 18.40 Eastleigh
18.05 Ludgershall	18.50	43xx 2-6-0	Swindon 75		19.05 19.15 Swindon
17.42 Eastleigh	18.50	T9 4-4-0	Eastleigh 282		19.25 19.35 Eastleigh
15.20 Cheltenham	19.55	43xx 2-6-0	249 (stale)		
17.25 Cheltenham	20.38	43xx 2-6-0	Swindon 76 (stale)		(Works Swindon 78)
16.49 Swindon Town	18.20	43xx 2-6-0	Cheltenham 23	20.40	20.55 Cheltenham
Yard Pilot	20.10	2MT 2-6-2T	Eastleigh 306 (Stale)		(Works 247)
19.04 S'ton Docks	20.50	43xx 2-6-0	250 (stale)		(Works 248)
19.45 Southampton	22.10	T9 4-4-0	B'mouth 403 (Stale)		(Works 248)
17.16 Fawley/Shunt	22.20	T9 4-4-0	280 (stale)		(Works 246)
Goods workings in italics					

WORTING JUNCTION : SALISBURY (EAST). 17.45

17.19 GRATELEY to SALISBURY. M7 0-4-4T

Worting Jcn

15.54 Clapham Jcn to Exeter (Milk). Merchant Navy 4-6-2

To Romsey   ANDOVER JCN

16.48 B'STOKE to SALISBURY. King Arthur 4-6-0

Whitchurch Hurstbourne   Grateley   Porton

Oakley   Overton

16.35 Amesbury to B'stoke. 700 0-6-0

17.15 SALISBURY to WATERLOO. King Arthur 4-6-0

Idmiston   SALISBURY

16.36 S'TON to CHELTENHAM. MANOR 4-6-0

To Bulford

To Waterloo

Appearance suggest that Andover Junction was having trouble with its 43xx 2-6-0's on 11th May 1957 as T9 30117 has been substituted to work the 07.30 to Romsey. The 4-4-0 is seen just prior to departure at the head of three very smart 'blood & custard' Bulleid coaches

the five engines involved in the down stopping service returned on an out and home basis.

The first of the class to work down, Nine Elms No.2, started its day with the 04.45 stopping train to Woking - the only inner-suburban local service not to be worked by a multiple unit - and proceeded westwards with the 06.33 to Yeovil Town; the engine working through. Returning to London in stages, the engine left Yeovil Junction at 15.00 after relieving the 13.06 stopping train from Exeter and arrived in Salisbury at 16.32. It berthed the stock in the carriage sidings, exchanging it for another set with which it worked up to Waterloo at 17.15, reaching London at 20.00.

The second Nine Elms N15, No.3 working, also went as far west as Yeovil, working the 07.20 Waterloo - Salisbury, but proceeded forward with the 12.46 slow train to Exeter - which included a through coach to Seaton off the down Atlantic Coast Express - as far as Yeovil Junction which it reached at 13.58. The afternoon was then spent in carriage shunting at Yeovil Town - where, incidentally, the two London King Arthur 4-6-0's could be seen side by side - before working the Yeovil - Gravesend Milk to Woking. The engine's last working of the day was a local goods from Woking to Nine Elms Goods, the engine returning to shed after some twenty hours in steam.

Nine Elms No.1 went no further west than Salisbury although the diagram included a wide range of trains, commencing with the 03.30 Nine Elms - Chertsey goods via Weybridge after which the en-

gine ran light to Woking for the 08.45 slow passenger to Basingstoke and the 10.45 on to Salisbury. The return working, the 15.15 from Salisbury, was the connection out of the 11.00 Plymouth -Brighton express and was a rather curious service, running as an express as far as Basingstoke, calling only at Andover Junction, but degenerating thereafter into a stopping service, reaching Waterloo at 17.35.

The 14.48 ex Basingstoke was worked by Nine Elms No.11 which started off from Waterloo at 12.54; the train recessing at Basingstoke (in the former Alton branch bay) for half an hour in order to connect with the 13.30 Waterloo - Bournemouth and the 13.48 Reading - Portsmouth services. At Salisbury the engine disposed of its empty stock before retiring to the loco where it sat for six hours before taking over the 17.18 Sidmouth Junction to Waterloo Milk and Parcels service from a Salisbury-based N15.

The rush hour contribution by Nine Elms, No. 10 duty, was a continuous headache for the operating staff, not from the locomotive point of view since the N15 simply worked the 17.39 to Salisbury and returned with the 12.45 Torrington to Nine

ENGINE WORKINGS : ANDOVER JCN MPD (1953)					
Dia	Class	Time	Train	To Shed	Rev miles
246	T9 4-4-0	05.00	*Goods shunting*		
			09.37 Andover Jcn - Fullerton		
			10.40 Fullerton - Long Parish		
			11.45 Long Parish - Fullerton		
			12.14 Fullerton - Romsey		
			14.35 Romsey - Nursling		
			15.14 Nursling - Romsey		
			Goods shunting		
			18.05 Romsey - Eastleigh		
			Eastleigh MPD	18.45	34
248	T9 4-4-0	06.20	06.45 Andover Jcn - S'ton terminus		
			08.33 S'ton Terminus - Andover Jcn		
			11.25 Andover Jcn - Eastleigh		
			13.05 Eastleigh - Portsmouth & S		
			15.45 Portsmouth & S - Romsey		
			17.50 Romsey - Eastleigh		
			19.22 Eastleigh - Portsmouth & S		
			21.49 Portsmouth & S - Eastleigh		
			Eastleigh MPD	22.40	185
247	2MT 2-6-2T	06.30	06.47 Andover Jcn - Tidworth		
			07.50 Tidworth - Andover Jcn		
			10.35 Andover Jcn - Ludgershall		
			12.35 Ludgershall - Tidworth		
			13.30 Tidworth - Ludgershall		
			14.00 Ludgershall - Andover Jcn		
			16.12 Andover Jcn - Romsey		
			17.03 Romsey - S'ton Terminus		
			18.58 S'ton Terminus - Alton		
			20.38 Alton - Eastleigh		
			Eastleigh MPD	21.45	114
249	43xx 2-6-0	07.15	07.30 Andover Jcn - Romsey		
			08.32 Romsey - Eastleigh		
			09.05 Eastleigh - S'ton terminus		
			10.10 S'ton Terminus - Cheltenham		
			15.20 Cheltenham - Andover Jcn	19.55	194
250	43xx 2-6-0	07.15	07.50 Andover Jcn - Cheltenham		
			13.56 Cheltenham - S'ton Terminus		
			19.04 S'ton Docks - Andover Jcn	20.50	194
77	45xx 2-6-2T	06.45	07.00 Andover Jcn - Marlborough		
			Works Marlborough - Savernake shuttle		
			20.15 Marlborough - Swindon		
			Swindon MPD	21.00	
					91
78	43xx 2-6-0	08.00	08.15 Andover Jcn - Swindon		
			Swindon MPD	14.00	34

Goods services in italics

Strictly speaking, Andover Junction was an MSWR shed with an allocation of two 43xx 2-6-0's for services to and from Cheltenham. However it also had five other engines, three of which rotated from Eastleigh and two from Swindon.

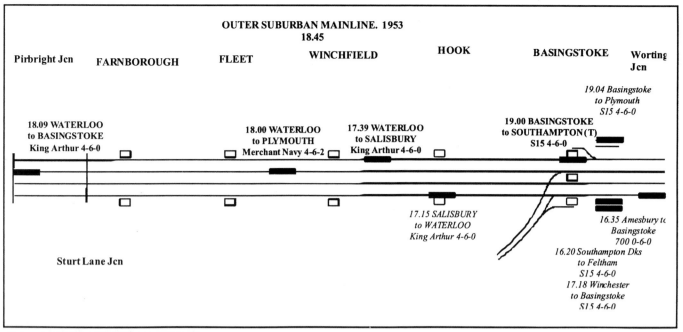

OUTER SUBURBAN MAINLINE. 1953
18.45

Pirbright Jcn	FARNBOROUGH	FLEET	WINCHFIELD	HOOK	BASINGSTOKE	Worting Jcn

19.04 Basingstoke
to Plymouth
S15 4-6-0

18.09 WATERLOO
to BASINGSTOKE
King Arthur 4-6-0

18.00 WATERLOO
to PLYMOUTH
Merchant Navy 4-6-2

17.39 WATERLOO
to SALISBURY
King Arthur 4-6-0

19.00 BASINGSTOKE
to SOUTHAMPTON (T)
S15 4-6-0

17.15 SALISBURY
to WATERLOO
King Arthur 4-6-0

16.35 Amesbury to
Basingstoke
700 0-6-0

16.20 Southampton Dks
to Feltham
S15 4-6-0

17.18 Winchester
to Basingstoke
S15 4-6-0

Sturt Lane Jcn

Although one of the finest designs produced by the Southern Railway - effectively a six-coupled engine with 4-4-0 dimensions - the Schools class did not have a lasting association with the South Western. During the 1930's a number had been used on the express services between Waterloo and Portsmouth and from Bournemouth to London but by nationalisation all forty engines had been transferred to the SECR where they monopolised the Charing Cross - Hastings duties together with a handful of workings to Ramsgate. Thus for many years they were strangers on the Western Section although there were occasions when odd members of the class, either displaced from a special working or ex-works from Eastleigh would be utilised for a rare trip between Salisbury and Waterloo en route to Bricklayers Arms. In their final days after the electrification of the system in Kent however, some of the survivors were moved across to the South Western where for a short period they could be found assisting with the stopping services between Waterloo and Salisbury. An unidentified and rather unkempt member of the class calls at Andover Junction with a slow train for Salisbury in 1962.

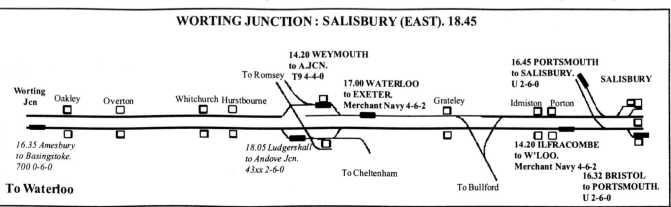

WORTING JUNCTION : SALISBURY (EAST). 18.45

Worting Jcn	Oakley	Overton	Whitchurch	Hurstbourne		Grateley	Idmiston	Porton	SALISBURY

14.20 WEYMOUTH
to A.JCN.
T9 4-4-0

To Romsey

17.00 WATERLOO
to EXETER.
Merchant Navy 4-6-2

16.45 PORTSMOUTH
to SALISBURY.
U 2-6-0

16.35 Amesbury
to Basingstoke.
700 0-6-0

18.05 Ludgershall
to Andove Jcn.
43xx 2-6-0

To Cheltenham

To Bullford

14.20 ILFRACOMBE
to W'LOO.
Merchant Navy 4-6-2

16.32 BRISTOL
to PORTSMOUTH.
U 2-6-0

To Waterloo

Elms Goods, but because of the crewing arrangements which were liable to collapse at the slightest provocation.

Departures from Waterloo were invariably worked by crews from main line sheds who arrived and remained in the station with their engine. The exceptions to the rule were men from sheds not normally associated with passenger duties but who were required to maintain route knowledge for which purpose they were allocated a small proportion of the main line services. By this means crews from such sheds could ease the burden on depots such as Salisbury and Nine Elms at the very busiest periods when engines and men were at a premium. (The arrangement was not always retained simply for operational expediency. Sheds were highly sensitive about the number of turns they had over each route and fought savagely against any proposals to limit them).

In the case of No.10 working the engine was booked to be worked light to Waterloo and coupled to the 17.39 by a set of Nine Elms men who then relieved the Merchant Navy Pacific which had arrived with the 15.05 from Bournemouth West. In the meantime a set of men from Feltham signed on duty at 16.05 and travelled passenger to Waterloo where they were booked to take over No.10 and work the 17.39 as far as Basingstoke after which they travelled passenger to Reading to relieve one of their own S15's and work the 21.03 goods goods to Feltham.

On arrival at Basingstoke the 17.39 was taken over by a pair of Salisbury men who had arrived with an Eastleigh Lord Nelson on the 16.05 from Salisbury and they in turn handed over to the Nine Elms crew who worked down to Salisbury with the 20.54 from Waterloo and returned on the 12.45 Torrington Goods.

It can be seen from the above that the scope for trouble was wide - it only needed a hiccup with the electric service from Feltham to guarantee that the Feltham men would not arrive in Waterloo before 17.30 in which case the locomotive inspector at Waterloo would have a mere nine minutes in which to realise that something had gone wrong and to scratch around for a spare set of men who almost certainly only work the first leg of the diagram.

Whilst the 17.39 was an extreme case of engine-manning, it demonstrates some of the complexities associated with railway operating. Controllers and Traffic Inspectors had - if they were to be any good at their jobs - to become very proficient in moving engines and men around at the drop of the hat and it was a poor man who did not carry most of the engine and crewing arrangements in his head. One of the great pleasures of observing railway life was to be present when a serious mishap occurred and to see how the most complex ad-hoc arrangements, effecting perhaps a dozen trains, were introduced purely from memory,as though from instinct. To have tried to reorganise using a notepad and the printed diagrams would have taken too long and when dealing with trains one always had to be mindful of which engines, men and guard were working each service and, most importantly, what they did next.

The third departure of the day from Salisbury (08.42) calling at the intermediate stations was little different from the first, except that it had an N15 4-6-0 on the front as opposed to the light Pacific of the earlier departure and took 154 minutes to reach London although the hand-ful of passengers who joined the train west of Salisbury - it started from Yeovil (Town) at 07.10) - could, if they were prepared to suffer for the sake of speed, decant at Salisbury and, after a fifty minute wait, pick up the 07.30 from Exeter which overtook the Yeovil train at Woking and got them to Waterloo a mere eight minutes earlier.

The final train of the morning was a mixed bag of assets and must have held the record for a stopping train, leaving Exeter behind a Merchant Navy 4-6-2 at 06.30 but calling at almost all stations to Basingstoke from which point it became an express, calling only at Woking but still requiring two hours and eighteen minutes to cover the Salisbury - Waterloo leg. (One suspected that somewhere in the timing office someone harboured an undying affection for the pre-1914 timetable and was determined at all costs to preserve at least one working which flew the pregrouping flag).

TRAIN MOVEMENTS : ANDOVER JUNCTION (1953)					
Train	Arr	Engine	Diagram	Dep	Destination
12.45 Torrington		*N15 4-6-0*	*N. Elms 10*	*00/53*	*Nine Elms*
17.00 Torrington		*MN 4-6-2*	*N. Elms 7*	*02/15*	*Nine Elms*
00.23 Woking	02.22	S15 4-6-0	Salisbury 441		(Fwd at 03.03)
01.25 WATERLOO	02.45	MN 4-6-2	Exmouth 498	02.48	PLYMOUTH
(00.23 Woking)		*S15 4-6-0*	*Salisbury 441*	*03.03*	*Exmouth Jcn*
13.55 Meldon		*H15 4-6-0*	*Salisbury 440*	*03/10*	*Woking*
14.58 Gravesend	03.08	*N15 4-6-0*	*Salisbury 432*	*03.25*	*Yeovil (T)*
23.58 Feltham		*S15 4-6-0*	*Feltham 115*	*03/48*	*Exmouth Jcn*
03.30 Basingstoke	04.30	S15 4-6-0	Salisbury 439	04.45	Salisbury
17.21 Plymouth	05.23	*N15 4-6-0*	*Salisbury 436*	*05.40*	*Feltham*
21.30 Okehampton		*H15 4-6-0*	*Salisbury 441*	*06/00*	*Woking*
		T9 4-4-0	Andover 248	06.45	Portsmouth
05.30 Basingstoke	06.26	700 0-6-0	B'stoke 242	06.46	Bulford
		2MT 2-6-2T	Andover 247	06.47	Tidworth
		45xx 2-6-2T	Swindon 77	07.00	Marlborough
06.45 Salisbury	07.17	WC 4-6-2	Salisbury 430	07.19	Waterloo
04.10 Cheltenham	07.28	43xx 2-6-0	Cheltenham 21		(Fwd at 08.04)
		43xx 2-6-0	Andover 249	07.30	Romsey
		43xx 2-6-0	Andover 250	07.50	Cheltenham
(04.10 Cheltenham)		*43xx 2-6-0*	*Cheltenham 21*	*08.04*	*S'ton Docks*
07.50 Tidworth	08.14	2MT 2-6-2T	Andover 247		
		43xx 2-6-0	Swindon 78	08.15	Swindon (T)
06.33 Woking	08.10	N15 4-6-0	N.Elms 2	08.17	Templecombe
08.15 SALISBURY	08.39	MN 4-6-2	Salisbury 431	08.40	WATERLOO
07.56 Eastleigh	08.54	M7 0-4-4T	Eastleigh 298		
07.05 Swindon Jcn	09.08	45xx 2-6-2T	Swindon 74		
07.10 Yeovil (T)	09.13	N15 4-6-0	Salisbury 432	09.16	Waterloo
07.20 Waterloo	09.25	N15 4-6-0	N. Elms 3	09.27	Salisbury
		M7 0-4-4T	Eastleigh 298	09.30	Eastleigh
		T9 4-4-0	Andover 246	09.37	Romsey
08.33 Southampton (T)	09.52	T9 4-4-0	Andover 248		
07.30 EXETER	09.57	MN 4-6-2	Exmouth 495	10.00	WATERLOO
05.42 Cheltenham	10.18	*43xx 2-6-0*	*Cheltenham 24*		
09.00 WATERLOO	10.27	MN 4-6-2	N. Elms 4	10.29	PLYMOUTH
06.30 EXETER	10.31	MN 4-6-2	Exmouth 494	10.35	WATERLOO
		2MT 2-6-2T	Andover 247	10.35	Tidworth
06.40 Eastleigh	*10.45*	*L1 4-4-0*	*Eastleigh 309*		
07.45 Basingstoke	*10.50*	*U 2-6-0*	*B'stoke 239*		
10.10 Southampton (T)	11.06	43xx 2-6-0	Andover 249	11.09	Cheltenham
10.45 Basingstoke	11.19	N15 4-6-0	N. Elms 1	11.21	Salisbury
		T9 4-4-0	Andover 248	11.25	Eastleigh
06.48 Cheltenham	*11.37*	*43xx 2-6-0*	*Cheltenham 23*		*(Fwd at 12.00)*
(06.48 Cheltenham)		*45xx 2-6-2T*	*Swindon 74*	*12.00*	*Romsey*
11.00 WATERLOO		MN 4-6-2	N.Elms 5	12/04	PLYMOUTH
10.42 Salisbury	12.45	*S15 4-6-0*	*Salisbury 438*		*(Fwd at 13.43)*
10.54 Waterloo	12.51	LN 4-6-0	Eastleigh 251	12.53	Salisbury
08.15 PLYMOUTH	12.58	MN 4-6-2	Exmouth 496	13.00	WATERLOO
10.11 Cheltenham	12.57	Manor 4-6-0	Cheltenham 22	13.03	Southampton (T)
		U 2-6-0	B'stoke 239	13.08	*Light to Overton*
11.30 Bevois Park	13.12	*43xx 2-6-0*	*Cheltenham 21*	13.30	*Washwood Heath*
11.19 Portsmouth	13.27	2MT 2-6-2T	Eastleigh 306		
12.54 Salisbury	13.31	S15 4-6-0	Salisbury 435	13.33	Waterloo
(10.42 Salisbury)		*S15 4-6-0*	*Salisbury 438*	*13.43*	*Basingstoke*
11.54 Waterloo	**13.47**	WC 4-6-2	Salisbury 430	13.49	Salisbury

Goods services in italics. "/" - passing time.

When it turned it's attention to the matter, the Southern could produce some pretty unappealing chimneys, a selection of which are reproduced on this page. The stovepipe chimney of the D15 4-4-0's never sat comfortably on their massive boilers whilst the spark-arresting arrangement fitted to King Arthur N15 4-6-0 30784 'Sir Nerovens' defies aesthetic description. The best that can be said is that such experiments paved the way for the Q1 0-6-0 whose performance was ahead of appearance by a considerable margin. The views were taken at Eastleigh in 1949 and to the surprise of many, D15 463 was resurrected from its oil-burning state and survived in traffic until the autumn of 1951. The Q1 0-6-0's were familiar in some parts of the system and rare in others. None worked regularly between Woking and Salisbury and only two - in the dead of night - could be seen on the secondary line between Eastleigh and Salisbury. The unhappily disfigured 30784 was a regular sight at Eastleigh for many years and was taken out of traffic in September 1959.

Local passengers may have grumbled at the fact the Bulleid revolution seemed to have left them in the cold but for the enthusiast the morning service from Salisbury held one gem - which was not advertised in the public book - in the shape of an M7 0-4-4 tank which ran the 07.20 workers train from Salisbury to Grateley each morning and represented the last opportunity to get a run behind one of these engines on a mainline service.

Services from London in the evening were very little better than those going up in the morning although the 17.00 Exeter express made calls at Overton and Whitchurch whilst the 17.39 Waterloo - Salisbury connected at Basingstoke with the 18.00 West of England service which lopped twenty minutes off the overall time and spared the passenger from the rigours of stopping everywhere beyond Woking.

For passengers who turned up at Waterloo after six o'clock nothing better than the 18.54 and 20.54 stopping trains were available, the only saving grace -from the enthusiasts point of view - of which was the S15 4-6-0 booked to work the earlier of the two; a class of engine not normally associated with passenger work.

This last gap in the timetable effected more than just the occasional passengers bound for rural Overton or Porton since neither Andover Junction or Salisbury had a fast service from Waterloo after the 18.00 departure and indeed the poor soul who arrived at Waterloo any later than 18.54 had to kick his heels until 01.25 in contrast to Wessex passengers who had a train to Southampton at 21.00 plus the 22.30 mail to Dorchester.

Of the intermediate stations on the main line the only location of significance was Andover Junction whose importance was rooted in the straggling MSW route to Swindon and Cheltenham and its LSWR 'continuation' to the south through Romsey, over which the GWR had gained direct access to Southampton.

The steeply graded single line Bulford branch which left the main line via the triangular layout at Amesbury Junction and Grateley had supported a rural service until early in the decade when the relatively generous service of seven trains to and from Salisbury in 1949 was pared to one return trip by 1952 in spite of the large military presence at Bulford camp station which lay on a private extension of the line, one and a quarter miles further on from Bulford proper.

The army being well mechanised found it a simple matter to ferry its personnel by road to and from either Porton or Salisbury and the Bulford service - which usually consisted of a single coach and a 700 0-6-0 - made its final run on the 28th June 1952 behind 0-6-0 30317. (The closure seems to have been rather peremptory since the service, such as it was, had been included in the summer 1952 timetable).

Freight traffic remained after the cessation of passenger services, the branch being worked by the two daily trips from Basingstoke and Salisbury, each being booked for 700 class - Black Motor - 0-6-0 goods engines.

After disposing of their respective loads both engines spent the rest of their shifts shunting the branch stations and military sidings before heading back from Amesbury at 14.45 and 16.35 to Salisbury and Basingtoke respectively. Of the pair only the Basingstoke train performed any mainline work, calling at Grateley and Andover Junction.

Occasionally traffic for the branch could be heavy and when the Basingstoke train required an assisting engine, it had to wait at Newton Tony Junction for the Salisbury 0-6-0 to arrive back, both engines working the train as far as Bulford. (In actual fact the Basingstoke service was the only train within the meaning of the act to regularly serve Bulford since the Salisbury train shed its load at Amesbury and proceeded forward with only a parcels van of letter-mail traffic and the like).

Because of the lack of mineral services, the volume of goods traffic between Basingstoke and Salisbury was not particularly impressive - there were about half a dozen services in each direction - whilst most of the trains ran at night, an operational factor that gave rise to the popularism amongst visiting enthusiasts of the day that the Southern did not run goods trains. A degree of experience - especially through a night spent on the line - gave the lie to the rumour and even if the number of trains was small, those services that existed were run with con-

TRAIN MOVEMENTS : ANDOVER JUNCTION (1953)					
Train	Arr	Engine	Diagram	Dep	Destination
14.00 Ludgershall	14.15	2MT 2-6-2T	Andover 247		
13.00 WATERLOO	14.16	MN 4-6-2	Salisbury 431	14.18	PLYMOUTH
		43xx 2-6-0	Cheltenham 23	14.35	Swindon (T)
10.30 ILFRACOMBE		MN 4-6-2	Exmouth 497	14/37	WATERLOO
10.45 Feltham		S15 4-6-0	Feltham 101	14/54	Exmouth Jcn
14.12 Romsey	15.05	45xx 2-6-2T	Swindon 74		
		L1 4-4-0	Eastleigh 309	15.11	Light to Andover (T)
14.25 Salisbury		S15 4-6-0	Feltham 106	15/12	Basingstoke
14.48 Basingstoke	15.24	N15 4-6-0	N. Elms 11	15.27	Salisbury
15.15 Salisbury	15.39	N15 4-6-0	Nine Elms 1	15.41	Waterloo
09.45 Tonbridge		H15 4-6-0	Salisbury 440	15/50	Exmouth Jcn
		2MT 2-6-2T	Andover 247	16.12	Romsey
15.00 WATERLOO	16.18	MN 4-6-2	N. Elms 7	16.20	PLYMOUTH
16.05 Salisbury	16.36	LN 4-6-0	Eastleigh 251	16.40	Waterloo
13.56 Cheltenham	16.37	43xx 2-6-0	Andover 250	16.43	Southampton (T)
17.00 Andover Town	17.05	L1 4-4-0	Eastleigh 309		
12.20 ILFRACOMBE	17.15	MN 4-6-2	Salisbury 461	17.17	WATERLOO
16.48 Basingstoke	17.24	N15 4-6-0	Salisbury 432	17.28	Salisbury
16.35 Amesbury	17.30	700 0-6-0	B'stoke 242		(Fwd at 18.00)
16.36 Southampton (T)	17.38	Manor 4-6-0	Cheltenham 22	17.42	Cheltenham
17.15 Salisbury	17.47	N15 4-6-0	N. Elms 2	17.51	Waterloo
15.54 Clapham Jcn		MN 4-6-2	Exmouth 494	18/00	Exeter
(16.35 Amesbury)		700 0-6-0	B'stoke 242	18.00	Basingstoke
16.49 Swindon	18.05	43xx 2-6-0	Cheltenham 23		
18.05 Ludgershall	18.38	43xx 2-6-0	Swindon 75		
17.00 WATERLOO	18.37	MN 4-6-2	Exmouth 496	18.39	EXETER
		L1 4-4-0	Eastleigh 309	18.40	Eastleigh
14.20 Weymouth	18.45	T9 4-4-0	Eastleigh 282		
14.20 ILFRACOMBE	18.57	MN 4-6-2	N. Elms 4	18.59	WATERLOO
		43xx 2-6-0	Swindon 75	19.15	Swindon Town
18.00 WATERLOO	19.20	MN 4-6-2	Exmouth 495	19.22	PLYMOUTH
		T9 4-4-0	Eastleigh 282	19.35	Eastleigh
15.20 Cheltenham	19.42	43xx 26-0	Andover 249		(Fwd at 20.50)
17.39 Waterloo	19.41	N15 4-6-0	N. Elms 10	19.47	Salisbury
17.16 Fawley	19.45	T9 4-4-0	Eastleigh 280		
19.04 Basingstoke	20.04	S15 4-6-0	Salisbury 438		(Fwd at 20.35)
19.30 light Salisbury	20.05	BR4 2-6-0	Eastleigh 316		(works 20.50)
17.25 Cheltenham	20.25	43xx 2-6-0	Swindon 76		
15.50 PLYMOUTH	20.33	MN 4-6-2	Exmouth 498	20.35	WATERLOO
(19.04 Basingstoke)		S15 4-6-0	Salisbury 438	20.35	Plymouth
19.04 S'ton Docks	20.41	43xx 2-6-0	Andover 250		(Fwd at 20.55)
(15.20 Cheltenham)		BR4 2-6-0	Eastleigh 316	20.50	Eastleigh
(19.04 S'ton Docks)		43xx 2-6-0	Cheltenham 23	20.55	Cheltenham
17.40 Yeovil (T)		N15 4-6-0	N. Elms 3	21/06	Gravesend
18.54 Waterloo	21.11	S15 4-6-0	Salisbury 435	21.14	Yeovil (T)
20.50 Salisbury	21.21	N15 4-6-0	Salisbury 432	21.23	Woking
19.45 Portsmouth	22.04	T9 4-4-0	B'mouth 403		
21.05 Templecombe		MN 4-6-2	N. Elms 5	22/38	Clapham Jcn
20.54 Waterloo	22.49	N15 4-6-0	Salisbury 436	22.51	Salisbury
21.10 Nine Elms		MN 4-6-2	Exmouth 497	23/08	Plymouth
17.18 Sidmouth Jcn	23.09	N15 4-6-0	N. Elms 11	23.16	Waterloo (Pcls)
22.50 Salisbury		S15 4-6-0	Salisbury 470	23/40	Basingstoke
22.00 Nine Elms	23.57	MN 4-6-2	Salisbury 461	00.05	Exmouth Jcn
Goods services in italics. "/" : passing time.					

Unnoticed by most visiting enthusiasts, Andover had a second station - Andover Town - which if short on trains was long on timelessness. Apart from minor detail, the scene could have happened at any time during the preceding half-century although change was in progress when the view was taken. To popularise the new English Electric diesel units, which started to appear in 1957, an interval service of trains was introduced in spite of the fact that there were insufficient units for the programme and thus the M7 tanks of the area found a new lease of life for a few years. M7 0-4-4T 30033 of Eastleigh pauses at Andover Town with the 10.42 Andover Junction - Eastleigh interval train on 19/2/59.

siderable expedition and, with no night passenger services competing for line occupation, were invariably punctual.

Not all the freight services earned an honest penny in the strictest sense of the expression since two of the workings came from Woking and Tonbridge and existed to return ballast hoppers to Meldon quarry for the needs of the Railway district engineer whilst a number of services in the opposite direction were dedicated to the import of stone from Meldon. (A colleague would watch an H15 4-6-0 tear westwards through Hampshire on its way from Tonbridge to Exmouth Junction and complain that for all its show it contributed not a penny to the railway's coffers....).

For the purposes of local goods workings the section was split into two, Andover Junction being the point of division. The stations to the

FREIGHT MOVEMENTS : ANDOVER JUNCTION YARD (1953)					
Inward		Arr	Loco	Diagram	Dep Destination
17.21 Plymouth		05.23	N15 4-6-0	Salisbury 438	05.40 Feltham
05.30 Basingstoke		06.26	700 0-6-0	Basingstoke 242	06.46 Bulford
04.10 Cheltenham		07.28	43xx 2-6-0	Cheltenham 21	08.04 S'ton Docks
			43xx 2-6-0	Swindon 78	08.15 Swindon Town
			T9 4-4-0	Andover 246	09.37 Romsey
05.42 Cheltenham		10.18	43xx 2-6-0	Cheltenham 24	
06.40 Eastleigh		10.45	L1 4-4-0	Eastleigh 309	
07.45 Basingstoke		10.50	U 2-6-0	Basingstoke 239	
06.48 Cheltenham		11.37	43xx 2-6-0	Cheltenham 23	(Fwd at 12.00)
(06.48 Cheltenham)			45xx 2-6-2T	Swindon 74	12.00 Romsey
10.42 Salisbury		12.45	S15 4-6-0	Salisbury 438	(Fwd at 13.43)
11.30 Bevois Park		13.12	43xx 2-6-0	Cheltenham 21	13.30 Washwood Heath
(10.42 Salisbury)			S15 4-6-0	Salisbury 438	13.43 Basingstoke
14.12 Romsey		15.05	45xx 2-6-2T	Swindon 74	
17.00 Andover Town		17.05	L1 4-4-0	Eastleigh 309	
16.35 Amesbury		17.30	700 0-6-0	Basingstoke 242	18.00 Basingstoke
18.05 Ludgershall		18.38	43xx 2-6-0	Swindon 75	
			43xx 2-6-0	Swindon 75	19.15 Swindon Town
15.20 Cheltenham		19.42	43xx 2-6-0	Andover 249	(Fwd at 20.50)
19.04 Basingstoke		20.04	S15 4-6-0	Salisbury 438	20.35 Plymouth
19.04 S'ton Docks		20.41	43xx 2-6-0	Andover 250	(Fwd at 20.55)
(15.20 Cheltenham)			BR4 2-6-0	Eastleigh 316	20.50 Eastleigh
(19.04 S'ton Docks)			43xx 2-6-0	Cheltenham 23	20.55 Cheltenham
22.00 Nine Elms		23.57	MN 4-6-2	Salisbury 461	00.05 Exmouth Jcn

Andover Junction goods yard was kept busy for nineteen hours a day and probably saw more goods trains per day than the entire Southern Region thirty years later. Most of the business was concerned with connections between the MSW and the LSW with London traffic being brought in by the 22.00 ex Nine Elms and West of England traffic being taken forward by the evening Basingstoke - Plymouth service. It is difficult to think of any other location where such a limited number of trains produced such a wide variety of motive power.

east were serviced by the morning Basingstoke - Andover Junction goods whilst those to the west were worked by the 10.42 from Salisbury to Basingstoke which, after remarshalling at Andover Junction, also served Overton.

With the exception of Overton, which also had a third service, none of the stations received a working in the opposite direction - a consignment from Whitchurch to Feltham, for example, had to be worked to Andover Junction before heading east - and the Basingstoke trip returned light from Andover Junction to Overton where it started an afternoon working back to Basingstoke.

So far as the passenger service was concerned the London traveller from most of the intermediate stations between Salisbury and Basingstoke - which the exception of those at Andover Junction where a proportion of the west of England trains paused - did not have a great deal to cheer about. One might have expected

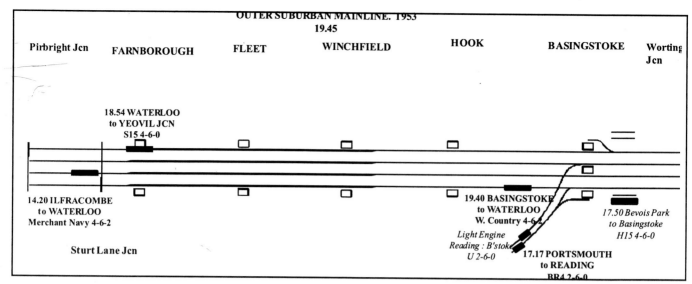

OUTER SUBURBAN MAINLINE. 1953

Pirbright Jcn   FARNBOROUGH   FLEET   WINCHFIELD   HOOK   BASINGSTOKE   Worting Jcn

19.45

18.54 WATERLOO to YEOVIL JCN S15 4-6-0

14.20 ILFRACOMBE to WATERLOO Merchant Navy 4-6-2

Sturt Lane Jcn

19.40 BASINGSTOKE to WATERLOO W. Country 4-6-2

Light Engine Reading : B'stoke U 2-6-0

17.17 PORTSMOUTH to READING BR4 2-6-0

17.50 Bevois Park to Basingstoke H15 4-6-0

BR5 4-6-0 73119. 11: 367/395 tons (1958)				
m.ch Point	1/in WTT	Actual	mph	dbhp pc
0.00 WATERLOO	0.00	0.00	-	- -
3.74 Clapham Jcn	-3642 7.00	6.52	50	793 3
7.19 Wimbledon	752	10.45	56	772 4
9.62 New Malden	-29773	13.21	64	928 5
12.03 SURBITON	7153 18.30	15.23	67	896 6
17.06 Walton	4242	19.46	74	993 7
19.12 Weybridge	-5242	21.31	70	230 2
24.27 WOKING	676 31.00	26.25	-	- -

Clapham Jcn to Walton 13.1 miles 1/2259
61 mph. 889 dbhp (pc 5)

Setting what may be a record for a local train, the class 5 engine with the eleven coaches of the 17.39 ex Waterloo not only managed to knock four and a half minutes off the booked timing but succeeded in beating the electric schedule by over half a minute.

- especially from a traffic management which alone of all the British systems had a greater stake in passenger matters than goods affairs - that the Salisbury to London slow trains would run in connection with the up Wessex expresses so that a convenient connection might have been available at Basingstoke. No-one seems to have given this possibility any thought (or action) and for the most part travellers between, say, Grateley and London were condemned to services which stopped, not merely as far as Basingstoke, but all the way to Woking taking over 150 minutes to cover the 84 miles from Salisbury.

One of the wayside points - Whitchurch - appears to have had a measure of influence since the Merchant Navy-hauled 08.15 Salisbury - Waterloo (10.08) made a call there and gave whatever regulars used the station a good run up to town - with an intermediate stop at Basingstoke - at an average speed of 47 mph which compared more than favourably with the 30-odd mph crawl of the normal workings. In the opposite direction the 17.00 express from Waterloo to Exeter acted as a balance and made calls at both Overton and Whitchurch.

By the 1950's it was difficult to guarantee a run over the main line behind anything that had not been either designed or rebuilt by Maunsell or his successor yet for those in the know - the working was unadvertised - it was possible to take an afternoon trip from Waterloo to Salisbury and back and include a run behind an M7 0-4-4 tank. This could be achieved by starting from Waterloo on the 13.30 Weymouth express (a West Country Pacific) as far as Basingstoke to connect with the 14.48 Salisbury stopper (an N15 4-6-0) to Idmiston where, after an hour and a half of watching trains, one could join the 17.30 workmans service to Salisbury which was the last scheduled train on the main line to be worked by an LSWR tank. It was not much of a run and, of course, it was not too difficult to get a ride behind an M7 on many of the secondary routes of the system. However to do so on the main West of England line in the 1950's gave the determined enthusiast rather more than an ordinary sense of deja-vu.

In spite of the fact that the Southern had a large fleet of 2-6-0's, only a single example - the U class of the Basingstoke - Andover Junction goods - was regularly used on the line and the most common type of 2-6-0 in the district was actually the GWR 43xx class which, although

WC. 4-6-2 34109 'Sir Trafford Leigh-Mallory'				
13: 430/465 tons (1955)				
m.ch point	1/in WTT	Actual	mph	dbhp pc
0.00 WATERLOO	- 0.00	0.00	-	- -
3.74 Clapham Jcn	-3642 7.00	8.01	45	610 2
10.78 Berrylands	1633	15.54	66	991 5
		pwc & signals		
24.27 WOKING	1521 28.00	31.35	11	- -
31.00 MP.31	312	41.37	47	1131 5
36.38 Fleet	-4581	46.57	68	1270 8
39.66 Winchfield	674	49.49	70	1307 9
42.13 Hook	1046	51.55	66	564 4
47.60 BASINGSTOKE	684 53.30	56.36	68	1300 9
50.23 Worting Jcn	260 56.00	58.57	54	410 3
52.43 Wootton	278	61.22	55	1270 7
58.09 Micheldever	-829	66.27	73	1099 7
61.60 Wallers Ash	-252	69.17	78	297 2
66.39 Winchester	-265	73.02	80	- -
		Signals		
79.19 SOUTHAMPTON	-388 91.00	89.16	-	- -

Woking to Micheldever. 33.8 miles 1/724
58 mph. 1122 dbhp (pc 7)

It is a matter for regret that the schedules laid down by the Southern did not match the capabilities of their engines as is witnessed by the performance of light Pacific 34109 on the 18.30 Waterloo - Weymouth when, in spite of three out of course delays plus a load of thirteen vehicles, it succeeded in reaching Southampton almost two minutes before time.

not having any turns of duty on the main line, could be seen at both Andover Junction and Salisbury; working off the MSW route from Cheltenham and the GWR route from Westbury.

To cover the MSWR duties which started at the southern end of the line, two 43xx locomotives were allocated to Andover Junction, ostensibly for northbound services although, since the down morning express started from Southampton Terminus, one of the pair worked southwards, well into LSWR country to get to

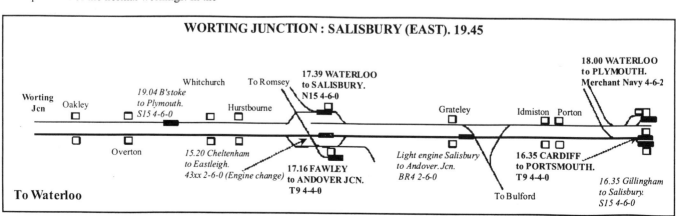

WORTING JUNCTION : SALISBURY (EAST). 19.45

Worting Jcn   Oakley   Whitchurch   To Romsey   Grateley   Idmiston   Porton

18.00 WATERLOO to PLYMOUTH. Merchant Navy 4-6-2

19.04 B'stoke to Plymouth. S15 4-6-0

17.39 WATERLOO to SALISBURY. N15 4-6-0

Hurstbourne

Overton

15.20 Cheltenham to Eastleigh. 43xx 2-6-0 (Engine change)

17.16 FAWLEY to ANDOVER JCN. T9 4-4-0

Light engine Salisbury to Andover. Jcn. BR4 2-6-0

16.35 CARDIFF to PORTSMOUTH. T9 4-4-0

16.35 Gillingham to Salisbury. S15 4-6-0

To Bulford

To Waterloo

74

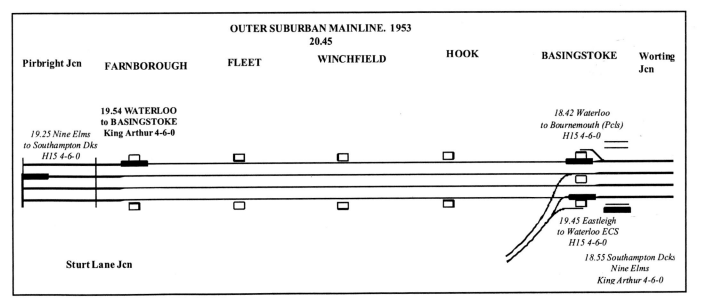

OUTER SUBURBAN MAINLINE. 1953
20.45

Pirbright Jcn   **FARNBOROUGH**   **FLEET**   **WINCHFIELD**   **HOOK**   **BASINGSTOKE**   Worting Jcn

19.25 Nine Elms to Southampton Dks
H15 4-6-0

19.54 WATERLOO to BASINGSTOKE
King Arthur 4-6-0

18.42 Waterloo to Bournemouth (Pcls)
H15 4-6-0

19.45 Eastleigh to Waterloo ECS
H15 4-6-0

18.55 Southampton Dcks Nine Elms
King Arthur 4-6-0

Sturt Lane Jcn

Southampton in order to work its train through. It was, of course, a legacy of the days when the MSWR had allowed the Great Western access to the Solent.

In addition to the two moguls, the shed also played host to a pair of other GWR locomotives: a 45xx 2-6-2T and a third 43xx, both from Swindon, which spent each night in the MPD.

The shed also had three SR engines - 2 T9 4-4-0's and an Ivatt LMS 2-6-2T - to book out each day although there were no engines permanently allocated to the depot for the diagrams. The locomotives instead worked to cyclic diagrams based at Eastleigh; each engine recessing overnight at a variety of sheds in the district. One of the curious features of Andover Junction MPD - especially in view of its size - was the fact that representatives of three of the four companies could be seen cheek by jowl, something that was distinctly unusual at that time. Adding to this variety a fourth dimension appeared each evening in the shape of a BR standard 2-6-0 which arrived light from Salisbury to relieve the 15 20 Cheltenham to Eastleigh goods. (For a short period in 1953,

when a number of LNER B1's and V2's were borrowed to cover a temporary shortage of Bulleid Pacifics, it was possible to see an ele-

35020 (MN/R) 'Bibby Line'. 432/465 tons. (1956)						
m.ch Point	1/in	WTT	Actual	mph	dbhp	pc
0 WATERLOO		0.00	0.00	-	-	-
3.74 Clapham Jcn	-3642	7.00	7.17	46.0	773	2
7.19 Wimbledon	752		11.15	57.0	1068	5
12.03 Surbiton	20774		15.56	64.5	915	6
19.12 Weybridge	8963		22.16	65.0	775	5
21.54 West Byfleet	6116		24.30	73.0	1529	10
24.27 WOKING	367	28.00	26.53	67.0	876	6
27.79 Brookwood	318		30.21	62.0	1088	7
31.00 MP 31	307		33.22	58.0	1043	6
33.17 Farnborough	-946		35.31	65.0	984	6
36.38 Fleet	2852		38.23	74.0	1499	10
42.13 Hook	789		43.14	70.0	953	7
50.23 WORTING JCN	435	51.00	50.07	64.0	1224	9
55.42 Overton	2921		54.52	71.5	1107	7
59.08 Whitchurch	-549		57.46	78.0	911	7
66.19 ANDOVER JCN	-369		63.03	90.0	860	7
72.49 Grateley	275		68.10	61.5	640	5
78.19 Porton	-571		73.22	86.0	1195	8
83.43 SALISBURY	-216	83.00	79.38	-	-	-

Weybridge - Porton. 59 miles 1/1400. 69 mph 1049 dbhp (pc 7)

Proof, if any were needed, that the running qualities of the Merchant Navy class had not been compromised by their rebuilding. 35020, fresh out of Eastleigh, had no difficulty in getting to Salisbury in under 80 minutes with a thirteen coach load. It is interesting to note the surge of power produced by the engine as the train left the 60 mph limit of the suburban area; the remainder of the run being punctuated by similar outbursts in order to keep the speed in the seventies.

35030 'Elder Dempster Lines'. (MN/R). 305/330 tons (1958)						
m.ch Point	1/in	WTT	Actual	mph	dbhp	pc
0.00 WATERLOO	-	0.00	0.00	-	-	-
3.74 Clapham Jcn	-3642	7.00	7.20	35.0	467	1
12.03 Surbiton	1750		16.19	70.5	929	5
17.06 Walton	1756		20.33	70.5	702	5
21.54 W. Byfleet	level		24.16	75.0	855	6
			Signals			
31.00 MP 31	326		33.42	62.5	728	4
33.17 Farnborough	-946		35.38	74.0	1309	9
36.38 Fleet	2852		38.13	79.0	1097	8
39.66 Winchfield	674		40.42	82.0	1356	11
42.13 Hook	1046		42.28	83.5	1122	9
47.60 BASINGSTOKE	684	48.30	46.42	65.0	-	-
50.23 Worting Jcn	260	51.00	49.06	61.5	932	6
55.42 Overton	2921		53.48	75.0	1034	7
59.08 Whitchurch	-549		56.44	69.0	-	-
66.19 ANDOVER JCN	-369		62.31	80.5	411	3
72.49 Grateley	275		67.43	65.0	868	6
78.19 Porton	-571		72.03	85.0	1181	9
83.43 SALISBURY	-216	83.00	78.04	-	-	-

MP 31 to Hook. 11.2 miles 1/1857/ 69 mph : 996 dbhp (pc 7)

The benefits of fast and powerful locomotives were not always understood by the operating department who, in the case above, ran the Atlantic Coast Express in two sections; each train being worked by a Pacific. The leading portion consisted of only nine vehicles: a plaything for the Merchant Navy locomotive which not only had to shut off steam several times in order to prevent early running but could probably have taken both sections of the train and run them without loss of time.

WORTING JUNCTION : SALISBURY (EAST). 20.45

Worting Jcn   Overton   Whitchurch   Hurstbourne   To Romsey   Idmiston   Porton   **SALISBURY**

18.54 WATERLOO to YEOVIL (T).
S15 4-6-0

19.04 S'ton Docks to Cheltenham.
43xx 2-6-2 (Engine change)

19.04 B'stoke to Plymouth.
S15 4-6-0

18.50 Wimborne to Salisbury.
700 0-6-0

Oakley

15.50 PLYMOUTH to WATERLOO.
Merchant Navy 4-6-2

15.20 Cheltenham to Eastleigh.
BR4 2-6-0

To Cheltenham

Grateley

To Bullford

17.40 Yeovil (T) to Gravesend (Milk).
King Arthur 4-6-0

20.50 SALISBURY to WOKING.
King Arthur 4-6-0

To Waterloo

Rushey Platt looking North with the MSWR to the left climbing to cross the GWR main line to Bristol and South Wales and then falling to burrow under the Swindon - Gloucester line. The route to the right is the connection to Swindon (GWR). Whilst the MSW had few pretensions to trunk status, it was nevertheless busier than is popularly supposed and at Rushey Platt, for example, the incidence of trains - 30 per day - amounted to more than one an hour which was not a bad average for a secondary line.

Guards-eye view of Marlborough (Low Level) from the 13.52 Cheltenham (St James') - Southampton (Terminus) on 5th September 1959. The use of modern BR coaches in the train give a misleading impression since, far from seeing improvements, the through service had been reduced to a single working which meant that passengers from the south were unable to spend more than three hours in Cheltenham. In addition the few remaining services had been moved from the Midland (Lansdown) station at Cheltenham to the remote St James', eliminating at a stroke the line's use as a North/South connection. The most obvious indication of the WR's loss of interest can be seen in the SR mogul, representatives of which replaced the familiar 43xx 2-6-0's during the route's last few years of operation.

Train	Engine	Andover Jcn	Weyhill	Ludgershall	C'bourne	Kingston	Grafton	Savernake	Marlborough	Destination
	LM 2-6-2T (AJ 247)	06.47	06.55	07.03						Tidworth
	45XX 2-6-2T (SWN 77)	07.00		07.22	07.29	07.32	07.40	07.46		
Mixed	45XX 2-6-2T (SWN 77)							08.20	08.35	
	43XX 2-6-0 (AJ 250)	07.50	07.58	08.08	08.16	08.28	08.35		08.45	Cheltenham
Mixed	45XX 2-6-2T (SWN 77)							09.40	09.55	
	45XX 2-6-2T (SWN 77)							11.08	11.18	
Goods	*43XX 2-6-0 (SWN 78)*	*08.15*	*09.15*	*10.50*	*11.07*		*11.27*	*11.36*		
	LM 2-6-2T (AJ 247)	10.35	10.48	10.55						Tidworth
10.10 Southampton	43XX 2-6-0 (AJ 249)	11.09	11.17	11.27				11.42	11.52	Cheltenham
	43XX 2-6-0 (Westbury)			*11.30*			*11/52*	*11/56*		Westbury
	LM 2-6-2T (AJ 247)			12.35						Tidworth
08.15 A. Jcn Goods	*43XX 2-6-0 (SWN 78)*							*11.54*	*12.11*	Swindon
	45XX 2-6-2T (SWN 77)							13.12	13.22	
11.30 Bevois Pk Goods	*43XX 2-6-0 (CHEL 21)*	*13.30*		*13/52*			*14/00*		*14.28*	Cheltenham
	45XX 2-6-2T (SWN 77)							14.32	14.42	
	43XX 2-6-0 (CHEL 23)	14.35	14.43	14.53	14.59	15.02	15.09	15.15	15.27	Swindon Town
	45XX 2-6-2T (SWN 77)							16.25	16.35	
	45XX 2-6-2T (SWN 77)							17.15	17.25	
	43XX 2-6-0 (SWINDON 75)			16.25						Tidworth
16.36 Southampton	78XX 4-6-0 (CHEL 22)	17.42	17.49	17.59	18.04	18.08	18.14	18.20	18.30	Cheltenham
Goods	*43xx 2-6-0 (SWN 75)*	*19.15*		*19.50*			*20/20*	*20/25*	*20/39*	Swindon
	45XX 2-6-2T (SWN 77)							19.50	20.00	Swindon
19.04 Southampton Docks	*43XX 2-6-0 (CHEL 23)*	*20.55*		*21/17*				*21/39*	*21.58*	Cheltenham

Goods trains in italics

ment of every pre-nationalisation railway at Andover Junction).

In addition to the GWR engines based at Andover Junction, a number of Cheltenham-based 43xx 2-6-0's worked in from the north, one of which had no booked return working and was used as a change-over engine to replace any other which required maintenance at Swindon. The SR engines generally worked from Andover towards Eastleigh or Southampton although the through services from Cheltenham were worked by GWR motive power throughout.

In its pre-war heyday the high point in the MSW's day came with the 10.42 Southampton (Terminus) to Cheltenham which conveyed a through coach to Sheffield (Midland) via Birmingham and Derby, thus affording a direct, if rather slow, service to the heart of the Midland Railway, something that was not easy to achieve from the LSWR without going in and across London. In common with many peculiarities of the timetable the through working did not survive the war although trains continued to operate between Southampton and Cheltenham

throughout most of the 1950's until the GWR decided to isolate the MSW from the rest of its system by diverting most of the services into Cheltenham St James', thus severing the links the line had with the Midland. The scheme - which was to drive traffic away before 'proving' that no-one used the services - was successful and the line closed to passenger traffic in 1961.

As well as possessing the rather cosmopolitan air derived from the mixture of engines to be found on the shed, Andover Junction had almost hourly visits from the biggest on the line and very few West of England expresses passed without making a stop. The Junction was ever a place for contrasts. For long periods an Edwardian atmosphere would reign as T9 4-4-0's shunted in and out of the station, the spell being broken by the arrival of a Merchant Navy Pacific - which at the time looked the most modern things on wheels - on one of the Exeter workings.

For the pre-grouping connoisseur there was still a touch of the London & South Western

influence to be sampled with five T9 'Greyhound' 4-4-0's making an appearance from the Romsey direction whilst an elderly 700 class 0-6-0 wheezed its way daily between Basingstoke and the Bulford branch.

On average Andover saw a train - excluding excursion and relief services - every fifteen minutes of the day and presented the spectator with over fifty different locomotives, most of which made more than one appearance. The most frequent visitors were the Merchant Navy Pacifics followed by Great Western 2-6-0's. Through goods traffic was almost completely monopolised by the S15 4-6-0's, in contrast to the H15 4-6-0's of which only one example was booked to make an appearance.

Whilst the mix of motive power to be seen at Andover Junction was enough to satisfy the most fastidious of observers, perhaps the best sighting of all came from the engine which shunted the yard for much of the day, the booked engine being an ex-SECR inside-cylinder 4-4-0; a number of the L class having been transferred to Eastleigh at the end of 1951 as replacements

Train	Engine	Marlborough	Savernake	Grafton	Kingston	C'bourne	Ludgershall	Weyhill	Andover Jcn	Destination
04.10 Cheltenham goods	*43xx 2-6-0 (Chel 21)*	*06/45*		*06/58*			*07.10*		*07.28*	S'ton Docks
07.50 Tidworth	2MT 2-6-2T (AJ 247)						07.59	08.07	08.14	
07.05 Swindon	45xx 2-6-2T (SWD 74)	07.56	08.29	08.35	08.41	08.45	08.53	09.01	09.08	
	45xx 2-6-2T (SWD 77)	09.06	09.17							
05.42 Cheltenham	*43xx 2-6-0 (Chel 24)*	*09.25*		*09/38*			*09.55*		*10.18*	
07.15 Westbury goods			*09.55*	*10.20*			*10.38*			
	45xx 2-6-2T (SWD 77)	10.08	10.19							
06.48 Cheltenham	*43xx 2-6-0 (Chel 23)*	*10/21*		*10/38*			*11.10*	*11.25*	*11.37*	Romsey
12.15 Tidworth	2MT 2-6-2T (AJ 247)						12.22			
10.11 Cheltenham	43xx 2-6-0 (Chel 22)	12.16	12.28				12.44		12.57	Southampton
	45xx 2-6-2T (SWD 77)	12.35	12.46							
13.30 Tidworth	2MT 2-6-2T (AJ 247)						13.40			
	2MT 2-6-2T (AJ 247)						14.00	14.08	14.15	
	45xx 2-6-2T (SWD 77)	14.05	14.16							
14.02 Swindon goods	*43xx 2-6-0 (SWD 75)*	*14.40*		*15.20*		*15.45*	*15.53*			
11.25 Cheltenham goods		*14.50*	*15/12*				*15/34*		*15.56*	
13.56 Cheltenham	43xx 2-6-0 (AJ 250)	15.50	16.02	16.07	16.12	16.15	16.22	16.30	16.37	Southampton
		16.00	16.11							
	45xx 2-6-2T (SWD 77)	16.47	16.58							
16.45 Tidworth							16.52			
16.49 Swindon Town	43xx 2-6-0 (Chel 23)	17.17	17.29	17.35	17.40	17.44	17.50	17.58	18.05	
15.20 Cheltenham goods	*43xx 2-6-0 (AJ 249)*	*18.00*		*18/13*			*19.00*	*19.45*	*19.55*	Eastleigh
	43xx 2-6-0 (SWD 75)						*18.05*		*18.38*	
Mixed	45xx 2-6-2T (SWD 77)	18.10	18.32							
17.25 Cheltenham	43xx 2-6-0 (SWD 76)	19.31	19.46	19.59	20.03	20.08	20.10	20.18	20.25	

Swindon was famous for its locomotive works and (in the 1950's) a rather out-of-gauge film actress. Rather less well known was the Town station which sheltered in the shadows of the town's more interesting products. The signalbox, carriage sidings and yard as seen from an MSW service in 1959.

for the elderly LSWR 4-4-0's which were rapidly disappearing to the breakers yard. For a short period these strangers became a familiar sight in the Eastleigh area, especially between Southampton and Bournemouth, but their presence was short-lived and the ten engines concerned all returned to their home metals within a year, their duties being largely taken over by new (LMS and BR) standard six-coupled tanks. As it happened the supply of new engines was insufficient to fill the vacuum and in December 1952 four L1 4-4-0's were despatched from Dover and Bricklayers Arms to make good the shortage.

The L1 4-4-0's remained at Eastleigh for eighteen months but were by no means intensively used, their only regular diagram being on the morning goods to Andover Junction - not the most suitable working for an express passenger engine - returning to Eastleigh with an evening passenger service; the intervening hours being spent in shunting and trip working in Andover Junction Yard.

Variety, albeit of a less remarkable nature, was also present on the MSWR whose Great Western atmosphere had been diluted by the transfer of the Ludgershall - Tidworth branch to the Southern in 1952 who diagrammed one of their new Ivatt 2-6-2T's - an instance of an LMS engine hauling GWR stock on a SR branch - to handle much of the traffic. The engine concerned was one of the Eastleigh diagrams which recessed the previous night at Andover Junction.

Passenger traffic between Ludgershall and Tidworth was light and one of the services, the 12.15 ex Tidworth, ran as a mixed train comprising a GWR two-coach 'B' set and up to fifteen or so goods wagons. (It was not unknown for freight traffic to exceed the tonnage permitted for mixed working and on occasions had to be worked independently by a 43xx 2-6-0, commandeered hurriedly by Andover Junction MPD).

During its last decade of existence, BR became obsessed with station names and secondary titles in particular. Cardiff General became Cardiff Central - for no good reason - whilst dual names such as Whitstable & Tankerton had to be truncated to show one or the other. To their credit the citizens of Edinburgh turned nasty when it was proposed to drop the designation 'Waverley' whilst one of the writers was castigated by the BRB because his station announcers routinely referred to Reading General. (It had to be pointed out that the train also called at Reading West....). What the latter-day men in grey suits would have made of Cirencester (MSW) with its non-enamel sign, secondary name, gas-lamp and barrow crossing beggars the imagination.

ROMSEY : SALISBURY

Romsey was a more cosmopolitan location that one might expect with locomotives being seen from three of the four companies plus a small number of BR standards. The London Midland element was the trio of Ivatt 2MT 2-6-2 tanks which took over a number of M7 0-4-4T duties and 41305 is seen running into Romsey with the 11.19 Portsmouth & Southsea to Andover Junction on 11 May 1957. On arrival at the Junction the engine spent the remainder of the day shunting the Yard, spending the first half of the following day on the Midland & South Western before returning to Eastleigh.

Although places like the Bulford branch could offer some escape from modernisation, in order to get as close to pregrouping conditions as it was possible to do in the 1950's, a trip to Romsey rarely disappointed especially since appearances by post-Maunsell locomotives was the exception rather than the rule whilst 4-4-0's and 0-4-4T's were commonplace on passenger trains.

Romsey's position as a junction of importance arose from the fact that neither the LSWR or its successors could decide whether Salisbury - Portsmouth trains should travel via Southampton or via Eastleigh and therefore had to provide connections for both together with the associated workings to Andover Junction and the MSW. For the enthusiast the great attraction of the line, and Romsey in particular, was that one never knew what sort of engine was going to turn up next since the variety was endless.

TRAIN MOVEMENTS : ROMSEY (1953)					
Train	Arr	Loco	Diagram	Dep	Destination
00.20 Eastleigh		Q1 0-6-0	Eastleigh 319	00/45	Salisbury
01.55 Eastleigh		U 2-6-0	Yeovil 482	02/14	Yeovil Town
01.35 Salisbury		U 2-6-0	Salisbury 450	02/30	Eastleigh
02.10 Bevois Park		S15 4-6-0	Salisbury 467	02/47	Salisbury
03.30 Salisbury		Q1 0-6-0	Guildford 214	04/25	Chichester
03.58 Bevois Park		H15 4-6-0	Eastleigh 311	04/45	Salisbury
04.25 Salisbury		Q1 0-6-0	Eastleigh 319	05/20	Eastleigh
06.07 Eastleigh	06.23	M7 0-4-4T	Eastleigh 300	06.43	Eastleigh
06.40 Eastleigh	07.05	L1 & M7	Eastleigh 309/329		
		L1 4-4-0	Eastleigh 309	07.30	Andover Jcn
06.45 Andover Jcn	07.30	T9 4-4-0	Andover Jcn 248	07.32	Portsmouth
07.30 Eastleigh	07.44	LM2 2-6-2T	Eastleigh 306		
05.58 Portsmouth	07.57	U 2-6-0	Salisbury 450	07.59	Salisbury
		LM2 2-6-2T	Eastleigh 306	08.00	Weymouth
07.30 Andover Jcn	08.08	43xx 2-6-0	Andover Jcn 249		
07.56 Eastleigh	08.11	M7 0-4-4T	Eastleigh 298	08.13	Andover Jcn
07.47 Salisbury	08.16	T9 4-4-0	Salisbury 445	08.19	Portsmouth
		43xx 2-6-0	Andover Jcn 249	08.32	Portsmouth
06.55 Portsmouth	08.32	T9 4-4-0	Fratton 365		
07.29 Portsmouth	08.41	H15 4-6-0	Nine Elms 72	08.43	Bristol
		T9 4-4-0	Fratton 365	08.52	Portsmouth
04.10 Cheltenham		43xx 2-6-0	Cheltenham 21	09/10	S'ton Docks
08.33 Southampton (T)	09.10	T9 4-4-0	Eastleigh 248	09.12	Andover Jcn
07.20 Chichester		S15 4-6-0	Feltham 106	09/15	Salisbury
09.30 Andover Jcn	10.08	M7 0-4-4T	Eastleigh 298	10.09	Eastleigh
09.47 Salisbury	10.17	U 2-6-0	Yeovil 465	10.19	Portsmouth
09.03 PORTSMOUTH	10.16	U 2-6-0	Fratton 368	10.18	SALISBURY
10.10 Southampton (T)	10.31	43xx 2-6-0	Andover Jcn 249	10.32	Cheltenham
		M7 0-4-4T	Eastleigh 329	10.35	Eastleigh
09.33 PORTSMOUTH	10.40	BR4 2-6-0	Eastleigh 270	10.42	CARDIFF
09.30 Eastleigh		BR4 2-6-0	Eastleigh 316	10/50	Salisbury
08.10 Bristol	11.07	U 2-6-0	Salisbury 450	11.09	Portsmouth
11.10 Eastleigh	11.25	M7 0-4-4T	Eastleigh 308		
Light engine		M7 0-4-4T	Eastleigh 308	11.35	Eastleigh
10.34 Portsmouth	11.46	BR4 2-6-0	Eastleigh 272	11.48	Bristol
Goods services in italics: "/" : passing time					

Working from Andover Junction MPD in lieu of a GWR 2-6-0, U class mogul 31802 of Eastleigh halts at Nursling with the 13.54 Cheltenham to Southampton Terminus on 7th September 1957. Principal services from the Andover direction took the Nursling route in order to be able to call at Southampton Central. The 2-6-0 had started life in August 1926 as 2-6-4 tank 'River Cuckmere' and was converted in July 1928.

T9 4-4-0 30732 of Salisbury blows off as it arrives at Dean with the 13.03 Portsmouth & Southsea to Salisbury stopping train in July 1957. Although the service called at all stations, because it was routed via Eastleigh the forty-five mile journey was accomplished in eleven minutes less than the preceding Pacific-hauled through express to Plymouth; the latter having to cover the greater distance via Southampton plus an eighteen minute pause at Fareham during which time the Brighton and Portsmouth portions were amalgamated. For all this it pleased the conservative elements in the area to claim that a fifty-year old Drummond 4-4-0 could show a clean pair of heels to a Pacific.

The core passenger service ran from Portsmouth & Southsea via Southampton Central to Salisbury, some trains - not always the fastest ones - being handed over to the Great Western at Salisbury and being taken forward to Bristol or South Wales. Connecting with the Salisbury trains were a group of workings which operated between Southampton (Terminus) and Andover Junction, via Eastleigh which included the MSW services from Southampton Terminus but which ran via the Central Station and Nursling. In addition to these services there was also a series of local trains which ran the short distance between Eastleigh and Romsey.

The motive power used in and out of Romsey was as varied as the train service and the direct Portsmouth and Salisbury trains were no exception; the nine trains in the westward direction, for example, requiring no less than six different classes which ranged from T9 4-4-0's to U class moguls plus one service booked to be worked by the H15 4-6-0 that had arrived in Portsmouth with the night goods from Nine Elms. (With so much electrification east of Portsmouth the diagrammers sometimes had to stretch their ingenuity to keep engines working and this particular example was given a filling-in turn to Salisbury before returning to London with a parcels train from Eastleigh).

Apart from the two light Pacifics which swept through with the through services between Brighton and Cardiff/Plymouth, the only sign of modernisation was seen in the form of one of the new BR4 2-6-0's which in early 1953 had displaced a D15 4-4-0 from the 09.33 Portsmouth - Cardiff. (It should not be thought that the arrival of the new era made the D15's redundant overnight since 1953 saw a number transferred to Nine Elms for the summer-only through service between Waterloo and Lymington Pier - no small compliment for a class that was, to say the least, getting a little long in the tooth by the Coronation year). The first of the replacement engines was BR 4MT 2-6-0 76005 which arrived at Eastleigh MPD on the 3rd January 1953 specifically for the Portsmouth - Salisbury workings. Further standard 2-6-0's, 76006-13, followed a month later although appearances by D15 4-4-0's on Portsmouth - Salisbury services continued well after a year following the arrival of the standard engines.

The D15 - massive looking 4-4-0's with a long association with the Portsmouth - Salisbury workings fought tenaciously to survive and two survivors were retained at Nine Elms for the Lymington service until June 1955 when the workings were taken over by U class 2-6-0's. Occasionally - when Nine Elms was especially pressed for motive power - a D15 could be found at the head of a Waterloo - Basingstoke stopper; an unusual occurrence but one which paled in contrast to the use of S11 4-4-0 30400 on the 12.39 Waterloo - Basingstoke on Saturday 12th June 1954, a month before its withdrawal. The D15's lingered on until the winter of 1955 when the last survivors were taken out of traffic from Eastleigh shed.

The new standard engines did not immediately reduce appearances by the old order and considerable excitement was generated locally in early 1953 by the loan of Brighton 4-4-2, 32421 'South Foreland', to Fratton who used it regularly on the 09.03 Portsmouth - Salisbury and the 18.57 (16.32 ex Bristol) return. The

penetration by a Brighton Atlantic so far as Salisbury would have been unique in itself but the engine was also employed on the intermediate stage of the duty, the 11.04 Salisbury to Yeovil Junction and the 16.05 Yeovil Town to Salisbury. The loan of the engine by Brighton MPD suggested a unusual degree of magnanimity since the depot was experiencing extraordinary problems with its allocation of Bulleid light Pacifics, it being nothing unusual to have all five out of action at the same time leaving the West Coast expresses - the through train to Bournemouth in particular - to be worked by either an Atlantic or a 2-6-4 tank. The situation eventually declined to such an extent that in the autumn of 1954 the Bournemouth train was diagrammed to be worked by a 4-4-2.

The greatest variety of trains and motive power was to be seen at the Eastern end of the line since many of the MSW services, which joined the route at Kimbridge Junction, were

powered by Great Western locomotives, the majority of which were 43xx moguls although a Manor 4-6-0 made a daily appearance on the 10.11 Cheltenham to Southampton Terminus and the 16.36 return. Another stranger was the Swindon-based 45xx 2-6-2T which recessed overnight at Andover Junction but penetrated SR territory by working the 06.48 Cheltenham - Romsey goods from Andover Junction.

Great Western locomotives were much less in evidence west of Kimbridge Junction and only one representative of the GWR was booked to make an appearance, a Bristol 43xx 2-6-0 working an afternoon goods from Salisbury to Eastleigh and returning with an evening passenger train.

Whilst the line played host to quite a busy service of passenger trains - services ran from Portsmouth to Salisbury at intervals of roughly ninety minutes - its role as a freight carrier was no less significant with ten daily goods services

TRAIN MOVEMENTS : ROMSEY (1953)					
Train	Arr	Loco	Diagram	Dep	Destination
11.25 Andover Jcn	12.03	T9 4-4-0	Eastleigh 248	12.04	Eastleigh
10.23 Bevois Park		H15 4-6-0	Eastleigh 312	12/06	Salisbury
11.30 Bevois Park		43xx 2-6-0	Cheltenham 21	12/21	Andover Jcn
11.27 Salisbury		S15 4-6-0	Feltham 116	12/22	Eastleigh
12.00 Southampton (T)	12.35	M7 0-4-4T	Fratton 371		
11.19 Portsmouth	12.44	LM2 2-6-2T	Eastleigh 306	12.47	Andover Jcn
10.27 BRISTOL		BR4 2-6-0	Eastleigh 270	13/06	PORTSMOUTH
11.00 BRIGHTON		WC 4-6-2	Brighton 731	13/08	CARDIFF
		M7 0-4-4T	Fratton 371	13.15	Portsmouth
06.48 Cheltenham		45xx 2-6-2T	Swindon 74	13.23	
11.30 BRIGHTON		WC 4-6-2	Brighton 732	13/35	PLYMOUTH
13.06 Salisbury	13.36	T9 4-4-0	Salisbury 443	13.37	Southampton (T)
12.24 Eastleigh	13.40	M7 0-4-4T	Eastleigh 329		
10.11 Cheltenham	13.42	Manor 4-6-0	Cheltenham 22	13.44	Southampton (T)
10.30 CARDIFF	13.50	BR4 2-6-0	Eastleigh 272	13.53	PORTSMOUTH
13.03 Portmouth	14.04	T9 4-4-0	Salisbury 445	14.05	Salisbury
		M7 0-4-4T	Eastleigh 329	14.05	Eastleigh
		45xx 2-6-2T	Swindon 74	14.12	Andover Jcn
12.14 Fullerton	14.16	T9 4-4-0	Andover Jcn 246		
		T9 4-4-0	Andover Jcn 246	14.35	Nursling
11.00 PLYMOUTH		WC 4-6-2	Brighton 731	15/17	BRIGHTON
15.14 Nursling	15.24	T9 4-4-0	Andover Jcn 246		
11.18 Salisbury	15.25	H15 4-6-0	Nine Elms 72		(Eastleigh)
14.33 Portsmouth	15.34	U 2-6-0	Yeovil 485	15.36	Bristol
(11.18 Salisbury)		H15 4-6-0	Nine Elms 72	15.45	Eastleigh
15.07 Salisbury		43xx 2-6-0	Bristol 365	16/02	S'ton Docks
13.00 CARDIFF		WC 4-6-2	Brighton 732	16/19	BRIGHTON
15.45 Portsmouth	16.49	T9 4-4-0	Andover Jcn 248		
16.12 Andover Jcn	16.50	LM2 2-6-2T	Andover Jcn 247		
16.36 Southampton (T)	16.58	Manor 4-6-0	Cheltenham 22	17.00	Cheltenham
		LM2 2-6-2T	Andover Jcn 247	17.03	Southampton (T)
16.18 Salisbury		H15 4-6-0	Eastleigh 312	17/13	Eastleigh
13.56 Cheltenham	17.22	43xx 2-6-0	Andover Jcn 250	17.23	Southampton (T)
17.16 Eastleigh	17.31	M7 0-4-4T	Eastleigh 305		
17.07 Salisbury	17.36	T9 4-4-0	Eastleigh 284	17.39	Portsmouth
		T9 & M7	248/305	17.50	Eastleigh
14.20 Weymouth	17.57	T9 4-4-0	Eastleigh 282	18.00	Andover Jcn
		T9 4-4-0	Andover Jcn 246	18.05	Eastleigh
16.45 Portsmouth	18.14	U 2-6-0	Salisbury 450	18.17	Salisbury
17.16 Fawley	18.45	T9 4-4-0	Eastleigh 280		
17.45 PORTSMOUTH	18.59	BR4 2-6-0	Eastleigh 272	19.01	CARDIFF
		T9 4-4-0	Eastleigh 280	19.07	Andover Jcn
18.40 Andover Jcn	19.17	L1 4-4-0	Eastleigh 309		
16.32 Bristol	19.25	U 2-6-0	Fratton 368	19.28	Portsmouth
		L1 4-4-0	Eastleigh 309	19.35	Eastleigh
19.20 Eastleigh	19.35	M7 0-4-4T	Eastleigh 298		
ECS		M7 0-4-4T	Eastleigh 298	19.50	Eastleigh
16.35 CARDIFF	20.08	U 2-6-0	Yeovil 482	20.09	PORTSMOUTH
19.04 Southampton (Docks)		43xx 2-6-0	Andover Jcn 250	20/09	Andover Jcn
19.35 Andover Jcn	20.18	T9 4-4-0	Eastleigh 282	20.21	Eastleigh
19.17 Portsmouth	20.43	T9 4-4-0	Salisbury 443	20.45	Salisbury
16.35 Exeter	20.46	S15 4-6-0	Feltham 101	20.48	Portsmouth
20.50 Eastleigh		Q1 0-6-0	Guildford 213	21/15	Salisbury
19.45 Portsmouth	21.23	T9 4-4-0	B'mouth 403	21.24	Andover Jcn
15.20 Cheltenham		BR4 2-6-0	Eastleigh 316	22/00	Eastleigh
21.44 Eastleigh	21.59	43xx 2-6-0	Bristol 31	22.03	Salisbury
19.10 Bristol	22.31	S15 4-6-0	Salisbury 467	22.34	Eastleigh
16.40 PLYMOUTH		BR4 2-6-0	Eastleigh 272	23/35	EASTLEIGH

M7 0-4-4T 30130 comes to a halt in Chandlers Ford with the 15.04 Romsey to Eastleigh on 7th September 1957 during the period when diesel units were starting to appear and an interval timetable had been introduced for the Hampshire local services. 30130 was something of a newcomer to rural workings and had for many years been a Nine Elms engine, tripping empty stock between Waterloo and Clapham Junction, being transferred to Eastleigh in August 1954. By coincidence, as if to cling on to its London past, the incorrect indicator suggests the train is the 08.45 Woking - Salisbury - a Nine Elms N15 duty.

Had history taken a different turn - or had the SECR main line been in better condition - 31808 might have spent most of its days as a top link 2-6-4T working London - Ramsgate express services. As things turned out the former 'River Char' only worked for nine months in its original form, reappearing in July 1928 as a U Class 2-6-0. It is seen thirty years after being rebuilt at the head of the 09.47 Salisbury - Portsmouth service whilst passing Kimbridge junction. The line diverging to the right is the branch to Andover Junction and, ultimately, Cheltenham.

31805, passing Dunbridge with the 10.30 Cardiff - Portsmouth express in July 1957, was the first of the U Class to make an appearance, taking to the rails in March 1928, having spent the previous year and a half as 2-6-4T 'River Camel'. The train was also of interest and had, until early 1953, been one of the last long distance workings for a D15 4-4-0.

T9 4-4-0 30300 of Eastleigh restarts the 06.45 Andover Junction to Eastleigh from Clatford on the Andover Junction to Kimbridge Junction branch. The train was part of a cyclic duty which saw the engine spending successive nights at Eastleigh, Bournemouth and Andover Junction.

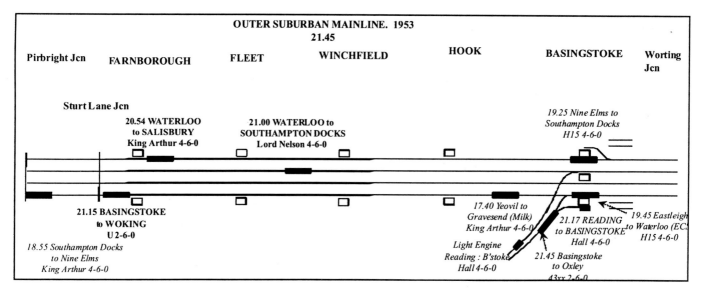

OUTER SUBURBAN MAINLINE. 1953
21.45

Pirbright Jcn   **FARNBOROUGH**   **FLEET**   **WINCHFIELD**   **HOOK**   **BASINGSTOKE**   Worting
Jcn

Sturt Lane Jcn

20.54 WATERLOO   21.00 WATERLOO to   19.25 Nine Elms to
to SALISBURY   SOUTHAMPTON DOCKS   Southampton Docks
King Arthur 4-6-0   Lord Nelson 4-6-0   H15 4-6-0

21.15 BASINGSTOKE   17.40 Yeovil to   19.45 Eastleigh
to WOKING   Gravesend (Milk)   to Waterloo (EC)
U 2-6-0   King Arthur 4-6-0   21.17 READING   H15 4-6-0
                                                                            to BASINGSTOKE
18.55 Southampton Docks   Light Engine   Hall 4-6-0
to Nine Elms   Reading : B'stoke   21.45 Basingstoke
King Arthur 4-6-0   Hall 4-6-0   to Oxley
                                                                             43xx 2-6-0

running eastwards from Salisbury; much of the traffic consisting of industrial and household coal from the South Wales coalfield to Hampshire and Sussex. In Edwardian times the volume of coal had been considerable with much of the steam coal for shipping based upon Southampton and Portsmouth coming from South Wales via Salisbury. This traffic, however, declined in the wake of a miners strike in 1910 which brought home to the Royal Navy the extent to which it was dependent upon coal and resulted in a change to oil fuel; a move imitated by the Merchant Navy a few years afterwards. Surprisingly this change had little effect on the number of goods trains on the line which in 1953 was the same as that of 1910.

Motive power used on the goods services which passed through Romsey was as varied as that of the passenger trains and ranged from the unlikely - M7 0-4-4 tanks and 'Greyhound' 4-4-0's - to the curiously shaped Q1 0-6-0's which were commonplace in London and parts of Kent but less often seen in east Hampshire. Eastleigh possessed three of the type - one of which worked a night goods to Salisbury and back - and a member of Guildford's eight-strong allocation could also be seen each evening as it headed west to work home with a through service to Chichester.

Further west towards Salisbury the eighteen mile single line branch between Alderbury Junction and West Moors, which allowed direct running from Salisbury to Bournemouth and Wey-

mouth, was probably the last remaining example of a route worked entirely by pre-Urie locomotives, a feature due more to the restricted nature of the line than a fondness for the products of Drummond.

All nine passenger workings (five up and four down) were booked to be handled by T9 4-4-0's (one from Eastleigh and three from Salisbury) with the two goods trains in each direction being worked by Salisbury-based '700' class 0-6-0's. Most of the passenger trains operated between Salisbury and Bournemouth West although one service, the 03.52 from Salisbury, operated through to Weymouth and could claim to be a through train from Waterloo given that its formation included a newspaper van transferred from the 01.25 Waterloo - West of England at Salisbury. The 01.25 was, in actual fact, the best way of making the overnight journey between London and Weymouth since the 22.30 from Waterloo pitched its passengers out at Dorchester in the middle of the night whilst

the 02.40 departure terminated at Bournemouth Central with over an hour to wait for the Weymouth connection which did not reach its destination until 08.50, six hours after leaving London. Those Weymouth passengers who knew about the 01.25 were not only able to complete their journey in four and three-quarter hours with only one change of train but were able to claim, if they had any interest in engines, that they had experienced extremes of the ancient and modern, the Salisbury T9 4-4-0 giving way to a Bulleid West Country 4-6-2 at Wimborne.

Finally there were the humble M7 0-4-4 tanks which bustled between Eastleigh and Andover Junction, occasionally terminating at Romsey. They were slowly being replaced by LMS 2MT 2-6-2T's but the pace of change was slow and the M7's remained in action well after the arrival of the Hampshire multiple-units and even by the end of 1961, ten of the 0-4-4T's remained on the books at Eastleigh. It was heartening to stand next to an M7 at somewhere like Romsey and reflect on the changes the engine had seen in its long existence - most of the class operated the pre-electrification London suburban service - and the different circumstances it had worked under.

TRAIN MOVEMENTS : FORDINGBRIDGE (1953)					
Train	Arr	Engine	Diagram	Dep	Destination
03.52 Salisbury	04.20	T9 4-4-0	Salisbury 443	04.23	Weymouth
04.05 Salisbury (Goods)	*05.08*	*700 0-6-0*	*Salisbury 452*	*05.18*	*Bournemouth (C)*
07.15 Salisbury	07.45	T9 4-4-0	Salisbury 444	07.50	Bournemouth (W)
07.14 Broadstone	07.48	T9 4-4-0	Eastleigh 294	07.49	Salisbury
07.42 Bournemouth (C)	08.39	T9 4-4-0	Salisbury 443	08.40	Salisbury
09.25 Salisbury	09.52	T9 4-4-0	Eastleigh 294	09.53	Bournemouth (W)
10.00 Salisbury (Milford)	*11.38*	*700 0-6-0*	*Salisbury 451*	*12.28*	*Wimborne*
13.20 Bournemouth (W)	14.22	T9 4-4-0	Eastleigh 294	14.24	Salisbury
17.20 Salisbury	17.48	T9 4-4-0	Salisbury 445	17.53	Bournemouth (W)
16.52 Bournemouth (W)	17.49	T9 4-4-0	Salisbury 444	17.52	Salisbury
17.26 Wimborne (Goods)	*18.23*	*700 0-6-0*	*Salisbury 451*	*18.43*	*Salisbury (Milford)*
18.40 Wimborne (Goods)	*19.52*	*700 0-6-0*	*Salisbury 452*	*20.07*	*Salisbury (GW)*
19.43 Bournemouth (W)	20.37	T9 4-4-0	Salisbury 445	20.38	Salisbury
Goods services in italics					

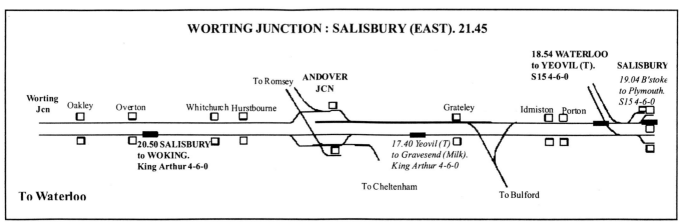

WORTING JUNCTION : SALISBURY (EAST). 21.45

18.54 WATERLOO
to YEOVIL (T).   **SALISBURY**
S15 4-6-0

To Romsey   **ANDOVER**   19.04 B'stoke
JCN   to Plymouth.
S15 4-6-0

Worting   Oakley   Overton   Whitchurch Hurstbourne   Grateley   Idmiston   Porton
Jcn

20.50 SALISBURY   17.40 Yeovil (T)
to WOKING.   to Gravesend (Milk).
King Arthur 4-6-0   King Arthur 4-6-0

To Cheltenham   To Bulford

To Waterloo

On the direct line from Salisbury to Dorset, T9 4-4-0 30300, above, arrives at Daggons Road with the 10.04 Bournemouth (West) to Salisbury on the 1st of October 1955 whilst, below, the T9 domination of the route is challenged by standard BR4 2-6-0 76008 as it emerges from Downton tunnel with the 17.20 Salisbury to Bournemouth on 25 June 1955. The standard 2-6-0's arrived on the South Western at Christmas 1952; a batch being allocated to Eastleigh in order to displace some of the elderly 4-4-0's in the district. 76008 moved to Salisbury in June 1955 and is seen on one of its first outings over the West Moors branch. Although the line was something of a backwater and a haunt of elderly 4-4-0's, during July and August it saw modernity in the form of a Bulleid light Pacific, one of the class being diagrammed for the 09.05 Salisbury - Weymouth and 18.20 return.

SALISBURY

In the light of the success of the Maunsell N15's, a larger four-cylinder 4-6-0 was produced in 1926 to handle the heavy west of England traffic between Waterloo and Exeter. It came therefore as a considerable disappointment to the Southern to learn that the new engines, the Lord Nelson 4-6-0's, were generally indistinguishable in performance from the much smaller King Arthur class. Numerous modifications, including the fitting of multiple jet blastpipes, were made to the class by both Maunsell and Bulleid and although some improvement in performance by the late 1930's was obtained, the war prevented any further developments whilst at the same time Bulleid preferred to pursue his own line of thought rather than to devote time and materials to a type of engine he regarded as obsolete. Although originally divided between the LSWR and SECR routes - working the Dover Continental services on the latter - the Lord Nelsons were congregated on the South Western for the last twenty years of their lives; half the allocation being based at Eastleigh for service on the Southampton boat trains and the balance being divided between Nine Elms (three engines) and Bournemouth. In the upper view 30853 'Sir Richard Grenville' of Eastleigh stands in the gloom of Salisbury loco after arriving with the 10.54 ex Waterloo. The Lord Nelson worked a long day - almost 23 hours - which commenced with the 06.04 from Southampton terminus to Waterloo and ended with the 23.25 express goods from Nine Elms. It returned to London from Salisbury with the 16.05 semi-fast to Waterloo. On the adjacent line is another Eastleigh 4-6-0, H14 30474, which is being prepared for the 16.18 goods to Eastleigh.

Understandably most of the activity towards the Western end of the district was overshadowed by the attractions of Salisbury which diverted attention from quieter but equally interesting locations with the result that there are rather more gaps than one would wish in the railway chronologies of places like Andover Junction and Romsey.

An old cathedral city largely ignored by the industrial revolution, Salisbury had railway importance thrust upon it by dint of the fact it was the cross-roads of the main line and the Portsmouth to Bristol route. It was also located half way between London and Exeter and because of this was the obvious point at which engines of through trains were changed and freight trains remarshalled.

There were four major goods yards at Salisbury, one - Fisherton - a Great Western facility where outward traffic was stabled prior to be

taken over the GWR via Westbury, and three belonging to the Southern: the East and West Yards which looked after up and down SR traffic respectively plus Milford goods yard which was situated some way from the passenger station on a branch off the Romsey line.

As a general rule GW goods services ran through the station and terminated in the East yard, the engines then running light to Fisherton to pick up their return workings. Up services from the Wilton direction also terminated in the East Yard whilst down workings from the east finished their journeys in the West Yard. There was, of course, a considerable amount of trip working between the four yards - most of it performed with train engines - whilst a large Z class 0-8-0T was engaged twenty-two hours a day in the East Yard. Terminating traffic for Salisbury was dealt with at Milford, trains from the Romsey and Wimborne lines detaching

whilst en route to the East Yard, traffic from other directions being tripped locally from the East Yard.

The greater part of the goods traffic worked into Salisbury came from the Great Western who operated a total of nine daily services, six coming from South Wales, two from Bristol and a local goods from Westbury. The variety of power used was as diverse as could be wished with five different classes of locomotive being diagrammed. 43xx moguls and a Grange 4-6-0 were employed on the Bristol and Westbury workings whilst most of the Welsh services used something heavier, usually a 2-8-2 tank or a 28xx 2-8-0.

The lack of through goods workings between the Great Western and Southampton - where most of the traffic was destined - is an interesting reminder of the barriers that not only existed between the pre-1948 companies but

The LBSCR electrification of the 1930's resulted in a surplus of locomotives some of which were transferred to other parts of the Southern Railway as replacements for more elderly indigenous engines. E4 0-6-2T 32506 (named 'Catherington' until 1910) was for many years a Littlehampton and Norwood Junction engine but in June 1951 moved to the LSWR at Salisbury for shunting in Fisherton Yard after the closure of the GWR motive power depot. It was not however the first time the engine had worked away from the LBSCR since in 1917 it, along with eleven other members of the class, had been seconded to the war effort, working on the Western Front until the armistice and subsequently in ordinary service in Belgium until being repatriated in the spring of 1919. Seen in 1952, it was regarded as a poor substitute for a GWR pannier 0-6-0T and aroused a great deal of adverse comment from the GWR footplate staff at Salisbury. Little notice was paid to these complaints, insult being added to injury when 32506 was joined by classmate 32486 in June 1952. 32506 remained at Salisbury until August 1955 when it was transferred to Guildford.

continued to persist a generation or more after nationalisation.

As mentioned above the GWR ran their goods trains as far as Salisbury - usually to the East Yard - and then scurried back to Fisherton sidings to pick up a train of empties and get back to civilisation as quickly as possible. Had the Great Western realised that life existed beyond Salisbury it should not have been the most difficult thing on earth to have worked most of their trains, probably with Westbury crews, through to Eastleigh or Southampton which would not only have saved a number of engines but might have allowed Salisbury to have concentrated all its freight operations in a single yard.

As it was the system carried on in a style that would have been recognisable half a century earlier and although it provided enthusiasts with a vista of entertainment (and kept those of us who were railwaymen happily occupied) the benefits that could have been realised had the regions recognised each other were innumerable.

It is generally believed that rationalisation on a large scale was deferred because of the historic sanctity attached to regional/railway boundaries and although conservatism played a part it was not by any means the principal brake on development. (All the same, an outsider would have been amazed to learn exactly how much of an alien someone from another railway (or region) was. Westbury, less than twenty fine miles from Salisbury, might as well have been in China: ones horizons were those of ones railway).

One of the deterrents was the volume of traffic that existed in the 1950's which was so great that most attempts to make improvements in the working very quickly became bogged down in a mass of detail. Most railwaymen, at all levels, had quite enough on their plate in keeping the existing railway running smoothly without wondering how changes - which would almost certainly run counter to traditional understandings - could be introduced.

But the greatest bar to change, especially as rationalisation invariably led to staff reductions, was the managerial salary structure which was based very largely on the number of people controlled or supervised. Any plans to reduce the complement automatically placed the

TRAINS MOVEMENTS : BULFORD BRANCH (1953)					
DOWN					
Train	Engine	Amesbury Jcn	Newton Tony	Amesbury	Bulford
06.10 Salisbury	700 0-6-0	6/35	06.40		
			6.55	07.10	
				07.18 (Pcls)	7.23
05.30 Basingstoke	700 0-6-0		7.36		
			7.51	8.05	
				8.45	8.51
Light ex Salisbury	700 0-6-0	13/30		13.44	
UP					
Engine	Bulford	Amesbury	Newton Tony	Amesbury Jcn	Destination
700 0-6-0		09.10		9.24	Salisbury mpd
700 0-6-0		14.45		15/05	Salisbury
700 0-6-0		16.35			Basingstoke

The train working on the Bulford branch after the withdrawal of passenger services. Two 700 0-6-0's were in daily use, one working in from Basingstoke and the other from Salisbury. The Salisbury service terminated at Amesbury, the engine proceeding forward to Bulford with a parcels vehicle before returning light to Salisbury. The Basingstoke train followed an hour later and picked up the Salisbury traffic at Amesbury before proceeding forward. The 0-6-0 remained on the branch for most of the day, shunting between Bulford and Amesbury as required and returned to Basingstoke with a local goods in the evening. Outward traffic for Salisbury was worked away in the afternoon by an 700 which ran light from Salisbury MPD. Shunting staff for the branch was provided by Porton, the shunter being picked up and returned by the Salisbury trip.

Before and after. With the evening sun reflecting from its casing, Rebuilt West Country 4-6-2 34046 'Braunton' eases the 13.00 Cardiff to Brighton away from Salisbury in 1952 having just taken the train over from a Canton Castle 4-6-0. 34046, together with four other members of the class, was a longtime exile at Brighton - the only Pacifics to be allocated to the LBSCR section - used for working the through trains to Plymouth, Cardiff and Bournemouth. The availability of the five engines was not good and although the Plymouth and Cardiff usually managed to have one of the Brighton Pacifics as far as Salisbury, the Bournemouth service was often given an Atlantic or 2-6-4T because of power shortages. 34046 was rebuilt in February 1959 and transferred to Bournemouth where it remained until withdrawal in October 1965 after a working life of twenty-one years. It is seen below on 4th July 1964 at Basingstoke with the 11.16 Bournemouth (West) to Newcastle express.

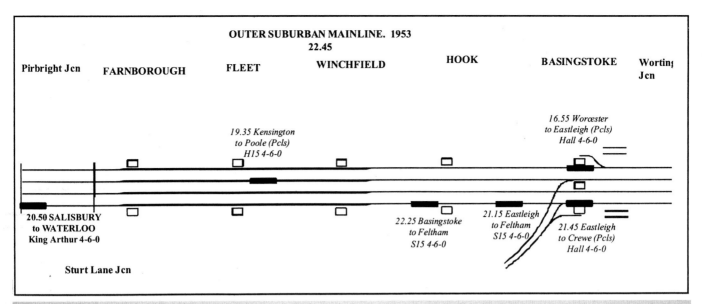

OUTER SUBURBAN MAINLINE. 1953
22.45

| Pirbright Jcn | FARNBOROUGH | FLEET | WINCHFIELD | HOOK | BASINGSTOKE | Worting Jcn |

16.55 Worcester to Eastleigh (Pcls) Hall 4-6-0

19.35 Kensington to Poole (Pcls) H15 4-6-0

20.50 SALISBURY to WATERLOO King Arthur 4-6-0

22.25 Basingstoke to Feltham S15 4-6-0

21.15 Eastleigh to Feltham S15 4-6-0

21.45 Eastleigh to Crewe (Pcls) Hall 4-6-0

Sturt Lane Jcn

BR standard locomotives did not appear in large numbers on the LSWR until very late in the day and for the first half of the 1950's were largely limited to a handful of 4MT moguls which could be seen on the Portsmouth - Salisbury workings as replacements for D15 4-4-0's. An unidentified representative of the Eastleigh allocation arrives at Salisbury with a through service for the Great Western in the mid-1950's.

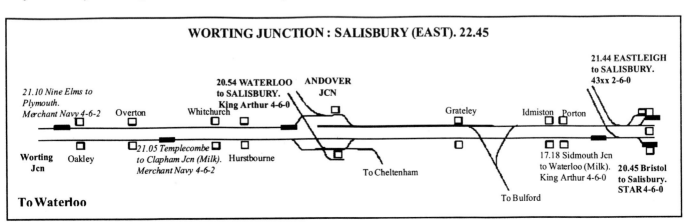

WORTING JUNCTION : SALISBURY (EAST). 22.45

21.44 EASTLEIGH to SALISBURY. 43xx 2-6-0

21.10 Nine Elms to Plymouth. Merchant Navy 4-6-2

Overton

Whitchurch

20.54 WATERLOO to SALISBURY. King Arthur 4-6-0

ANDOVER JCN

Grateley

Idmiston Porton

Worting Jcn

Oakley

21.05 Templecombe to Clapham Jcn (Milk). Merchant Navy 4-6-2

Hurstbourne

To Cheltenham

17.18 Sidmouth Jcn to Waterloo (Milk). King Arthur 4-6-0

20.45 Bristol to Salisbury. STAR 4-6-0

To Bulford

To Waterloo

Train	Arr	Engine	Diagram	Dep	Destination
19.10 Bristol		S15 4-6-0	Salisbury 467*	22.00	Eastleigh
21.05 Templecombe	21.50	MN 4-6-2	N. Elms 5	22.05	C. Jcn (Milk)
20.56 Eastleigh	22.18	Q1 0-6-0	Guildford 236	22.20	Fisherton Yard
21.44 Eastleigh	22.36	43xx 2-6-0	Bristol 365		
17.18 Sidmouth Jcn	22.25	N15 4-6-0	Salisbury 432/2*		Waterloo (Milk)
17.18 Sidmouth Jcn		N15 4-6-0	N. Elms 11*	22.40	Waterloo (Milk)
20.45 Bristol	22.41	Star 4-6-0	Bristol 121		
(From East Yard)		H15 4-6-0	Salisbury 470	22.50	Basingstoke
16.40 Plymouth	22.52	MN 4-6-2	Salisbury 431*		Eastleigh
16.40 Plymouth		BR4 2-6-0	Eastleigh 272*	23.10	Eastleigh
20.54 WATERLOO	23.20	N15 4-6-0	Salisbury 436		
22.20 Templecombe	23.20	S15 4-6-0	Salisbury 467*	23.30	Fisherton Yard
21.10 Nine Elms	23.37	MN 4-6-2	Exmouth 497	23.45	Plymouth
12.45 Torrington	23.43	WC 4-6-2	Salisbury 432/2*		East Yard
12.45 Torrington		N15 4-6-0	N. Elms 10*	00.13	Nine Elms
21.50 Bristol East		Grange 4-6-0	Bristol 366	00/20	East Yard
22.00 Nine Elms	00.40	MN 4-6-2	Salisbury 461	00.41	Exmouth Jcn
00.20 Eastleigh	01.30	Q1 0-6-0	Eastleigh 319	01.31	West Yard
(From East Yard)		U 2-6-0	Salisbury 450	01.35	Eastleigh
17.00 Torrington	01.32	MN 4-6-2	N. Elms 7	01.40	Nine Elms
13.55 Meldon	02.03	H15 4-6-0	Salisbury 440	02.20	Woking
17.21 Plymouth	02.37	S15 4-6-0	Salisbury 471	02.40	East Yard
01.55 Eastleigh	02.36	U 2-6-0	Salisbury 482	02.50	Yeovil (T)
01.25 WATERLOO	03.11	MN 4-6-2	Exmouth 498	03.19	Plymouth
(From East Yard)		Q1 0-6-0	Guildford 237	03.30	Chichester
02.10 Bevois Pk (S'ton)	03.43	S15 4-6-0	Salisbury 467	03.44	West Yard
00.23 Woking	03.48	H15 4-6-0	Salisbury 441	03.55	Exmouth Jcn
		T9 4-4-0	Salisbury 443	03.52	Weymouth
(From East Yard)		700 0-6-0	Salisbury 452	04.05	Bournemouth (C)
(From East Yard)		S15 4-6-0	Salisbury 471	04.15	Milford Yard
22.00 Avonmouth		43xx 2-6-0	Bristol 365	04/23	East Yard
(From East Yard)		Q1 0-6-0	Eastleigh 319	04.25	Northam (S'ton)
(From East Yard)		N15 4-6-0	Salisbury 436	04.35	Feltham
23.58 Feltham	04.35	S15 4-6-0	Feltham 115*		Exmouth Jcn
23.58 Feltham		S15 4-6-0	Salisbury 467*	04.55	Exmouth Jcn
21.30 Okehampton	04.33	H15 4-6-0	Salisbury 441	04.55	Woking
05.05 West Yard		700 0-6-0	Salisbury 454	05/10	Milford Yard
14.58 Gravesend (Milk)	04.07	N15 4-6-0	Salisbury 432	05.15	Yeovil (T)
03.58 Bevois Pk (S'ton)	05.30	H15 4-6-0	Eastleigh 311	05.32	Fisherton Yard
19.45 Bassaleg		28xx 2-8-0	STJ 351	05/40	East Yard
03.30 Basingstoke	05.40	H15 4-6-0	Salisbury 439	05.42	West Yard
(From East Yard)		700 0-6-0	Salisbury 454	06.10	Bulford
16.40 Wadebridge	06.25	S15 4-6-0	Salisbury 435	06.27	East yard
		WC 4-6-2	Salisbury 430	06.45	WATERLOO
07.00 East Yard		S15 4-6-0	Salisbury 435	07/05	West Yard
		T9 4-4-0	Salisbury 444	07.15	B'mouth (W)
		M7 0-4-4T	Salisbury 447	07.20	Grateley
07.37 West Yard		700 0-6-0	Salisbury 451	07/42	Wimborne
		T9 4-4-0	Salisbury 445	07.47	Portsmouth
01.00 Cardiff		Hall 4-6-0	Canton 354	08.06	East Yard
Light engine Grateley		M7 0-4-4T	Salisbury 447	08/10	MPD
		MN 4-6-2	Salisbury 431	08.15	WATERLOO
07.14 Broadstone	08.19	T9 4-4-0	Eastleigh 284		
05.25 Swindon	08.25	Hall 4-6-0	Bristol 64		
05.58 Portsmouth & S	08.31	U 2-6-0	Salisbury 450		
07.10 YEOVIL (T)	08.33	N15 4-6-0	Salisbury 432	08.42	WATERLOO
(From East Yard)		H15 4-6-0	Eastleigh 311	08.45	Fratton
06.33 Woking	08.49	N15 4-6-0	N. Elms 2	09.24	Templecombe
07.42 Bournemouth	09.10	T9 4-4-0	Salisbury 443		
07.29 PORTSMOUTH	09.16	H15 4-6-0	N. Elms 72	09.34	BRISTOL
		T9 4-4-0	Eastleigh 284	09.25	B'mouth (W)
07.30 EXETER	09.27	MN 4-6-2	Exmouth 495	09.33	WATERLOO
21.15 Aberdare		Hall 4-6-0	Aberdare 353	09/40	East Yard
Light engine Amesbury		700 0-6-0	Salisbury 454	09/44	MPD
		U 2-6-0	Yeovil 485	09.47	Portsmouth
09.45 East yard		S15 4-6-0	Salisbury 435	09/50	West Yard
07.20 WATERLOO	09.58	N15 4-6-0	N. Elms 3		
06.30 EXETER	09.53	MN 4-6-2	Exmouth 494	10.01	WATERLOO
03.00 Brighton		S15 4-6-0	Feltham 106	10/22	Fisherton Yard
08.10 BRISTOL	10.27	Star 4-6-0	Bristol 120*		PORTSMOUTH
08.10 BRISTOL		U 2-6-0	Salisbury 450*	10.37	PORTSMOUTH
09.03 Portsmouth	10.41	U 2-6-0	Fratton 368		
(From East Yard)		S15 4-6-0	Salisbury 438	10.42	Basingstoke
09.00 WATERLOO	10.50	MN 4-6-2	N. Elms 4	10.56	PLYMOUTH
02.35 Radyr		72xx 2-8-2T	Radyr 352	10/54	East Yard

Goods trains in italics. * = engine change. "/" = passing time.

manager's own salary and status in question and keen though most were on the need to introduce working improvements, a line was drawn at kamikaze tactics. (To be generally condemnatory about the railway's reluctance to change rapidly is to misunderstand the ethos of the 1950's. Most large organisations had changed but little in half a century - very few people saw any reason why they should - and structural emphasis tended more towards tradition rather than the sort of dynamism that became a way of life ten years later).

Not everything remained static and perhaps the most momentous change in the working of the district came in 1950 with the decision to cease the engine change that had traditionally been made to the Waterloo - Exeter expresses. No attempt however was made to extend the limits worked by train crews who continued to relieve at Salisbury and in fact the savings made from the increased locomotive utilisation were compromised to some extent by an agreement which provided for additional sets of men located at the passenger station whose principal duty was to shovel coal from the rear to the front of engine tenders whilst the crews were being relieved. Of greater concern to the footplatemen was the overall loss of jobs such as those concerned with the preparation and disposal of express engines which, combined with the duties lost following the run-down of the Bulford branch, cast something of a pall in the messroom. Motive power personnel were always more sensitive to the loss of jobs rather than locomotives.

The arrangements had the effect of putting Salisbury rather in the shade so far as the prestige locomotive duties were concerned and after the implementation of the through working the shed was left with only three express workings per day - two Merchant Navy and one light Pacific - together with a pair of King Arthur 4-6-0's, one of which worked a goods service to Feltham.

Other traffic was unaffected, apart from the small number of goods trains which balanced the Merchant Navy duties by running through, and ten goods or mixed traffic 4-6-0's were booked off the shed in the course of a normal day. Traffic towards Romsey and Wimborne was catered for by a batch of T9 4-4-0's whilst an M7 0-4-4T was retained for carriage shunting and the unadvertised workmans service to and from Grateley.

The allocation of engines to Salisbury declined from 66 to 56 locomotives between 1949 and 1954, the greater part of the loss coming from the smaller and older types - M7 0-4-4T's no longer being required for the Bulford branch whilst the loss of five Pacifics following the through running arrangements between London and Exeter was balanced by the addition of six S15 4-6-0's. Full details of movements over the period are given in the accompanying table.

Although the loss of its involvement with most of the long distance express traffic appeared as a move to downgrade the status of the shed, in fact the workings effected had only been a small proportion of Salisbury's motive power activities and the shed continued to work to a very exacting schedule, details of which can be seen in the accompanying booking out arrangement, showing the engines that were booked off the shed to take up workings together with the time stale engines (i.e. locomo-

90

Train	Arr	Engine	Diagram	Dep	Destination
09.33 PORTSMOUTH	11.05	BR4 2-6-0	Eastleigh 270	11.17	CARDIFF
(From East Yard		S15 4-6-0	*Feltham 116*	*11.27*	*Chichester*
10.45 Basingstoke	11.52	N15 4-6-0	N. Elms 1		
09.30 Eastleigh	*12.05*	*BR4 2-6-0*	*Eastleigh 316*		*(Arrives Milford)*
07.35 Westbury		*43xx 2-6-0*	*Westbury 28*	*12/20*	*East Yard*
10.34 PORTSMOUTH	12.18	BR4 2-6-0	Eastleigh 272*	12.35	BRISTOL
11.00 WATERLOO	12.23	MN 4-6-2	N.Elms 5	12.28	PLYMOUTH
08.15 PLYMOUTH	12.28	MN 4-6-2	Exmouth 496	12.34	WATERLOO
10.27 BRISTOL	12.37	Hall 4-6-0	Canton 38*		PORTSMOUTH
10.27 BRISTOL		BR4 2-6-0	Eastleigh 270*	12.44	PORTSMOUTH
10.23 Bevois Park	*12.52*	*H15 4-6-0*	*Eastleigh 312*	*13.08*	*Rogerstone*
		S15 4-6-0	Salisbury 435	13.00	WATERLOO
		T9 4-4-0	Salisbury 443	13.06	S'ton (T)
10.30 BRISTOL	13.21	Castle 4-6-(	Bristol 10		PORTSMOUTH
10.54 WATERLOO	13.24	LN 4-6-0	Eastleigh 251		
10.30 BRISTOL		BR4 2-6-0	Eastleigh 272*	13.28	PORTSMOUTH
06.45 S. T. Junction		*72xx 2-8-2TSTJ 363*		*13/40*	*East Yard*
11.00 BRIGHTON	13.31	WC 4-6-2	Brighton 731	13.52	CARDIFF
11.30 BRIGHTON	13.58	WC 4-6-2	Brighton 732	14.03	PLYMOUTH
10.30 ILFRACOMBE	14.09	MN 4-6-2	Exmouth 497	14.15	WATERLOO
11.54 WATERLOO	14.20	WC 4-6-2	Salisbury 430		
(Ex East Yard)		*S15 4-6-0*	*Feltham 106*	*14.25*	*Basingstoke*
13.03 Portsmouth	14.35	T9 4-4-0	Salisbury 445		
13.00 WATERLOO	14.39	MN 4-6-2	Salisbury 431	14.45	PLYMOUTH
11.00 PLYMOUTH	14.49	WC 4-6-2	Brighton 731	14.55	BRIGHTON
13.20 Bournemouth (W)	14.59	T9 4-4-0	Eastleigh 284		
(Ex East Yard)		*43xx 2-6-0*	*Bristol 365*	*15.07*	*S'ton Docks*
		N15 46-0	N. Elms 1	15.15	WATERLOO
14.45 Amesbury	*15.25*	*700 0-6-0*	*Salisbury 454*	*15.28*	*Fisherton Yard*
15.30 East Yard		*S15 4-6-0*	*Salisbury 475*	*15/33*	*West Yard*
10.45 Feltham	*15.44*	*S15 4-6-0*	*Feltham 101*	*15.45*	*West Yard*
13.00 CARDIFF	15.47	Castle 4-6-0	Canton 11*		BRIGHTON
13.00 CARDIFF		WC 4-6-2	Brighton 732*	15.57	BRIGHTON
14.48 Basingstoke	16.00	N15 46-0	N. Elms 11		
		LN 4-6-0	Eastleigh 251	16.05	WATERLOO
10.55 Bristol East		*Hall 4-6-0*	*Old Oak C. 1*	*16/10*	*East Yard*
(Ex East Yard)		*U 2-6-0*	*Yeovil 482*	*16.10*	*Milford Yard*
14.33 PORTSMOUTH	16.08	U 2-6-0	Yeovil 485	16.20	BRISTOL
(Ex East Yard)		*H15 4-6-0*	*Eastleigh 312*	*16.18*	*Eastleigh*
		M7 0-4-4T	*Salisbury 447*	*16/37*	*Light Grateley*
15.00 WATERLOO	16.42	MN 4-6-2	N. Elms 7	16.49	PLYMOUTH
12.20 ILFRACOMBE	16.45	MN 4-6-2	Salisbury 461	16.51	WATERLOO
15.40 Bradford on Avon	16.56	Hall 4-6-0	Westbury9*		Portsmouth
15.40 Bradford on Avon		T9 4-4-0	Eastleigh 284*	17.07	Portsmouth
17.00 Milford Yard	*17.10*	*BR4 2-6-0*	*Eastleigh 316*	*17.16*	*Fisherton Yard*
		N15 4-6-0	N. Elms 2	17.15	WATERLOO
		T9 4-4-0	Salisbury 445	17.20	Bournemouth (W)
09.45 Tonbridge	*17.19*	*H15 4-6-0*	*Salisbury 440*	*17.21*	*West Yard*
17.19 Grateley	17.41	M7 0-4-4T	Salisbury 447		
16.48 Basingstoke	18.00	N15 4-6-0	Salisbury 432		
17.58 Milford Yard	*18.07*	*U 2-6-0*	*Yeovil 482*	*18.09*	*East Yard*
16.52 Bournemouth (W)	18.22	T9 4-4-0	Salisbury 444		
15.54 Clapham Jcn	*18.27*	*MN 4-6-2*	*Exmouth 494*	*18.40*	*Exeter (Milk)*
14.20 ILFRACOMBE	18.27	MN 4-6-2	N. Elms 4	18.33	WATERLOO
16.32 BRISTOL	18.45	Hall 4-6-0	Bristol 64*		PORTSMOUTH
16.45 Portsmouth	18.49	U 2-6-0	Salisbury 450		
16.32 BRISTOL		U 2-6-0	Fratton 368*	18.57	PORTSMOUTH
17.00 WATERLOO	19.00	MN 4-6-2	Exmouth 496	19.06	EXETER
17.45 PORTSMOUTH	19.25	BR4 2-6-0	Eastleigh 272	19.38	CARDIFF
Light engine		*BR4 2-6-0*	*Eastleigh 316*	*19/32*	*Andover Jcn*
16.35 CARDIFF	19.37	Hall 4-6-0	Bristol 64/2*		PORTSMOUTH
16.35 CARDIFF		U 2-6-0	Yeovil 482*	19.45	PORTSMOUTH
18.00 WATERLOO	19.44	MN 4-6-2	Exmouth 495	19.50	PLYMOUTH
16.35 Gillingham	*19.45*	*S15 4-6-0*	*Salisbury 467*	*19.48*	*East Yard*
15.50 PLYMOUTH	20.03	MN 4-6-2	Exmouth 498	20.09	WATERLOO
16.35 EXETER	19.54	S15 4-6-0	Fratton 101	20.16	PORTSMOUTH
17.39 WATERLOO	20.18	N15 4-6-0	N. Elms 10		
15.35 Wimborne	*20.33*	*700 0-6-0*	*Salisbury 452*	*20.35*	*East Yard*
17.40 Yeovil (T)	*20.27*	*N15 4-6-0*	*N. Elms 3*	*20.37*	*Gravesend (Milk)*
		N15 4-6-0	Salisbury 432	20.50	Woking
18.50 Wimborne	*20.58*	*700 0-6-0*	*Salisbury 451*	*21.00*	*Fisherton Yard*
19.43 Bournemouth (W)	21.10	T9 4-4-0	Salisbury 445		
19.17 Portsmouth	21.17	T9 4-4-0	Salisbury 443		
19.04 Basingstoke	21.25	S15 4-6-0	Salisbury 438	21.30	West Yard
19.10 Bristol	21.38	Hall 4-6-0	Canton 38*		Eastleigh
18.54 WATERLOO	21.46	S15 4-6-0	Salisbury 435	21.55	YEOVIL (T)

Goods trains in italics. * = engine change. "/" = passing time.

tives that had finished their spell of duty) were due back onto the depot. Also shown are the foreign engines which came onto the shed for short periods of time - usually for coal and turning - and added in no small way to the highly varied movements that made up the routine activity of this strategic shed.

Another change introduced in 1950 was the closure of the Great Western shed and the transfer of its locomotive servicing to the Southern depot which resulted in locomotives of both companies sharing the same facilities. The Great Western went to considerable lengths to rediagram their engines so that Salisbury could be operated on an out and home basis but the incidence of trains did not always lend itself to tidy engine workings and seven GW locomotives had to stable in the LSWR shed whilst the number of programmed light engine movements between Salisbury and Westbury, because of traffic imbalances, increased considerably. The engines that recessed in the Southern shed were worth chasing by the enthusiast since, in addition to four Halls and a 28xx 2-8-0, two Severn Tunnel Junction 2-8-2 tanks could usually be found; one waiting to work the 01.10 to Westbury and the other the 10.23 Bevois Park - Rogerstone which it took over from an H15 4-6-0 in Fisherton Yard.

Amongst the pick of the Great Western crop which visited the station were a pair of Star class 4-6-0's - forerunners of the Castle's - which were booked to work in and out of Salisbury each day. One arrived with the 08.10 from Bristol and returned west with the 10.34 from Portsmouth whilst the other, more difficult to see, arrived late at night with the 20.45 from Bristol and left with the 02.55 for Temple Meads. The late morning was an especially interesting time for GW movements and in addition to the Star 4-6-0 which waited to take over the Portsmouth service, two 2-8-2 tanks made an appearance: One to re-engine the Southampton - Rogerstone empties and the other arriving with the 02.35 coal ex Radyr and returning as required, which usually entailed running light to Westbury for a train of empties to Cardiff. Curiously, given the GW's addiction to complex engine workings, the same pair of engines - 7202 and 7205 - alternated on this working for almost the entirety of the 1950's.

One used to wonder at the time why, with so many large engines on its books, the Southern did not employ some of its light Pacifics on the Salisbury - Portsmouth workings, duties which were probably far more consistent with

SALISBURY MPD DEPOT ANALYSIS (1953)			
Class	Diagrams	Allocation	Spare
MN	2	4	2
WC	2	7	5
N15	3	7	4
S15	6	12	6
H15	4	6	2
U	1	4	3
T9	4	4	0
M7	1	2	1
700	3	4	1
Z	1	1	0
E4	1	2	1
TOTAL	28	53	25
HALL	4		
43xx	3		
72xx	1		

Radical changes to the SR motive power department came during the last years of the 1950's with the rebuilding of the Bulleid Pacifics and the gradual replacement of the N15 4-6-0's by BR 5MT locomotives, some of which came new to Nine Elms in the summer of 1955; others following from the SECR after the Kent Coast electrification of 1959. Although handsome in a utilitarian way, the BR standard 4-6-0's lacked the stately dignity of the engines they replaced and efforts to popularise them with the public by bestowing upon them names from withdrawn King Arthur locomotives made no impact whatsoever. 73110 'The Red Knight', one of the original Nine Elms allocation, runs forward to the MPD after arriving at Salisbury with a semi-fast from Waterloo. The smaller 4MT version also arrived on the Southern in 1955, five examples being sent to Dover and seven to Exmouth Junction. A further batch of six engines was allocated to Basingstoke in May 1956 to assume the duties formerly covered by the N15X 'Remembrance' 4-6-0's. 75068, a former Dover engine, runs into Salisbury station to take up a working to Portsmouth.

Train	Arr	Loco	Diagram	Off Shed	Working
ENGINE MOVEMENTS : SALISBURY MPD (1953)					
06.45 Severn Tunnel Jcn	14.00	72xx 2-8-2T	STJ 363	00.35	01.10 Severn Tunnel Jcn
		S15 4-6-0	470	00.55	01.10 Exmouth Jcn
		U 2-6-0	450	01.00	01.35 Eastleigh
22.00 Nine Elms	01.03	MN 4-6-2	461 (stale)		
15.35 Wimborne/shunt	01.05	700 0-6-0	452 (stale)		
Pilot	01.35	M7 0-4-4T	447 (stale)		
		H15 4-6-0	440	01.50	02.20 Woking
20.45 Bristol	22.50	Star 4-6-0	Bristol 121	02.15	02.55 Bristol
		T9 4-4-0	444	02.25	03.52 Wimborne
21.50 Bristol	00.30	Grange 4-6-0	Bristol 366	02.40	03.10 Avonmouth
20.50 Eastleigh	22.25	Q1 0-6-0	Guildford 214	02.50	03.30 Chichester
21.44 Eastleigh	23.05	43xx 2-6-0	Bristol 365	03.00	03.30 Avonmouth
Fisherton Pilot	03.05	E4 0-6-2T	458 (stale)		
		N15 4-6-0	432	03.10	03.30 Yeovil Jcn
		700 0-6-0	452	03.35	04.05 B'mouth (C)
		S15 4-6-0	438	03.40	West Yard shunt
0.20 Eastleigh	02.50	Q1 0-6-0	Eastleigh 319	03.45	04.25 Northam
00.23 Woking	04.00	H15 4-6-0	441 (stale)		
		N15 4-6-0	436	04.05	04.35 Feltham
		H15 4-6-0	441	04.25	04.45 Woking
		700 0-6-0	454	04.45	05.05 Bulford
		E4 0-6-2T	458	05.55	Fisherton Pilot
03.30 Basingstoke	06.00	H15 4-6-0	439 (stale)		
		WC 4-6-2	430	06.10	06.45 WATERLOO
		M7 0-4-4T	447	06.10	07.20 Grately
		T9 4-4-0	443	06.30	07.15 Bournemouth (W)
20.38 Westbury	21.45	Hall 4-6-0	Cardiff 38	06.50	07.25 Bristol
02.10 Exeter	06.50	S15 4-6-0	475 (stale)		
		T9 44-0	445	07.10	07.47 Portsmouth
		700 0-6-0	451	07.20	07.37 Wimborne
		MN 4-6-2	461	07.40	08.05 EXETER
		MN 4-6-2	431	07.40	08.15 WATERLOO
21.45 Exmouth Jcn	08.07	S15 4-6-0	471 (stale)		
03.55 Eastleigh	05.55	H15 4-6-0	Eastleigh 311	08.20	08.45 Eastleigh
07.14 Broadstone	08.25	T9 4-4-0	Eastleigh 284	08.55	09.25 Bournemouth (W)
07.20 Westbury	08.55	Hall 4-6-0	Bristol 64/1	09.10	09.34 Bristol
07.42 B'mouth (C)	09.20	T9 4-4-0	446 (stale)		
07.27 Southampton (T)	09.00	U 2-6-0	450/2	10.04	10.37 Portsmouth
03.55 Yeovil Jcn	10.05	S15 4-6-0	435 (stale)		
23.58 Feltham	04.35	S15 4-6-0	Feltham 116	10.06	11.27 Chichester
West Yard Shunt	07.00	S15 4-6-0	438/2	10.15	10.42 Basingstoke
16.32 Bristol	18.55	Hall 4-6-0	Bristol 64	10.35	11.17 Cardiff
07.29 Portsmouth	09.25	H15 4-6-0	Nine Elms 72	10.55	11.18 Salisbury
07.42 Bournemouth (C)	10.35	T9 4-4-0	444/2	11.25	12.58 Bournemouth (W)
09.33 Portsmouth	11.15	BR4 2-6-0	Eastleigh 270	12.14	12.44 Portsmouth
08.10 Bristol	10.40	Star 4-6-0	Bristol 120	12.15	12.45 Bristol
16.10 Severn Tunnel Jcn	23.40	72xx 2-8-2T	Severn T.J. 363A	12.20	13.08 Rogerstone
07.20 Waterloo	10.16	N15 4-6-0	Nine Elms 3	12.26	12.46 Yeovil Junction
		S15 4-6-0	435	12.30	12.54 Waterloo
10.04 Bournemouth (W)	11.47	T9 4-4-0	443/2	12.35	13.06 Southampton (T)
		S15 4-6-0	471	12.35	12.55 Yeovil Junction
10.34 Portsmouth	12.30	BR4 2-6-0	Eastleigh 272	13.00	13.28 Portsmouth
		S15 4-6-0	475	13.15	17.15 Exmouth Junction
East Yard Pilot	13.20	Z 0-8-0T			
16.35 Cardiff	19.45	Hall 4-6-0	Bristol 64/2	13.30	13.52 CARDIFF
07.20 Chichester	11.25	S15 4-6-0	Feltham 106	14.00	14.25 Basingstoke
11.00 BRIGHTON	13.40	WC 4-6-2	Brighton 731	14.30	14.55 BRIGHTON
22.00 Avonmouth	04.40	43xx 2-6-0	Bristol 365	14.40	15.07 Southampton Docks
11.30 BRIGHTON	14.10	WC 4-6-2	Brighton 732	15.20	15.57 BRIGHTON
10.54 Waterloo	13.30	LN 4-6-0	Eastleigh 251	15.30	16.05 Waterloo
		Z 0-8-0T	457	15.30	East Yard pilot
10.23 Bevois Park	13.00	H15 4-6-0	Eastleigh 312	15.45	16.18 Eastleigh
10.30 CARDIFF	13.35	Castle 4-6-0	Bristol 110	15.50	16.20 Bristol
19.45 Bassaleg	06.00	28xx 2-8-0	Severn T.J. 351	16.05	16.35 Severn Tunnel Jcn
10.27 Bristol	12.50	Hall 4-6-0	Cardiff 38	16.10	17.02 Cardiff
13.03 Portsmouth	14.50	T9 4-4-0	445/2	16.35	17.20 Bournemouth (W)
13.20 Bournemouth (W)	15.20	T9 4-4-0	Eastleigh 284	16.35	17.07 Portsmouth
07.35 Westbury	12.30	43xx 2-6-0	Westbury 28	17.30	18.00 Westbury
14.02 Woking	17.50	H15 4-6-0	440 (stale)		
15.40 Bradford on Avon	17.05	Hall 4-6-0	Westbury 9	18.35	Shunt/20.15 Westbury
13.00 Cardiff	16.10	Castle 4-6-0	Cardiff 11	19.15	19.38 Cardiff
12.52 Yeovil Junction	18.30	T9 4-4-0	Yeovil 482	19.30	19.45 Portsmouth
17.00 Milford trip	18.05	BR4 2-6-0	Eastleigh 316	19.30	Light to Andover Jcn
16.47 Bournemouth (W)	18.40	T9 4-4-0	444/2	19.40	20.22 Bournemouth (C)
10.45 Feltham	16.50	S15 4-6-0	Feltham 101	19.40	20.16 Portsmouth
16.35 Gillingham	20.15	S15 4-6-0	467 (stale)		
16.48 Basingstoke	18.17	N15 4-6-0	432/2	20.30	20.50 Woking
16.45 Portsmouth	21.05	U 2-6-0	450/2 (stale)		
18.50 Wimborne	21.15	700 0-6-0	451 (stale)		
		S15 4-6-0	467	21.30	22.00 Eastleigh
19.43 Bournemouth (W)	21.31	T9 4-4-0	445/2 (stale)		
19.04 Basingstoke	22.00	S15 4-6-0	438/2 (stale)		
14.48 Basingstoke	16.15	N15 4-6-0	Nine Elms 11	22.10	22.40 Waterloo
17.45 Portsmouth	19.37	BR4 2-6-0	Eastleigh 272	22.25	23.10 Eastleigh
		H15 4-6-0	439	22.30	22.50 Basingstoke
17.18 Sidmouth Junction	22.30	N15 4-6-0	473 (stale)		
21.15 Aberdare	10.00	Hall 4-6-0	Aberdare 353	22.45	23.15 Aberdare
19.50 Exeter	22.57	MN 4-6-2	431 (stale)		
20.54 Waterloo	23.25	N15 4-6-0	436 (stale)		
17.39 Waterloo	20.30	N15 4-6-0	Nine Elms 10	23.29	00.13 Nine Elms
21.10 Yeovil Junction	23.30	S15 4-6-0	470 (stale)		
20.28 Eastleigh	23.35	T9 4-4-0	443/2 (stale)		
18.31 Yeovil Junction	20.35	WC 4-6-2	430/2	23.55	00.15 Exmouth Junction

the engine's abilities than pottering about the West Country, as many of the class did, with three and four coach stopping trains. The view, however, did not allow for the fact that the West Country trains expanded by a factor of two or three at peak times which did not apply to the Salisbury - Portsmouth services and the T9 4-4-0's survived in spite of the Bulleid era until ousted from 1957 by multiple units.

The Great Western on the other hand was handsome to the point of generosity in repowering some of the Portsmouth trains, allocating nothing less than Castle class 4-6-0's to take over the 14.33 and 16.45 Portsmouth trains from nothing more grand than a brace of U class moguls. (Some of the engine changing at Salisbury exhibited some bizarre contrasts such as the 10.34 Portsmouth - Bristol which, until a BR 4MT 2-6-0 took over the working in 1953, arrived behind a D15 4-4-0 and departed with a Star class 4-6-0.)

Unlike the Great Western (and LMS), the Southern disliked complicated cyclic engine diagrams and preferred to keep engines, so far as it was possible, to well worn tracks so that each could get back to its home shed at the close of play. The advantage was that engines were less likely to get lost since, apart from the Merchant Navy Pacifics, the majority of engines which worked on the out and home principle rarely strayed far from their local area and could be depended upon to return to their point of origin at the end of each turn of duty. Most Nine Elms locomotives, for example, came off their trains as soon as Salisbury was reached and the incidence of 'strange' engines on any SR line was - to the irritation of enthusiasts who needed a constant supply of foreign engines to maintain interest - minimal. There were, however, a few exceptions to the rule such as the Nine Elms King Arthur 4-6-0's which worked as far as Yeovil Junction and a Fratton 2-6-0 which strayed through the border in the late morning with a local train from Salisbury to Yeovil Junction.

On peak summer Saturdays the out and home system could not be maintained and on Sundays and Mondays it was quite common to find a respectable number of unbalanced Exmouth Junction light Pacifics sitting about at Nine Elms waiting for someone to think of a way of getting them back to their home station without incurring too much light engine mileage. Usually special freight trains from Feltham, empty stock workings to Exeter and a modicum of double heading resolved the problem by the middle of the week and whilst wearied MPD clerks would be sending out telegrams by the dozen in order to locate - and get something done about - their missing engines, the presence of such rarities in the home counties perked up many a local observer whose tally of Exmouth Junction engines was never what it ought to have been.

Foreign engines also loomed large in the thoughts and actions of the shed staff since the booking-out of home engines - 31 per day - was markedly less that of Salisbury engines, of which 39 were booked off the depot each weekday. This was a proportion which could lead to problems at times since, from the shed perspective, engines fell into one of two categories: your own and other peoples. Foreign engines arrived on shed in the middle of a diagram and had to go out to continue the same working

A fitters nightmare. WC Pacific 34051 'Winston Churchill' receives mechanical attention in Salisbury MPD. 34051 was a long term resident of Salisbury, arriving there in June 1951 and remaining at the depot until its withdrawal in September 1965. Although having seven light Pacifics on its books in 1953, very little booked work was diagrammed for the engines and their regular duties consisted of a stopping train to Waterloo and a night goods to Exmouth Junction. This contrast between allocation and duties was by no means untypical of the class in its unrebuilt state.

The Maunsell 2-6-0's saw little regular mainline work on the route to London but were extensively used on the Portsmouth services and on the stopping trains to Exeter and the twenty intermediate stations. U class 2-6-0 31792 of Yeovil backs onto the 15.05 all stations to Exeter Central, a journey that took exactly three hours for the eighty-eight miles leaving Salisbury in the wake of the 13.00 express from Waterloo and arriving just ahead of the 15.00. 31792 was another 2-6-4T conversion, appearing as A792 'River Arun' in May 1925 and being rebuilt in July 1928.

Dia	Class	Time	Train	To Shed	Rev Miles
431	MN 4-6-2	07.25	ECS to station for:		
			08.15 Salisbury : Waterloo		
			Nine Elms MPD		
			13.00 Waterloo - Exeter		
			Exmouth Jcn MPD		
			19.50 Exeter - Salisbury	22.57	343
461	MN 4-6-2	07.40	**08.05 Salisbury : Exeter**		
			Exmouth Jcn MPD		
			14.30 Exeter : Waterloo		
			Nine Elms MPD		
			22.00 Nine Elms : Salisbury	01.03	343
430/1	WC 4-6-2	05.45	ECS to station for:		
			06.45 Salisbury : Waterloo		
			Nine Elms MPD		
			11.54 Waterloo : Salisbury		
			14.55 Salisbury : Yeovil Jcn		
			Yeovil MPD		
			18.31 Yeovil Jcn : Salisbury		
			Salisbury MPD	20.35	245
430/2	WC 4-6-2	23.55	00.15 Salisbury : Exmouth Jcn		
			Exmouth Jcn MPD		
			20.50 Exmouth Jcn : Salisbury	00.10	174
432	N15 4-6-0	03.10	ECS to station for:		
			03.30 Salisbury : Yeovil Jcn		
			07.10 Yeovil (T) : Waterloo		
			Nine Elms MPD		
			14.54 Waterloo : Basingstoke		
			16.48 Basingstoke : Salisbury		
			Salisbury MPD	18.17	249
473	N15 4-6-0	20.30	**20.50 Salisbury : Woking**		
			01.25 Woking : Yeovil (T)		
			Yeovil MPD		
			12.14 Yeovil Jcn : Exeter		
			Exmouth Jcn MPD		
			15.29 Exeter - Sidmouth Jcn		
			16.20 Sidmouth Jcn - Honiton		
			17.18 Sidmouth Jcn : Salisbury	22.35	301
436	N15 4-6-0	04.05	04.35 Salisbury : Feltham		
			Feltham MPD		
			14.47 Feltham : Nine Elms		
			Nine Elms MPD		
			20.54 Waterloo : Salisbury	23.25	176
440	H15 4-6-0	01.50	02.20 Salisbury : Woking		
			Guildford MPD		
			14.02 Woking : Salisbury	18.00	112
441	H15 4-6-0	04.25	04.55 Salisbury : Woking		
			Guildford MPD		
			00.23 Woking : Salisbury	04.00	112
439	H15 4-6-0	22.30	22.50 Salisbury : Basingstoke		
			Basingstoke MPD		
			03.30 Basingstoke : Salisbury	06.00	71
435	S15 4-6-0	12.30	ECS to station for:		
			13.00 Salisbury : Waterloo		
			Nine Elms MPD		
			18.54 Waterloo : Yeovil (T)		
			Shunt Yeovil Jcn		
			03.55 Yeovil Jcn : Salisbury		
			West Yard shunt		
			09.45 East - West trip	10.05	248
470	S15 4-6-0	00.55	01.10 Salisbury : Exmouth Jcn		
			Exmouth Jcn MPD		
			13.20 E. Jcn : Templecombe		
			21.10 Yeovil Jcn : Salisbury	23.30	184
438	S15 4-6-0	03.40	West Yard shunt		
			10.42 Salisbury : Basingstoke		
			Basingstoke MPD		
			19.04 Basingstoke : Salisbury	22.00	71
471	S15 4-6-0	12.40	12.55 Sal'y : Templecombe		
			14.55 T'combe : Yeovil Jcn		
			16.21 Yeovil Jcn : Exeter		
			21.45 Exmouth Jcn : Salisbury		
			04.15 East : Milford trip		
			Milford shunt	08.07	176
475	S15 4-6-0	13.20	East Yard shunt		
			15.30 East : West trip		
			17.15 Salisbury : Exmouth Jcn		
			Exmouth Jcn MPD		
			02.10 Exeter : Salisbury	07.00	177
467	S15 4-6-0	21.30	**22.00 Salisbury : Eastleigh**		
			Eastleigh MPD		
			02.10 Bevois Park : Yeovil Jcn		
			Shunt		
			11.45 Y. Jcn : Templecombe		
			Gillingham shunt		
			Semley shunt		
			16.35 Semley : Salisbury	20.00	96
444	T9 4-4-0	02.25	carriage shunt		
			03.52 Salisbury : Wimborne		
			05.17 Wimborne : B'mouth (C)		
			07.42 B'mouth (C) : Salisbury		
			Carriage shunt		
			12.58 Salisbury : B'mouth (W)		
			16.52 B'mouth (W) : Salisbury		
			ECS to sidings	18.40	156
446	T9 4-4-0	19.40	**20.22 Salisbury : B'mouth (C)**		
			Bournemouth MPD		
			07.42 B'mouth (C) : Salisbury	09.20	79
443	T9 4-4-0	06.30	ECS to station for:		
			07.15 Salisbury : Bournemouth		
			10.04 Bournemouth : Salisbury		
			ECS to station for:		
			13.06 Salisbury : S'ton (T)		
			Southampton MPD		
			15.46 S'ton (C) : Bevois Park		
			Woolston shunt		
			18.42 Woolston : Bevois Park		
			20.28 Eastleigh : Salisbury		
			ECS to sidings	23.35	134
445	T9 4-4-0	07.10	ECS to station for:		
			07.47 Salisbury : Portsmouth		
			Fratton MPD		
			13.03 Portsmouth : Salisbury		
			17.20 Salisbury : B'mouth (W)		
			19.43 B'mouth (W) : Salisbury		
			ECS to sidings	21.31	173
450	U 2-6-0	01.00	01.35 Salisbury : Eastleigh		
			03.40 Eastleigh : S'ton Docks		
			05.10 Docks : S'ton (T)		
			07.27 S'ton (T) : Salisbury		
			ECS to sidings		
			10.37 Salisbury : Portsmouth		
			12.45 Portsmouth : Fratton		
			16.45 Portsmouth : Salisbury		
			West Yard shunt	21.05	146
447	M7 0-4-4T	06.10	Carriage shunt		
			07.20 Salisbury : Grateley		
			Light engine Salisbury		
			Carriage shunt		
			Light engine Grateley		
			17.19 Grateley : Salisbury		
			Carriage shunting	01.35	22
452	700 0-6-0	03.35	04.05 Salisbury : Bournemouth		
			11.35 B'mouth : Poole		
			Light engine Wimborne		
			Shunt		
			15.35 Wimborne : Salisbury		
			West Yard shunt	01.05	73
454	700 0-6-0	04.45	05.05 West : Milford trip		
			Light to East Yard		
			06.10 Salisbury : Bulford		
			1440 Amesbury : Salisbury	15.50	30
45i	700 0-6-0	07.20	07.37 Salisbury : Wimborne		
			16.25 Hamworthy Jcn : W'brne		
			18.50 Wimborne : Salisbury	21.30	64
457	Z 0-8-0T	15.30	East Yard shunt	13.20	
458	E4 0-6-2T	05.55	Fisherton Shunt	03.05	

Passenger services in bold type

Unrebuilt West Country 34107 'Blandford Forum', a Bournemouth engine of many years standing until transferred to Exmouth Junction in March 1959, runs into Salisbury with an express from the West. 34107 was one of the light Pacifics which remained in its original form and had a wider route availability west of Exeter, hence the transfer. It was withdrawn in September 1964.

Although some drivers considered the rebuilt Merchant Navy's to be less free in their steaming than in their original form, general opinion favoured the reconstruction programme, not least amongst the maintenance staff who were spared the difficulties of internal oil-baths and air smoothed casing. The rebuilds also lost the mystique they had held for enthusiasts and from 1956 onwards had too much of a 'BR standard' appearance for many peoples taste. There was however no doubting their power and the way they could master a heavy express made the rebuilds the envy of many parts of BR. 35029 'Ellerman Lines' pauses at Salisbury with a Waterloo - West of England express. To the enthusiast in the picture 35029 is evidently just another Spam.

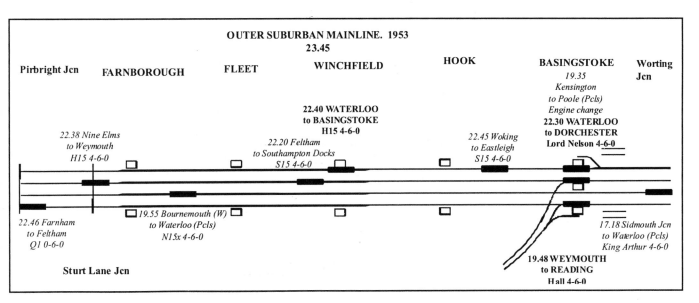

OUTER SUBURBAN MAINLINE. 1953
23.45

Pirbright Jcn — FARNBOROUGH — FLEET — WINCHFIELD — HOOK — BASINGSTOKE — Worting Jcn

22.38 Nine Elms to Weymouth H15 4-6-0

22.40 WATERLOO to BASINGSTOKE H15 4-6-0

22.20 Feltham to Southampton Docks S15 4-6-0

22.45 Woking to Eastleigh S15 4-6-0

19.35 Kensington to Poole (Pcls) Engine change
22.30 WATERLOO to DORCHESTER Lord Nelson 4-6-0

22.46 Farnham to Feltham Q1 0-6-0

19.55 Bournemouth (W) to Waterloo (Pcls) N15x 4-6-0

17.18 Sidmouth Jcn to Waterloo (Pcls) King Arthur 4-6-0

Sturt Lane Jcn

19.48 WEYMOUTH to READING Hall 4-6-0

whereas there was considerable elasticity to juggle around your own engines - provided each working had the appropriate (or an appropriate) type of engine allocated to it. If, for example, Salisbury found itself short of H15 4-6-0's, the running foreman was quite at liberty to hack his diagrams around or make sensible substitutions in order to get over the temporary shortage. (In fact he was expected to do so). On the other hand if the Canton Castle 4-6-0 due off shed at 19.15 to take over the 17.45 Portsmouth - Cardiff failed and was unable to work, the scope for improvisation was limited.

If the engine failed in sufficient time - which normally they didn't - the first avenue of attack was to contact Westbury MPD and ask them to send a replacement engine all speed to take up the working. Defects however were not usually discovered until the final check was being done, minutes before coming off shed and leaving very little time for the provision of a substitute.

The first and perhaps most obvious step would be to consider letting the engine which brought the train in from Portsmouth continue forward but such a solution not only meant the loss of an engine - it would mean, for example, that the 23.10 would be without an engine unless as engine change could be effected by Westbury and the Eastleigh locomotive returned light to Salisbury in time to be prepared for the rest of its diagram. Steps also had to be taken to ensure that

Rebuilt MN 35002 'Union Castle'. 15:517/555 tons (Pullman)				
m.ch point	1/in WTT	ctual mph	dbhp pc
0.00 SOUTHAMPTON	-	0.00	0 -	- -
1.05 Northam Jcn	560999	3.30	3.40 20	417 1
2.09 Swaythling	864		7.38 43.5	1238 5
5.64 EASTLEIGH	570	10.00	10.30 52.5	1298 6
9.49 Shawford	281		14.40 55.5	1532 8
14.63 Winchester	260		18.09 53	1291 7
21.30 Micheldever	259		27.26 56.5	1479 8
22.77 Roundwood	252		29.27 56.5	1479 8
26.56 Wootton	-6534		33.00 71.5	1660 10
28.76 Worting Jcn	-278	37.00	34.57 65	- -
31.39 BASINGSTOKE	-260	39.30	37.09 75	961 7
37.06 Hook	-684		41.36 75	583 4
39.33 Winchfield	-1046		43.28 80.5	1588 12
42.61 Fleet	-674		45.57 80.5	809 7
46.02 Farnborough	-2852		48.30 78	788 6
48.19 MP.31	946		50.14 76.5	1269 10
51.20 Brookwood	-307		52.33 81	672 5
54.72 WOKING	-318	60.30	55.09 85	781 7
57.45 West Byfleet	-367		57.01 86.5	754 6
60.07 Weybridge	-6116		58.48 80.5	406 3
65.72 Hampton Ct Jcn	-2348	69.30	63.10 79	1036 8
		Signals		
79.19 WATERLOO	-711	86.00	95.32 -	- -

Swaythling to Wootton. 23.2 miles 1/336. 55 mph 1467dbhp
Worting Jcn to H.C. Jcn. 36.9 miles 1/-657. 79 mph 863dbhp

A further example of the Southern's failure to recognise the mile-a-minute potential it had in its Pacifics. Had it not been for problems of congestion on the approach to Waterloo Rebuild 35002 would have reached London in about 79 minutes from Southampton - with a trailing load of over 550 tons. The highest output of the journey was produced on the climb of Wallers Ash bank with the engine managing about 1500 dbhp; the equivalent of a 2000hp diesel-electric. After passing Basingstoke the only time the locomotive was extended was to inch the speed into the 80's - standard LSW driving - yet time was picked up hand over fist.

the correct type of engine - a BR 4MT 2-6-0 - was actually in the working. The 2-6-0 could run over the GWR without restriction but a D15 4-4-0 - and in 1953 the class were still in occasional use on their former workings - was subject to a number of speed restrictions between Salisbury and Westbury whilst it was a good man who knew (or even knew where to look) what the limitations on D15's north of Westbury were.

So the foreman would have to find out from Eastleigh what type of engine was working in, make provision for its next working, ascertain what restrictions applied, get some sort of a guarantee from Westbury that they would re-engine the train and return the Eastleigh engine, all speed, to Salisbury, advise the district control of what was happening, telephone the station inspector to say that a small engine was being turned out for the Cardiff, tell the clerk to 'wire' Canton with details of the change and finally advise the Bristol driver of any restrictions he had to observe and prepare for an unholy row because he hadn't been given his booked type of engine.

An alternative was to step up the GWR engines on the shed until either the Castle was repaired or Westbury sent a replacement. The problem, however, was the very limited number of GWR engines at Salisbury to juggle with although, in the example used, there were two Hall 4-6-0's on shed: one for the 23.15 Aberdare goods and the other for

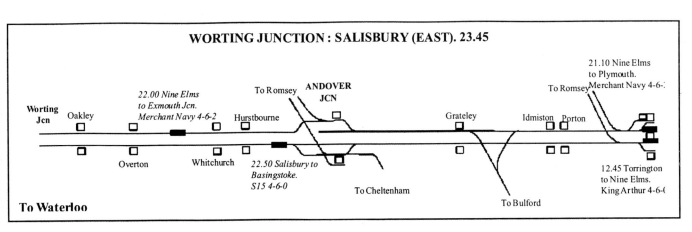

WORTING JUNCTION : SALISBURY (EAST). 23.45

Worting Jcn — Oakley — Overton — Whitchurch — Hurstbourne — ANDOVER JCN — Grateley — Idmiston — Porton

To Waterloo

22.00 Nine Elms to Exmouth Jcn. Merchant Navy 4-6-2

To Romsey

21.10 Nine Elms to Plymouth. Merchant Navy 4-6-2

To Romsey

22.50 Salisbury to Basingstoke. S15 4-6-0

To Cheltenham

To Bulford

12.45 Torrington to Nine Elms. King Arthur 4-6-0

LOCOMOTIVE ALLOCATION SALISBURY : 1949 - 1960

Left section

Mar-49	Apr-50	Mar-53	Apr-54	Nov-55	Jan-57	Mar-59	Feb-60
204HP diesel							
							D2274
G6 0-6-0T (1894)							
30238	30238		30270	30266	30266	30266	30266
30274			30266	30270	30270		
'0395' 0-6-0 (1881)							
30577	30577						
'700' 0-6-0 (1897)							
30315	30315	30315	30315	30309	30309	30315	30309
30317	30317	30317	30317	30317	30317	30309	30315
30355	30355	30690	30690	30327	30327	30692	30692
30690	30690	30691	30691				
30691	30691						
E4 0-6-2T (1897)							
		32486	32486	32486			
		32506	32506				
Z 0-8-0T (1929)							
30957	30957	30957	30957	30956	30954	30954	30957
				30957	30957	30957	
M7 0-4-4T (1897)							
30023	30023	30673	30673	30673	30025	30025	30025
30041	30041	30674	30674	30674	30374	30673	30673
30127	30127				30673	30674	30674
30243	30243				30674		
30675	30675						
L12 4-4-0 (1904/15)							
30421	30421						
E1 4-4-0 (1919)							
							31019
							31067
							31497
							31507
T9 4-4-0 (1899/1922)							
30122	30122	30304	30301	30301	30301	30301	30729
30288	30288	30301	30304	30304	30304	30313	
30289	30289	30702	30702	30313	30313	30729	
30709	30301	30721	30721	30702	30702		
30715	30706			30721	30721		
30727	30709						
	30715						
	30719						
	30724						
	30727						
N 2-6-0 (1917)							
31836	31836		31813	31813	31813	31813	31813
31846	31846		31814	31814	31814	31814	31814
31872	31872						
31873	31873						
U 2-6-0 (1928)							
31612	31612	31626	31635				
31618	31618	31635	31636				
31626	31626	31636	31639				
31630		31639					
31636							
U 2-6-0 (R/B 2-6-4T) 1928							
	31795						
BR4 4-6-0							
				76005	76005	76005	76005
				76006	76006	76006	76007
					76008	76007	76008
						76008	76017
						76009	76066
						76059	76067
						76060	

Right section

Mar-49	Apr-50	Mar-53	Apr-54	Nov-55	Jan-57	Mar-59	Feb-60
H15 4-6-0 (1907/14)							
30330	30330	30330	30330	30330	30330	30331	30331
30331	30332	30331	30331	30331	30331	30334	30334
30332	30333	30332	30332	30332	30333	30335	
30333		30333	30333	30333	30334		
30334		30334	30334	30334	30335		
30335		30335	30335	30335			
30475							
H15 4-6-0 (1924)							
							30522
							30523
							30524
S15 4-6-0 (1897/1927)							
30828	30827	30823	30823	30823	30823	30823	30823
30829	30828	30824	30824	30824	30824	30824	30824
30830	30829	30825	30825	30825	30825	30825	30825
30831	30830	30826	30826	30826	30826	30826	30826
30832	30831	30827	30827	30827	30827	30827	30827
	30832	30828	30828	30828	30828	30828	30828
		30829	30829	30829	30829	30829	30829
		30830	30830	30830	30830	30830	30830
		30831	30831	30831	30831	30831	30831
		30832	30832	30832	30832	30832	30832
S15 4-6-0 (1927)							
		30846	30847	30847	30847	30847	
		30847					
N15 4-6-0 (1918)							
	30739	30748	30748	30748	30748		
	30741						
	30744						
N15 4-6-0 (1925)							
30448	30448	30448	30448	30448	30448	30448	30448
30449	30449	30449	30449	30449	30449	30449	30450
30450	30450	30450	30450	30450	30450	30450	30453
30451	30452	30452	30452	30452	30452	30452	
30452	30453	30453	30453	30453	30453	30453	
30453	30454	30454	30454	30454	30454		
30454	30455						
30455	30457						
30456							
N15 4-6-0 (1926)							
							30796
							30798
							30799
WC 4-6-2 (1945)							
34032	34022	34032	34032	34049	34049	34049	34049
34034	34023	34050	34050	34050	34050	34051	34051
34035	34033	34051	34051	34051	34051	34054	34054
34042	34034	34052	34052	34052	34052	34055	34059
34049	34042	34053	34053	34053	34053	34059	34099
34050	34043	34054	34054	34054	34054		
34051		34055	34055	34055	34055		
34052				34059	34059		
34053							
34054							
34055							
WC/R (1957)							
						34050	34048
						34052	34050
						34053	34052
MN 4-6-2 (1941)							
35004	35006	35006	35006	35006	35006	35006	
35006	35007	35007	35007	35007	35007		
35007	35008	35008	35009	35009	35009		
35008	35009	35009					
35009							
35010							
MN/R (1956)							
						35004	35004
						35007	35006
							35007
68	**62**	**53**	**54**	**54**	**55**	**51**	**54**

Rebuilt MN 35009 'Shaw Savill'. 12:390/415 tons (1958)						
m.ch point	1/in	WTT	Actual	mph	dbhp	pc
0.00 SALISBURY	-	0.00	0.00	-	-	-
5.24 Porton	216		8.55	52	1336	5
10.74 Grateley	571		14.36	64	1210	7
17.24 ANDOVER JCN	-275	22.00	19.39	75	388	3
22.36 Hurstbourne	401		23.36	66	1075	8
24.35 Whitchurch	307		25.30	69	1538	10
28.01 Overton	549		28.29	75	1611	12
31.12 Oakley	2937		30.55	80	1433	11
33.20 Worting Jcn	-734	36.00	32.28	82	924	8
35.63 BASINGSTOKE	-260	38.30	34.16	84	263	2
41.30 Hook	-684		38.21	85	676	6
43.57 Winchfield	-1046		40.08	81	178	1
47.05 Fleet	-674		42.33	78	348	3
50.26 Farnborough	-2852		44.57	80	1105	9
52.43 MP.31	946		46.34	82	1606	13
55.44 Brookwood	-307		48.45	86	347	3
59.16 WOKING	-318	58.00	51.27	75	-	-
61.69 West Byfleet	-367		53.33	78	468	4
64.31 Weybridge	-6116		55.30	74	412	3
71.40 Surbiton	-8963		60.58	82	1207	9
			pwc			
83.43 WATERLOO	-3384	85.00	77.16	-	-	-

Andover Jcn to Worting Jcn. 15.1 miles 1/664
75 mph. 1322 dbhp (pc 10)

Even this run by rebuild 35009 falls short of the maximum that a Merchant Navy could produce since the engine was eased considerably once Basingstoke had been passed. Had it not been for a permanent way slack the train would probably have arrived in Waterloo ten minutes earlier than scheduled - and this at speeds well below what the engine was capable of.

the 11.17 (09.33 ex Portsmouth) to Cardiff. The best bet was the second of these engines which came onto the shed after arriving with the 16.32 ex Bristol and was worked by the same men who were booked to man the Castle. All they had to do was keep the engine they already had and return, after turning, to the station whilst the running foreman sent to Westbury for an engine for the next day's 11.17 Cardiff.

This sort of move was known as a clean move in that it was relatively simple to arrange and involved a minimum of other engines and depots. More importantly it kept paperwork down to a minimum and this was a feature that loomed high in the order of things at a running shed.

Although running foremen were salaried - and at large sheds, of relatively senior grade - they were nonetheless promoted from the wages grades, usually with a mechanical and driving background, and as a result often stood in awe of paperwork and those associated with it. At the London sheds, the running foremen, by and large, treated most paperwork with the sort of contempt that Ghengis Khan reserved for civil rights but their counterparts at country depots seemed to live in a fear of magisterial scrutiny and any course of action that would draw the attention of the 'clerical' was to be avoided.

What appears to be the obvious option - that of substituting a spare Southern engine - was in fact out of the question and anyone suggesting such a thing would be thought unsound. The first objection was straightforward one of route availability and although the position was clear enough so far as the line to Westbury was concerned, beyond that point it was by no means easy to tell whether or not it was safe to send a Southern engine over the route. The second objection concerned the loss of an engine and the effect it could have on meeting diagrammed and special train needs the following day. The

greatest deterrent to adventurousness was the simple fact that, in spite of 1948, the route to Westbury was a foreign railway and Southern engines were not supposed to work over it. If the Great Western wanted trains running from Salisbury to Bristol, they should jolly well ensure that a proper supply of engines, including contingencies, was provided. There was, of course, a strong feeling that by closing the Great Western shed, the Western only had themselves to blame for any problems that arose.

Another important circumstance was the fact that most Running Foremen - and most senior railwaymen - were in the last decade or so of their working lives of which almost all had been spent with the Railway Companies whose boundaries had been etched into the subconscious for so many years that something far more than an act of nationalisation was needed to erase them.

Matters were not much more simple in the event of a 'foreign' Southern engine failing and having to be replaced. There was no fixed provision - as was the case at Peterborough, for example, where a V2 was on hand twenty-four hours a day to take over from any ailing Pacific - for main line engine failures and if a Nine Elms Merchant Navy failed with a Waterloo - West of England train, the Running Foreman at Salisbury had to make the best use of whatever he had on hand and ready to go.

If the failed Pacific could be patched up fairly quickly then it was a simple matter to find out what the replacement engine was going to return with and effect a changeover in the station when it arrived. If, on the other hand, the failure had to be towed away to Eastleigh or its home depot and Nine Elms appeared unwilling to return the engine promptly then action had to be taken.

Initially a report would be submitted to the shedmaster and the clerk instructed to telegraph Nine Elms with a standard request to cut the engine out of the working and return it as quickly as possible to Salisbury.

What then happened would depend on the state of play at Nine Elms and if they happened at the time to be short of power then, human nature being what it is, they would try and keep the engine on their diagrams for as long as they could get away with it and eventually the matter would have to be referred to the regional authority for resolution and the Shed Master instructed to get the engine back to Salisbury.

The instruction would be relayed to the Running Foreman and almost certainly result in the well worn exchange:

"Get 34053 back to Salisbury."
"But Guv', we're already five engines short...."

"Tonight if you please."
"But Guv. Feltham's got two of ours and Bournemouth three...."
"Tonight!"
"All right but if we're cancelling trains tomorrow it won't be my responsibility....."

It was possible for a shed to keep an unbalanced engine for a few days, perhaps a week if it belonged to another region, but tales of engines being held for weeks and months can be taken, by and large, to be apocryphal. Discipline within the running department was tight and the organisation effective.

Even without engine failures, the work of the Running Foreman called for a considerable organisational talent; a blessing that was usually referred to as 'keeping two engines ahead'. His first duty would be to see that all the foreign engines - turn-rounds - were in place and then to arrange engines for his own workings. This would be done by looking at the engines available for work, allocating each to an appropriate duty and arranging for them to be prepared in good time. Any gaps would be plugged by looking at the arrival times of inward engines, establishing whether or not they would be arriving on time and estimating what sort of condition they would be in, in order to gauge how long it would take to turn them round. A shortage of one particular class could be made good by substituting something similar - an H15 in lieu of an S15 for example - so long as the difference was not too marked. In any event whenever the booked type of engine could not be used it was necessary to forewarn the traffic department so that steps to reduce loads could be taken.

Load reductions apart there were hidden perils in substituting one sort of engine for another. There was a temptation to look at the train the engine worked from Salisbury and, when the booked engine could not be provided, to make a local arrangement to turn out some-

MN 4-6-2 (R/B) 35024 'East Asiatic Company'. 13:430/460						
m.ch Point	1/in	WTT	Actual	mph	dbhp	pc
0 WATERLOO		0.00	0.00	-	-	-
			signals			
3.74 Clapham Jcn	-3642	7.00	7.22	30	539	2
7.19 Wimbledon	752		11.30	60	1660	8
12.03 Surbiton	20774		15.50	70	1185	8
21.54 West Byfleet	7988		23.27	77	1194	9
24.27 WOKING	367	27.00	25.30	76	1663	13
27.79 Brookwood	318		28.28	74	1585	12
31.00 MP.31	307		31.00	71	1415	10
33.17 Farnborough	-946		32.50	75	1054	8
36.38 Fleet	2852		35.20	78	1401	11
39.66 Winchfield	674		39.55	77	1330	10
47.60 BASINGSTOKE	761	47.30	44.05	65	893	7
50.23 Worting Jcn	260	50.00	46.27	63	1396	9
55.42 Overton	2923		50.47	78	1710	12
59.08 Whitchurch	-549		53.27	82	912	7
61.07 Hurstbourne	-307		54.50	84	620	5
66.19 ANDOVER JCN	-401		58.40	86	478	4
72.49 Grateley	275		63.38	67	1102	8
78.19 Porton	-571		67.48	86	1704	14
82.48 Tunnel Jcn	-190		71.35	15	-	-
83.43 SALISBURY	-580	80.00	74.03	-	-	-

Clapham Jcn to Overton. 51.6 miles 1/857
71 mph. 1367 dbhp (pc 10)

Confirming that the run by 35009 was no flash in the pan, 35024 later ran with thirteen vehicles to Salisbury, gaining six minutes on an already fast schedule in spite of signal delays in the early stage of the run. Had the Southern Region used these engines to the extent of their capacity their timetable could have been the envy of Europe. The run was made in 1962.

thing smaller. If traffic was light and the engine situation poor, the use of a 700 0-6-0 in place of the booked S15 for the 12.55 West Yard to Yeovil Junction goods might, with the agreement of the traffic department, seem a good way of keeping things moving. (The Foreman probably remembered a time when most main line goods trains were worked by 700's and still considered them strong engines). Problems of some magnitude would arise later in the day when the 0-6-0 presented itself for the 14.55 Salisbury - Exeter passenger, which the 12.55 engine was booked to take over from Yeovil Junction, and there would either be a considerable loss of time involved or Yeovil would lose an engine. Either way there would be a few letters to answer and a grim reckoning: It paid to scrutinise an entire diagram when booking out engines. (The writer incidentally speaks from experience, having fallen into the trap and been made to suffer, quite rightly, for it afterwards. It was not a mistake one made twice and it was better not to make it in the first place). Fortunately Salisbury was well stocked with 4-6-0's of one sort or another and the need to use a '700' in lieu did not often arise.

Having allocated engines to workings, the next task was to arrange the roads, positioning engines in the order they were to leave the shed and making sure they were the right way round. It was also necessary to use some imagination as to where engines were positioned whilst waiting to leave the shed. There were ten shed roads to choose from but most of these had to be reserved for incoming engines, some of which remained on the shed for some time whilst others were to be handed over to the fitting staff for attention. Generally roads one to five (numbered, as usual, from the running lines) were reserved for outgoing engines whilst arriving engines used the remainder.

In addition to arranging the outgoing engines strategically, 'setting out your stall', a close watch had to be maintained over incoming engines which, as they arrived, had to be parked with the time they spent on shed uppermost

in the Foreman's mind. Some engines came on shed to turn, coal and water and had to be kept apart from those which either spent some time on shed before their next working or, in the case of local engines, had not yet been given a duty. Most important of all was the need to keep foreign engines apart from local ones and visiting engines were usually allocated to a shed road of their own to prevent them from getting mixed up - and blocked in - with a miscellany of Salisbury engines. Neither was there much time to

make decisions since an engine waiting for instructions prevented others from moving; a blockage that could quickly react back onto the running lines.

To complicate an already complex job, it could never be assumed that one day was going to be like the one before since there were always a number of special workings being arranged and, not infrequently, the booked workings were altered to cater for these additional trains. Thus, whilst for time immemorial the 04.35 goods to Feltham (17.21 ex Plymouth) had been worked by a Salisbury N15 4-6-0, the duty for a single day might be altered so that the engine instead worked a special empty stock service at 07.30 to Yeovil followed by an excursion to Wembley via Clapham Junction and the West London Extension; the engine returning light from Kensington to Nine Elms and picking up its normal working in the evening with the 20.54 Waterloo - Salisbury.

Attention to such amendments was not drawn by illuminated writing in the sky but instead by some small print on a circular headed 'Salisbury duty 436 amended....'. Elsewhere on another piece of paper would be the arrangements for the 04.35 ex Salisbury (probably a Nine Elms 4-6-0 booked to bring ECS from Clapham Junction to Salisbury - the same stock that 436 engine re-engined for Yeovil - which then returned with the Plymouth goods, finishing with the 14.47 Feltham to Nine Elms). The altered arrangements for the train crews and guards would have to be found on separate circulars and the whole scrutinised in order to ensure that headquarters had not left anything out. (Generally the diagramming sections were pretty adroit at carving up diagrams in order to run addition trains without extra engines and men being used but it was not wholly unknown for something to be overlooked).

Even when the paper work had been brought together and everything appeared to be watertight, things could still go wrong and it paid to be able to keep the details of the altered workings in one's head together with those of the normal service. As sure as eggs are eggs the phone would ring half an hour before the Plymouth goods was due to leave...

"East box. Where's the engine for the Feltham?"

"Off the special stock from London. I'll find out if its turned here yet...."

Train	Arrive	Yard	Loco	Depart	Destination
(Torrington)		East	N15 4-6-0 (Nine Elms 10)	00.13	Nine Elms
		West	WC 4-6-2 (Salisbury 430/2)	00.15	Torrington
21.50 Bristol	00.23	East	Grange 4-6-0 (Bristol 366)		
22.00 Nine Elms	00.55	West	MN 4-6-2 (Salisbury 461)		(Exmouth Jcn)
19.05 Exmouth Jcn	01.05	East	WC 4-6-2 (Salisbury 430/2)		
(Nine Elms)		West	S15 4-6-0 (Salisbury 470)	01.10	Exmouth Jcn
		Fisherton	72xx 2-8-2T (STJ 363)	01.10	Severn T. Jcn
		East	U 2-6-0 (Salisbury 450)	01.35	Eastleigh
00.20 Eastleigh	01.45	West	Q1 0-6-0 (Eastleigh 319)		(Exmouth Jcn)
17.21 Plymouth	02.45	East	S15 4-6-0 (Salisbury 471)		(Feltham)
(Templecombe)		Fisherton	Grange 4-6-0 (Bristol 366)	03.10	Avonmouth
		Fisherton	43xx 2-6-0 (Bristol 365/2)	03.30	Avonmouth
		East	Q1 0-6-0 (Guildford 237)	03.30	Chichester
02.10 Bevois Pk	03.58	West	S15 4-6-0 (Salisbury 467)		
		East	700 0-6-0 (Salisbury 452)	04.05	B'mouth (Cent)
		East	S15 4-6-0 (Salisbury 471)	04.15	Milford Trip
		East	Q1 0-6-0 (Eastleigh 319)	04.25	Northam
22.00 Avonmouth	04.28	East	43xx 2-6-0 (Bristol 365)		
(Plymouth)		East	N15 4-6-0 (Salisbury 436)	04.35	Feltham
		West	700 0-6-0 (Salisbury 454)	05.05	East Yard
05.05 West Yard	05.14	East	700 0-6-0 (Salisbury 454)	05.25	Milford Trip
03.58 Bevois Pk	05.37	Fisherton	H15 4-6-0 (Eastleigh 311)		
19.45 Bassaleg	05.44	East	28xx 2-8-0 (STJ 351)		(Loco coal)
03.30 Basingstoke	05.50	West	H15 4-6-0 (Salisbury 439)		
		East	700 0-6-0 (Salisbury 454)	06.10	Bulford
16.40 Wadebridge	06.32	East	S15 4-6-0 (Salisbury 435)		
		West	700 0-6-0 (Salisbury 451)	07.37	East Yard
07.37 West Yard	07.45	East	700 0-6-0 (Salisbury 451)	08.00	Wimborne
01.00 Cardiff	08.10	East	Hall 4-6-0 (Canton 354)		
		East	H15 4-6-0 (Eastleigh 311)	08.45	Fratton
21.15 Aberdare	09.44	East	Hall 4-6-0 (Aberdare 353)		
		East	S15 4-6-0 (Salisbury 435)	09.45	West Yard
09.45 East Yard trip	09.53	West	S15 4-6-0 (Salisbury 435)		
03.00 Brighton	10.29	Fisherton	S15 4-6-0 (Feltham 106)		
		East	S15 4-6-0 (Salisbury 438)	10.42	Basingstoke
02.35 Radyr	10.57	East	72xx 2-8-2T (Radyr 352)		
		East	H15 4-6-0 (Nine Elms 72)	11.18	Eastleigh
		East	S15 4-6-0 (Feltham 116)	11.27	Chichester
09.30 Eastleigh	12.05	Milford	BR4 2-6-0 (Eastleigh 316)		
07.35 Westbury	12.24	East	43xx 2-6-0 (Westbury 28)		
10.23 Bevois Park	12.52	Fisherton	H15 4-6-0 (Eastleigh 312)		(Rogerstone)
		West	S15 4-6-0 (Salisbury 471)	12.55	Templecombe
(Bevois Park)		Fisherton	72xx 2-8-2T (STJ 363/2)	13.08	Rogerstone
06.45 Severn T. Jn	13.44	East	72xx 2-8-2T (STJ 363)		
		East	S15 4-6-0 (Feltham 106)	14.25	Basingstoke
		East	43xx 2-6-0 (Bristol 365)	15.07	S'ton Docks
		East	S15 4-6-0 (Salisbury 475)	15.30	West Yard
14.45 Amesbury	15.33	Fisherton	700 0-6-0 (Salisbury 454)		
15.30 East Yard trip	15.35	West	S15 4-6-0 (Salisbury 475)		
10.45 Feltham	15.59	West	S15 4-6-0 (Feltham 101)		(Exmouth Jcn)
		East	U 2-6-0 (Yeovil 482)	16.10	Milford Trip
		East	H15 4-6-0 (Eastleigh 312)	16.18	Eastleigh
		Fisherton	28xx 2-8-0 (STJ 351)	16.35	Severn T. Jcn
		Milford	BR4 2-6-0 (Eastleigh 316)	17.00	Fisherton
(Feltham)		West	S15 4-6-0 (Salisbury 475)	17.15	Exmouth Jcn
09.45 Tonbridge	17.25	West	H15 4-6-0 (Salisbury 440)		(Exmouth Jcn)
17.00 Milford Trip	17.35	Fisherton	BR4 2-6-0 (Eastleigh 316)		
		East	43xx 2-6-0 (Westbury 28)	18.00	Westbury
17.58 Milford Trip	18.11	East	U 2-6-0 (Salisbury 482)		
16.35 Gillingham	19.52	East	S15 4-6-0 (Salisbury 467)		
15.35 Wimborne	20.37	East	700 0-6-0 (Salisbury 452)		
18.50 Wimborne	21.20	Fisherton	700 0-6-0 (Salisbury 451)		
19.04 Basingstoke	21.50	West	S15 4-6-0 (Salisbury 438)		(Plymouth)
20.56 Eastleigh	22.25	Fisherton	Q1 0-6-0 (Guildford 236)		
		East	H15 4-6-0 (Salisbury 439)	22.50	Basingstoke
		Fisherton	Hall 4-6-0 (Aberdare 353)	23.15	Aberdare
16.10 Severn T. Jn	23.20	Fisherton	72xx 2-8-2T (STJ 363/2)		
22.20 T'combe	23.35	Fisherton	S15 4-6-0 (Salisbury 470)		(Avonmouth)

What might have been... During the early days of the grouping the Southern was keen to use large 2-6-4T locomotives for many of its medium-distance express services and although the preponderance would have operated in the LBSCR and SECR districts, had the scheme proved a success it is probable that some LSWR workings, possibly the Salisbury semi-fasts, would have been effected. River class 2-6-4T is seen in its original condition as 797 'River Mole' at the head of the 17.05 London Bridge - Eastbourne service in the summer of 1925. The engine was rebuilt as a U class 2-6-0 in July 1928 and spent much of the 1950's at Guildford where it regularly covered the two main line workings between Woking and Basingstoke.

"The Yeovil stock's not passed Woking yet. Blocked in at Clapham or somewhere. Don't anyone talk to you?"

".......just hang on."

Some pretty furious thinking would follow.

"Right then. Engine 30450 is out their somewhere waiting to take over the Yeovil stock. Send it back here to turn and it can do the Feltham. Tell the West to keep the London engine going on the stock and I'll send a set out to relieve it."

"30450 for the goods, Righto then..."

After the thinking followed a considerable amount of action. A set of men would have to be scraped together to work the Plymouth goods whilst the booked men could wait at the station and relieve the London men when they eventually arrived with the Yeovil stock - or would it be better to let the men already on the engine stay with it and work the goods whilst a buck-shee set did the Yeovil passenger. And what about the loose ends such as the Feltham - Nine Elms leg? Would whoever worked the special know the road to Kensington or would they be eager and alert (pilotmen needed front and back) at Clapham Junction?

These problems were usually resolved almost instinctively, the individual receiving the problem taking the initiative and doing whatever was necessary to put thing right. The astonishing aspect of shed working was that most of the ad hoc planning was done on a scrap of paper with an absolute minimum of clerical assistance and had anyone suggested at the time that miracles of administration were being produced by the hour, those in the hot-seat would have been the first to express astonishment.

Thirty-five years later a very much smaller number of engines were being allocated to trains by a computer. The problems were - and probably still are - immense - not because of any especial operating difficulties - which have all but disappeared - but because the computer software is too complicated for the operators to understand thoroughly and frequently fails to cope with the amount of detail being typed in: expensive high technology which achieves less than used to be accomplished on the back of a used envelope.....

The allocation of 53 locomotives to work 28 daily diagrams seems at first glance to be on the generous side although with an average of about fifteen engines out of traffic at any one time plus the need to service a timetable which fluctuated according to the time of year, Salisbury was not, if fact, as well endowed as appearances suggest.

The position can be demonstrated by reference to the Merchant Navy allocation which consisted of four engines (35006-9) but only two duties (the 13.00 Waterloo - Exeter and the 16.30 Exeter - Waterloo). One might well ask why, with only a 50% utilisation (or 25% if one accepts the third engine as a contingency), it was necessary to denude Bournemouth of its allocation in order to provide Stewarts Lane with Merchant Navy engines for its boat trains. The answer lies in the fact that there was an additional turn of duty at the weekends (the Devon Belle between Wilton and Exeter) whilst the fourth engine was retained as a standby for failures, maintenance and special traffic requirements.

With four engines having to be provided for two permanent diagrams plus one weekend/special workings; only one engine was available to provide cover in the event of problems which meant, in practical terms, that there were occasions when demand for Merchant Navy engines came perilously close to the level of supply.

To some extent salvation could be obtained from the five theoretically spare light Pacifics although the two basic workings (which in fact was one two-day cyclic diagram) were expanded by one during the summer when the 09.05 Salisbury to Weymouth via Verwood operated. (Apart from bringing a Pacific onto territory normally inhabited only by T9's and 700 0-6-0's, the working was remarkable in that of the twelve hours the engine was away from Salisbury, almost seven and a half were spent doing nothing on Weymouth MPD whilst the train required no less than four sets of men).

On summer Saturdays the Weymouth train was extended back to Bristol Temple Meads but worked from Salisbury by a T9 4-4-0, the light Pacific working instead the 09.03 Portsmouth to Exeter and the 16.05 Exeter - Waterloo - the engine working through on both trains and amassing a respectable mileage of 309 - whilst another West Country was turned out

There was very little on the Southern that was not scheduled on paper and the working arrangements even included the supply of heating coal to signalboxes. It kept an HQ clerk in work but most railwaymen were cheerfully unaware of such small-print instructions - at least until one of the trains concerned was diverted and the signalman started howling.

for the 09.00 Waterloo to Sidmouth Junction and the milk train back to Basingstoke. The second part of 430 diagram did not operate on Saturdays but there were still three engines out of the seven at work whilst the remainder were kept available as substitutes for any Pacific shortcomings and to work any special diagrams, of which in the summer there were a great many. (The Southern was very liberal when it came to party bookings and where the other regions might reserve a coach or two the Southern would tend to think in terms of additional trains and this of course called for a high proportion of 'spare' engines, although by any reckoning the ratio of work to engines was, in the case of the light Pacifics, low).

More realistic targets were set for the King Arthur 4-6-0's and not only were six out of the seven engines diagrammed for Saturday work (throughout the year) but two were booked to head express services (the 08.40 and 10.48 from Torrington) through to Waterloo from Exeter whilst a third worked from Templecombe to London.

For not the first time in these ages, the question might be asked what three such veterans were doing on front rank work when Bulleids in excelsis had saturated the fleet but for railwaymen they represented times when engines had been built solidly and reliably whilst to the enthusiast they brought a whiff of nostalgia and a sense of continuity: perhaps the world was not changing as fast as people feared.

The drawback of being employed at a busy location such as Salisbury was that one rarely had time to sit back and absorb all that was going on and thus it was that many railwaymen, the author included, spent almost as many hours sitting on the end of a platform as they did on duty. Movement economics and budgetary considerations were what one was paid to put into effect but, at the end of the day, the railway - pre-Beeching - could never be as dry as a bank to work in and, in a deep recess of one's soul, it was a vi-

The ones that were difficult to catch. Although Exmouth Junction had an enormous allocation of locomotives, the bulk of the shed's responsibilities lay with trains to the west and, the Merchant Navy's apart, few of its fleet regularly worked as far east as Salisbury. The light Pacifics could be counted upon to stray from Devon with relief expresses from time to time but the smaller stuff was all but impossible to find without making a long trip west. The table above shows the allocation at Exmouth Junction during the 1950's, the accompanying table on the following train listing the larger classes of engine.

EXMOUTH JUNCTION : 1949-60

M7 0-4-4T (1897)

Jun-49	Apr-50	Apr-53	May-54	Nov-55	Jan-57	Mar-59	Feb-60
30024	30024	30021	30024	30030	30030	30027	30048
30025	30025	30024	30030	30034	30041	30030	30055
30030	30030	30025	30034	30041	30042	30034	30105
30032	30032	30030	30041	30042	30055	30041	30252
30034	30034	30034	30044	30055	30105	30055	30323
30039	30039	30041	30045	30105	30252	30105	30356
30046	30046	30045	30055	30252	30323	30252	30357
30049	30049	30055	30105	30323	30356	30323	30375
30055	30055	30105	30252	30356	30357	30356	30667
30105	30105	30252	30323	30357	30667	30357	30670
30124	30124	30323	30356	30375	30669	30375	
30133	30133	30356	30357	30378	30670	30667	
30245	30245	30357	30375	30667	30671	30670	
30252	30252	30375	30378	30669	30676	30671	
30253	30253	30378	30667	30670			
30255	30255	30667	30668	30671			
30256	30256	30668	30668	30676			
30320	30320	30669	30669				
30323	30323	30670	30670				
30374	30377	30671	30671				
30376	30668	30676	30676				
30377	30669						
30668	30671						
30669							
30671							

O2 0-4-4T (1889)

Jun-49	Apr-50	Apr-53	May-54	Nov-55	Jan-57	Mar-59	Feb-60
30192	30192	30199	30199	30199	30183	30182	30199
30193	30193	30224	30224	30224	30199	30199	30224
30199	30199	30230	30230	30230	30224	30224	30230
30224	30224	30232	30232		30230	30230	
30230	30230						
30232	30232						

GWR 57xx 0-6-0PT

Jun-49	Apr-50	Apr-53	May-54	Nov-55	Jan-57	Mar-59	Feb-60
							3679
							9756

'0415' 4-4-2T (1882)

Jun-49	Apr-50	Apr-53	May-54	Nov-55	Jan-57	Mar-59	Feb-60
30582	30582						
30583	30583						
30584							

'0395' 0-6-0 (1881)

Jun-49	Apr-50	Apr-53	May-54	Nov-55	Jan-57	Mar-59	Feb-60
30564	30581	30575	30580	30580			
		30580	30581	30581			
		30581					

'700' 0-6-0 (1897)

Jun-49	Apr-50	Apr-53	May-54	Nov-55	Jan-57	Mar-59	Feb-60
				30315	30315	30317	30317
				30691	30691	30327	30327
						30691	30691

E1/R 0-6-2T (1927)

Jun-49	Apr-50	Apr-53	May-54	Nov-55	Jan-57	Mar-59	Feb-60
32124	32124	32124	32124	32124	32124	32135	32135
32135	32135	32135	32135	32135	32135		
32695	32695						
32697	32697						

BR3 2-6-2T

Jun-49	Apr-50	Apr-53	May-54	Nov-55	Jan-57	Mar-59	Feb-60
		82010	82010	82017	82017	82017	82017
		82011	82011	82018	82018	82018	82018
		82013	82013	82019	82019	82022	82022
		82017	82017	82022	82022	82023	82023
		82018	82018	82023	82023	82024	82024
		82019	82019	82024	82024	82024	82024
				82025	82024	82025	82025
					82025		

LMS 2MT 2-6-2T (1946)

Jun-49	Apr-50	Apr-53	May-54	Nov-55	Jan-57	Mar-59	Feb-60
		41313	41313	41306	41306	41306	41306
		41314		41307	41307	41307	41307
				41313	41313	41313	41308
						41318	41309
							41318

Z 0-8-0T (1929)

Jun-49	Apr-50	Apr-53	May-54	Nov-55	Jan-57	Mar-59	Feb-60
30954	30954	30954	30954	30954	30950	30950	30950
					30954	30953	30951
					30956	30954	30952
						30955	30953
						30956	30954
							30955
							30956

L11 4-4-0 (1903)

Jun-49	Apr-50	Apr-53	May-54	Nov-55	Jan-57	Mar-59	Feb-60
30408	30408						
30409	30409						
30436	30436						
30439	30439						

T9 4-4-0 (1899/1922)

Jun-49	Apr-50	Apr-53	May-54	Nov-55	Jan-57	Mar-59	Feb-60
30283	30283	30703	30703	30703	30703	30708	30313
30702	30702	30706	30706	30706	30706	30712	30338
30716	30703	30707	30707	30707	30707	30717	30708
30723	30707	30708	30708	30708	30708	30723	30712
30724	30716	30709	30709	30709	30709	30725	30717
30725	30717	30711	30711	30711	30712	30726	30718
30730	30723	30712	30712	30712	30716		30719
	30724	30715	30716	30716	30717		30723
	30725	30716	30717	30717	30723		30725
	30730	30717	30723	30723	30725		
		30723	30724	30725			
		30724	30725				
		30725					

BR4 4-6-0

Jun-49	Apr-50	Apr-53	May-54	Nov-55	Jan-57	Mar-59	Feb-60
			75070				
			75071				
			75072				
			75073				
			75074				
			75075				

brant and exciting spectator sport. Those, whatever their jobs, who could simply walk away from their place of work and go home without a second thought, were to be wondered at and the author pitied them since he found the temptation to hang about the railway after a stint of duty not only irresistible but rewarding. Several hours watching trains at a busy station was always enjoyable but much more so if one knew by heart the timetable and engine workings since each movement could be anticipated and every unexpected operation explained. (It was also great fun to impress visiting trainspotters to announce well in advance the engines that were going to arrive for an hour ahead without, of course, saying how it was done: few if any of them understood that locomotives operated to a rigid sequence of trains. Most seemed to cherish the notion that the shed authorities allocated engines to trains according to whim).

Most of the action and interest at major locations such as Salisbury centred on the motive power or in the goods yards but the district produced at least one gem from another direction when (in the judgement of one of the writers who was a station master in the district) it was responsible for discovering what in more recent years has come to be known as dyslexia.

One of the smaller stations - which had better remain nameless - in the district only had its booking office manned by a full-blown clerk on the morning shift whilst for the rest of the time the porters held the fort. If the truth be told, the porters generally took to their clerical functions like ducks to water and - if the truth be extended further - were probably better (certainly more conscientious) at tackling the voluminous accountancy work that lay behind the simple issuing of tickets than many of their salaried betters.

With one exception. One of the porters couldn't spell. In every other respect he excelled: he bowed and scraped to the passengers, he freely volunteered information, carried luggage without thought of gratuities, was never late for duty, his arithmetic was first class and he would sooner have died than skived off ten minutes early yet for all these admirable qualities and more, he could not comprehend the slightest alphabetical principle. In those days before excuses became a way of life, opinion was divided on his trouble. Close relatives described him as being confused whilst the clerk said he was bloody thick. The truth probably lay somewhere in between.

There was no question of sacking him since he not only relished his booking office duties but spent his waking off-duty hours poring over the accountancy instructions - it was even said that he made his wife question him from the conditions of carriage manual before going to sleep at night - and all in all he was so proud of his additional duties that he completely disarmed the stationmaster from criticising him for his unconscious illiteracy.

The SM was not the most cheerful of souls - few were - but the sight of the blank card sheets with a hundred or more long distance destinations written in anagram was more than the poor soul could keep a straight face at and on more than one occasion he would disappear at speed from the booking office clutching the blank card sheets, convulsed in silent laughter. How the porter concerned could see nothing strange in a ticket being issued to PYLMTHOU via EXRET had to be a matter for mirth whilst a return to Penzance produced more contiguous consonants than anything in any Welsh dictionary.

And so it went on, the SM paying a visit whenever he was in need of a laugh and the porter happily mutilating the alphabet, until one day he surpassed himself and became a legend for a week.

The normal clerk went on leave for a day and was replaced, rather unusually, by the senior relief clerk of the district who arrived none too happy at having to spend eight hours of his life at such a one-horse location. He glared at the porter who, unconscious of the great man's grade and seniority, was trying to tell him the difference between a cheap day and an ordinary return.

"Just find something to do."

"All right, chief." said the porter quite unabashed, "I know - there's engineering work this weekend. I'll draw up a poster and pin it up."

"You do that." replied the clerk wondering where the tea was kept.

Within minutes the porter had a double-royal poster unrolled on the floor and armed with more set squares, protractors and coloured pencils than Brunel had used in the Tamar Bridge, set to work on the reverse side.

"Watch your spelling" growled the clerk as he glanced over some of the station's accountancy but the porter laboured away, rigid with concentration and effort.

An hour or two later he announced the end of the project and

it is no lie to say that he had engineered a work of art. It was a marvel of beauty: wonderfully coloured with lettering so skilfully drawn that one could only stand silent in admiration. It was unquestionably a new dimension in the art of calligraphy and really ought to have been framed and it was the glorious colour and magnitude of the thing that drew attention away from its one weakness.

Uncensored it was pinned up on the outside of the office for the benefit of weekend travellers. Whether it served it's purpose of warning passengers about the Sunday diversions has to be taken for granted but there is no doubt that it contributed handsomely to the old man's hernia when he spotted it earlier in the following week.

Creased up and weak with laughter he pointed out the message on the poster to those standing around. **ATTENTION,** *it ran in huge letters,* **TRAINS ARE BEING DIVERTED** *via* **ROSMEY.** Some time later the SM was walking down the platform when a hot box had to be removed from a train. The guard set to but the porter - the man of letters - got there first and tackled it with all his usual enthusiasm. Of course, never having touched a coupling or vacuum hose before he made a complete horlicks of the thing but the Station Master knew the hand of providence when he saw it. (He also knew the auditors were on their way and were unlikely to be impressed by the blank card returns).

Calling him into his office he grasped the porter by the hand and shook it vigorously.

"In all my career I have never seen anyone uncouple a van the way you have just done it."

"Well, sir, I...."

"No, no, no. It was excell...it was...Look, I have a vacancy for a shunter at Eastleigh. I need someone like you to show the others how to do it. Will you take it. PLEASE..."

So the porter was transferred to Eastleigh and is probably still telling anyone prepared to listen that he was hand-picked for the job.

"No-one else knows how to do it so my guv'nor said to me..."

For years afterwards the SM wondered how many wagons a day were being labelled for places such as Dreagni or Cralsiel. God help Europe if he every found his way into the Continental Yard. Still...Rosmey!

Whilst the days of steam cannot be restored, it is to be hoped that the tables showing the arrivals

EXMOUTH JUNCTION : 1949-60							
Jun-49	Apr-50	Apr-53	May-54	Nov-55	Jan-57	Mar-59	Feb-60
N 2-6-0 (1917)							
31407	31407	31407	31407	31407	31407	31407	31407
31408	31408	31830	31830	31830	31836	31836	31830
31409	31409	31828	31836	31836	31838	31838	31836
31828	31828	31831	31838	31838	31839	31839	31838
31831	31831	31832	31839	31839	31840	31840	31839
31832	31832	31833	31840	31840	31841	31841	31840
31833	31833	31835	31841	31841	31842	31842	31841
31834	31834	31837	31842	31842	31843	31843	31842
31835	31835	31838	31844	31844	31844	31844	31843
31837	31837	31839	31845	31845	31845	31845	31844
31838	31838	31840	31846	31846	31846	31846	31845
31839	31839	31841	31847	31847	31847	31847	31846
31840	31840	31845	31848	31848	31848	31849	31847
31841	31841	31846	31849	31849	31849	31855	31848
31845	31845	31848	31855		31855		31849
31847	31847	31849					31855
31853	31853	31855					31860
31855	31855						
31856							
31869							
31871							
31874							
31875							
U 2-6-0 (1928)							
31628	31628				31790		
31634	31634				31791		
31635	31635						
S15 4-6-0 (1897/1927)							
30823	30823	30823	30823	30823	30823	30823	30823
30824	30824	30824	30824	30824	30824	30825	30825
30825	30825	30825	30825	30825	30825	30827	30842
30826	30826	30826	30826	30826	30826	30842	30843
30827	30827	30827	30827	30827	30827		
30841	30841	30841	30841	30841	30841		
30842	30842	30842	30842	30842	30842		
30843	30843						
30844	30844						
30845	30845						
30846	30846						
30847	30847						
WC 4-6-2 (1945)							
34001	34001	34003	34003	34003	34003	34003	34003
34002	34002	34004	34004	34004	34004	34004	34004
34004	34004	34005	34005	34006	34006	34006	34006
34005	34005	34006	34006	34007	34007	34011	34011
34006	34006	34007	34007	34014	34014	34014	34014
34007	34007	34021	34021	34015	34015	34021	34027
34008	34008	34023	34024	34019	34019	34027	34035
34009	34009	34024	34033	34021	34021	34035	34036
34010	34010	34033	34041	34023	34023	34036	34038
34014	34014	34034	34043	34024	34024	34038	34056
34015	34015	34041	34044	34027	34027	34043	34057
34016	34016	34043	34045	34033	34043	34044	34058
34017	34017	34044	34048	34043	34044	34056	34059
34018	34018	34045	34049	34044	34056	34057	34061
34019	34019	34048	34056	34056	34057	34058	34063
34020	34020	34056	34057	34057	34058	34059	34064
34024	34024	34057	34058	34058	34059	34061	34065
34025	34027	34058	34059	34059	34061	34063	34069
34026	34028	34059		34061	34069	34069	34072
34027	34029			34069		34072	34074
34028	34030					34074	34075
34029	34031					34075	34076
34030	34032					34076	34079
34041	34041					34079	34080
34043	34043					34080	34081
34044	34044					34081	34096
34045	34045					34096	34104
34046	34046					34104	34106
34047	34047					34106	34107
34048	34048					34108	34108
						34109	34109
						34110	34110
MN 4-6-2 (1941)							
35001	35001	35001	35001	35001	35001	35001	35001
35002	35002	35002	35002	35002	35002	35002	35002
35003	35003	35003	35003	35003	35003	35003	35005
35021	35004	35025	35005	35005	35005	35004	35014
35022	35021		35013	35008	35008	35005	35023
35023	35022		35014	35013	35014	35014	
35024	35023		35023	35014	35023	35025	
			35025	35023			
				35025			
MN/R (1956)							
					35013	35008	35003
					35026	35009	35009
						35011	35010
						35013	35013
						35023	35022
							35024
							35025

With so many six-coupled engines in its books, 4-4-0's were a sought-after sight on the South Western main line, none more so than the D15 class which always tended to be overshadowed by the more celebrated T9 engines. Ten of the class entered the 1950's, all being allocated to Eastleigh, but started to disappear from December 1951 until 30465 became, in August 1955, the sole survivor. Massive looking engines with large, high-pitched boilers, representative of the class could be seen daily at Salisbury on a Portsmouth - Bristol service until early 1953 after which the three remaining engines were transferred to Nine Elms for a brief season on the Lymington boat trains. 30465 returned to Eastleigh in November 1955 and was withdrawn a month later.

and departures at Salisbury will act as an aide-memoire to those who wish to recreate those happy years in their mind's eye. There is no especial memory that stands out but, instead, a happy kaleidoscope of activity which no amount of time can blot from the imagination. An unrebuilt Merchant Navy arriving from Exeter, only half its journey done on a dark and cold winter's evening, being relieved in the platform whilst coal is pushed from the rear to the front of the tender. The asthmatic sound of the blower on and the rising crescendo of escaping steam all but drowning out the sound of carriage doors being slammed. The driver standing back from the engine, looking down the platform until the right-away is given followed by a quick sprint and a jump onto the footplate. A burst of exhaust like rifle fire as the Pacific slips wildly, steadies, slips and steadies again until the yellow glow of the cab disappears into the night and the coaches, more than a dozen, follow slowly; the efforts of the engine to get hold of its trains echoing back until drowned by the sound of the next arrival.

One missed the engine change on the West of England trains - two Merchant Navy Pacifics for one train made Salisbury seem even more important than it was but other trains continued to change engines, the most interesting being the Great Western workings which always seem to arrive far more sedately than the Southern trains. The engines - usually a Castle or a Hall - maintained a gleam that most SR locomotives lacked - not that the Southern passenger engines were in any way filthy - and ran like sewing machines. In contrast the BR4 2-6-0 which backed on for the continuation to Portsmouth was usually lacking any sort of shine and blowing off furiously although they could get anything up to ten bogies away from the station and round the curve with far less fuss than the Pacifics. The rear coach, however, was still doing a pedestrian rate when it cleared the station and made one wonder anew why some West Country's were not allocated to the route. The change from a GWR class 7P to a 4MT seemed a curious exchange.

Between passenger trains the main running lines were usually occupied with a freight trip transferring wagons from the West to the East sidings, or vice versa, with many of the engines used thus being H15 or S15 4-6-0's finishing a turn of duty.

The sight that drew forth cheers though was that of an N15 'King Arthur' preparing to leave for London. These were the talismen of the Southern and although they had some of their gloss taken away by the new Pacifics, they could still be found on passenger trains from Exeter in the west to Deal in the east and even though they were more often than not to be found on the slower LSWR services, on the neighbouring London Chatham & Dover they were still the kingpin of the Kent coast services to Ramsgate. They still had Saturday express workings to the West of England but even if it was a stopping train to Basingstoke and Waterloo that you saw one leave Salisbury with, the steady confident bark and the acceleration reminded you that the King Arthurs were still the aristocrats of the system. (But if only one could read the nameplates from any distance......).

The variety went on continuously - Salisbury never slept - and to witness it all, knowing what the trains and engines were and knowing you played a part in the operation, was like watching over the world's largest model railway system but without the need for imaginative improvisation. To watch the South Western at work was an experience - to work on it was a job you would have paid to do. Let us hope these pages have rekindled a little life in it.

PERFORMANCE SUMMARY					
Class	Engine	Section	mph	dbhp	pc
D15 4-4-0	30464	Hook - Porton	57	327	2
H15 4-6-0	30475	Clapham Jcn - West Byfleet	59	523	3
N15 4-6-0	30450	Worting Jcn - Woking	75	529	4
LN 4-6-0	30865	Basingstoke - Brookwood	74	594	4
N15 4-6-0	30777	Worting Jcn - West Byfleet	83	581	5
H15 4-6-0	30475	MP.31 - Overton	59	666	4
BR5 4-6-0	73110	Clapham Jcn - West Byfleet	61	815	5
LN 4-6-0	30860	Weybridge - Porton	62	829	5
N15 4-6-0	30450	Porton - Oakley	65	833	5
V 4-4-0	30932	Wimbledon - Worting Jcn	59	887	5
BR5 4-6-0	73119	Clapham Jcn - Walton	61	889	5
WC 4-6-2	34044	Worting Jcn - Brookwood	80	690	6
BR5 4-6-0	73111	Clapham Jcn - West Byfleet	65	938	6
V2 2-6-2	60893	Weybridge - Farnborough	57	977	6
MN/R 4-6-2	35018	Eastleigh - Roundwood	54	1182	6
MN/R 4-6-2	35002	Worting Jcn - Hampton Ct Jcn	79	863	7
N15 4-6-0	30777	Porton - Oakley	72	961	7
MN 4-6-2	35005	Wimbledon - Andover Jcn	72	977	7
MN 4-6-2	35030	MP.31 - Hook	69	996	7
MN/R 4-6-2	35020	Weybridge - Porton	69	1049	7
WC 4-6-2	34109	Woking - Micheldever	58	1122	7
WC 4-6-2	34041	Eastleigh - Roundwood	59	1176	7
LN 4-6-0	30865	Eastleigh - Roundwood	53	1307	7
Diesel	10201	Esher - Overton	72	1106	8
MN 4-6-2	35001	Clapham Jcn - West Byfleet	64	1303	8
MN/R 4-6-2	35002	Swaythling - Wootton	55	1467	8
MN 4-6-2	35001	Brookwood - Basingstoke	66	1337	9
MN/R 4-6-2	35009	Andover Jcn - Worting Jcn	75	1322	10
MN/R 4-6-2	35024	Clapham Jcn - Overton	71	1367	10

The table above summarises the performance logs in the book, selecting the hardest part of each journey and listing the output figures for each locomotive.